Rogue State

A Guide to the World's Only Superpower

William Blum

Zed Books Ltd
London

David Philip
Cape Town

Rogue State: A Guide to the World's Only Superpower, 3rd edition, was first published in the United Kingdom by Zed Books Ltd, 7 Cynthia Street, London N1 9JF, UK in 2006.

Published in the United States by Common Courage Press, Box 702, Monroe, ME 04951 in 2005.

Published in South Africa by David Philip Publishers, a division of New Africa Books, PO Box 23408, Claremont 7735.

Cover design by Andrew Corbett, Cambridge

Printed and bound in the United Kingdom by Cox & Wyman Ltd, Reading, Berkshire

A catalogue record for this book is available from the British Library

ISBN 1 84277 826 9 hb
ISBN 1 84277 827 7 pb

ISBN 978 1 84277 826 5 hb (from 2007)
ISBN 978 1 84277 827 2 pb (from 2007)

Third Edition, First Impression

Contents

A Rogue State versus the world

Author's Note

The first edition of this book was written during 1999-2000 and published in 2000. It was inspired by the brutal US bombing of Yugoslavia in the spring of 1999. For this 2005 edition, most chapters as well as the Introduction, have been revised and updated to reflect many of the events since 2000. However, several sections of the book still reflect the fact that they were first written during the Clinton administration and its bombing of Yugoslavia because the text is as applicable today as it was then.

The United States is good.
We try to do our best everywhere.

Secretary of State Madeleine Albright, 1999[1]

> *Never before in modern history has a country dominated the earth*
> *so totally as the United States does today.... America is now the*
> *Schwarzenegger of international politics: showing off muscles,*
> *obtrusive, intimidating.... The Americans, in the absence of limits*
> *put to them by anybody or anything, act as if they own a kind of*
> *blank check in their 'McWorld.'*

Der Spiegel, Germany's leading newsmagazine, 1997[2]

A world once divided into two armed camps now recognizes one sole and
pre-eminent power, the United States of America. And they regard this
with no dread. For the world trusts us with power, and the world is right.
They trust us to be fair, and restrained. They trust us to be on the side of
decency. They trust us to do what's right.

President George H.W. Bush, 1992[3]

> *How can they have the arrogance to dictate to us where we should*
> *go or which countries should be our friends? Gadhafi is my friend.*
> *He supported us when we were alone and when those who tried*
> *to prevent my visit here today were our enemies. They have no*
> *morals. We cannot accept that a state assumes the role of the*
> *world's policeman.*

South African President Nelson Mandela, 1997[4]

When I came into office, I was determined that our country would go into
the 21st century still the world's greatest force for peace and freedom, for
democracy and security and prosperity.

President Bill Clinton, 1996[5]

> *Throughout the world, on any given day, a man, woman or child*
> *is likely to be displaced, tortured, killed or "disappeared", at the*
> *hands of governments or armed political groups. More often than*
> *not, the United States shares the blame.*

Amnesty International, 1996[6]

INTRODUCTION

This book could be entitled: Serial chain-saw baby killers and the women who love them.

The women don't really believe that their beloved would do such a thing, even if they're shown a severed limb or a headless torso. Or if they believe it, they know down to their bone marrow that lover-boy really had the best of intentions; it must have been some kind of very unfortunate accident, a well-meaning blunder; in fact, even more likely, it was an act of humanitarianism.

For more than 70 years, the United States convinced much of the world that there was an international conspiracy out there. An *International Communist Conspiracy*, seeking no less than control over the entire planet, for purposes which had no socially redeeming values. And the world was made to believe that it somehow needed the United States to save it from communist darkness. "Just buy our weapons," said Washington, "let our military and our corporations roam freely across your land, and give us veto power over who your leaders will be, and we'll protect you."

It was the cleverest protection racket since men convinced women that they needed men to protect them, for if all the men vanished overnight, how many women would be afraid to walk the streets?

And if the people of any foreign land were benighted enough to not realize that they needed to be saved, if they failed to appreciate the underlying nobility of American motives, they were warned that they would burn in Communist Hell. Or a CIA facsimile thereof. And they would be saved nonetheless.

More than 15 years after the fall of the Berlin Wall, America is still saving countries and peoples from one danger or another. The scorecard reads as follows: Between 1945 and 2005 the United States has attempted to overthrow more than 50 foreign governments, and to crush more than 30 populist-nationalist movements struggling against intolerable regimes. In the process, the US has caused the end of life for several million people, and condemned many millions more to a life of agony and despair.

In April 1999 the United States was busy saving Yugoslavia, bombing a modern, sophisticated society back to a near-third-world level. And The Great American Public, in its infinite wisdom, was convinced that its government was motivated by "humanitarian" impulses.

At that time Washington was awash with foreign dignitaries come to celebrate the 50th anniversary of the North Atlantic Treaty Organization; three days of unprecedented pomp and circumstance. The prime ministers, presidents and foreign ministers, despite their rank, were delighted to be included amongst the close friends of the world's only superpower. Private corporations funded the opulent weekend; a dozen of them paying $250,000 apiece to have one of their executives serve as a director on the NATO Summit's host committee. Many of the same firms lobbied hard to expand NATO by adding the Czech Republic, Hungary and Poland, each of which would be purchasing plentiful quantities of military hardware from these companies.

This marriage of NATO and the transnationals was the foundation of the New World Order, the name George Bush, Sr. gave to the American Empire. The credibility of the New World Order depended upon the world believing that the new world would be a better one for the multitude of humanity, not just for those for whom too much is not enough; and believing that the leader of the New World Order, the United States, meant well for the planet and its people.

Let's have a short look at some modern American history, which may be instructive in this regard. A report of the US congress in 1994 informed us that:

Approximately 60,000 military personnel were used as human subjects in the 1940s to test two chemical agents, mustard gas and lewisite [blister gas]. Most of these subjects were not informed of the nature of the experiments and never received medical followup after their participation in the research. Additionally, some of these human subjects were threatened with imprisonment at Fort Leavenworth if they discussed these experiments with anyone, including their wives, parents, and family doctors. For decades, the Pentagon denied that the research had taken place, resulting in decades of suffering for many veterans who became ill after the secret testing.[1]

In the decades between the 1940s and 1990s, we find a remarkable variety of government programs, either formally, or in effect, using soldiers as guinea pigs—marched to nuclear explosion sites, with pilots then sent through the mushroom clouds; subjected to chemical and biological weapons experiments; radiation experiments; behavior modification experiments that washed their brains with LSD; exposure to the dioxin of Agent Orange in Korea and Vietnam...the list goes on...literally millions of experimental subjects, seldom given a choice or adequate information, often with disastrous effects to their physical and/or mental health, rarely with proper medical care or even monitoring.[2]

Proceeding now to the 1990s: Many thousands of American soldiers came home from the Gulf War with unusual, debilitating ailments. Exposure to harmful chemical or biological agents was suspected, but the Pentagon denied that this had occurred. Years went by while the GIs suffered terribly: neurological problems, chronic fatigue, skin problems, scarred lungs, memory loss, muscle and joint pain, severe headaches, personality changes, passing out, and much more. Eventually, the Pentagon, inch by inch, was forced to move away from its denials and admit that, yes, chemical weapon depots had been bombed; then, yes, there probably were releases of the deadly poisons; then, yes, American soldiers were indeed in the vicinity of these poisonous releases, 400 soldiers; then, it might have been 5,000; then, "a very large number", probably more than 15,000; then, finally, a precise number—20,867; then, "The Pentagon announced that a long- awaited computer model estimates that nearly 100,000 U.S. soldiers could have been exposed to trace amounts of sarin gas."[3]

Soldiers were also forced to take vaccines against anthrax and nerve gas not approved by the FDA as safe and effective, and punished, sometimes treated like criminals, if they refused. (During World War II, US soldiers were forced to take a yellow fever vaccine, with the result that some 330,000 of them were infected with the hepatitis B virus.[4]) Finally, in late 1999, almost nine years after the Gulf War's end, the Defense Department announced that a drug given to soldiers to protect them against a particular nerve gas, "cannot be ruled out" as a cause of lingering illnesses in some veterans.[5]

The Pentagon brass, moreover, did not warn American soldiers of the grave danger of being in close proximity to expended depleted uranium weapons on the battlefield. Depleted uranium is a radioactive metal associated with a long list of rare and gruesome illnesses and birth defects.

If the Pentagon had been much more forthcoming from the outset about what it knew all along about these various substances and weapons, the soldiers might have had a proper diagnosis early on and received appropriate care sooner. The cost in terms of human suffering was incalculable. One gauge of that cost may lie in the estimate that one-third of the homeless in America are military veterans.

This scenario is in danger of being repeated to a distressing degree for the veterans of the invasion of Afghanistan beginning in 2001 and Iraq two years later. Depleted uranium, for example, has again been widely used by the United States in both countries.

(See chapter 12.)

Soldiers serving in Iraq or their families have reported purchasing with their own funds bullet-proof vests, better armor for their vehicles, medical supplies, and global positioning devices, all for their own safety, which were not provided to them by the army.

And throughout all these years, and all these wars, the numerous complaints by servicewomen of sexual assault and rape at the hands of their male counterparts were routinely played down or ignored by the military brass..."boys will be boys".

The moral of this little slice of history is simple: If the United States government does not care about the health and welfare of its own soldiers, if American leaders are not moved by the prolonged pain and suffering of the wretched warriors they enlist to fight the empire's wars, how can it be argued, how can it be believed, that they care about foreign peoples? At all.

When the Dalai Lama was asked by a CIA officer in 1995: "Did we do a good or bad thing in providing this support [to the Tibetans]?", the Tibetan spiritual leader replied that though it helped the morale of those resisting the Chinese, "thousands of lives were lost in the resistance" and that "the U.S. Government had involved itself in his country's affairs not to help Tibet but only as a Cold War tactic to challenge the Chinese."[6]

"Let me tell you about the very rich," wrote F. Scott Fitzgerald. "They are different from you and me."

So are American leaders.

Consider Zbigniew Brzezinski, national security advisor to Jimmy Carter. In a 1998 interview he admitted that the official story that the US gave military aid to the Afghanistan opposition only *after* the Soviet invasion in 1979 was a lie. The truth was, he said, that the US began aiding the Islamic fundamentalist *moujahedeen* six months *before* the Russians made their move, even though he believed—and told this to Carter, who acted on it—that "this aid was going to induce a Soviet military intervention".

Brzezinski was asked whether he regretted this decision.

> Regret what? That secret operation was an excellent idea. It had the effect of drawing the Russians into the Afghan trap and you want me to regret it? The day that the Soviets officially crossed the border, I wrote to President Carter: We now have the opportunity of giving to the USSR its Vietnam War. Indeed, for almost 10 years, Moscow had to carry on a war unsupportable by the government, a conflict that brought about the demoralization and finally the breakup of the Soviet empire.[7]

Besides the fact that there is no demonstrable connection between the Afghanistan war and the breakup of the Soviet empire, we are faced with the consequences of that war: the defeat of a government committed to bringing the extraordinarily backward nation into the 20th century; the breathtaking carnage; *moujahedeen* torture that even US government officials called "indescribable horror"[8]; half the population either dead, disabled or refugees; the spawning of thousands of Islamic fundamentalist terrorists who have unleashed atrocities in numerous countries; and the astounding repression of women in Afghanistan, instituted by America's wartime allies.

And for playing a key role in causing all this, Zbigniew Brzezinski has no regrets. Regrets? The man is downright proud of it! The kindest thing one can say about such a person—as about a sociopath—is that he's amoral. At least in his public incarnation, which is all we're concerned with here. In medieval times he would have been known as Zbigniew the Terrible.

In the now-famous exchange on TV between Madeleine Albright and reporter Lesley Stahl, the latter was speaking of US sanctions against Iraq, and asked the then-US ambassador to the UN: "We have heard that a half million children have died. I mean, that's more children than died in Hiroshima. And—and you know, is the price worth it?"

Replied Albright: "I think this is a very hard choice, but the price—we think the price is worth it."[9]

One can give Albright the absolute full benefit of any doubt and say that she had no choice but to defend administration policy. But what kind of person is it that takes a job appointment knowing full well that she will be an integral part of such ongoing policies and will be expected to defend them without apology? It is a person who expects to be rewarded for such unquestioning loyalty. Not long afterwards, Albright was appointed Secretary of State.

Lawrence Summers, currently the president of Harvard, is another case in point. In December 1991, while chief economist for the World Bank, he wrote an internal memo saying that the Bank should encourage migration of "the dirty industries" to the less-developed countries because, amongst other reasons, health-impairing and death-causing pollution costs would be lower. Inasmuch as these costs are based on the lost earnings of the affected workers, in a country of very low wages the computed costs would be much lower. "I think," he wrote, "the economic logic behind dumping a load of toxic waste in the lowest-wage country is impeccable and we should face up to that."[10] Despite this memo receiving wide distribution and condemnation, in 1993 the Clinton administration appointed Summers Undersecretary of the Treasury, for international affairs no less, and then Secretary of the Treasury.

There's also President Clinton himself, who on day 33 of the aerial devastation of Yugoslavia—33 days and nights of destroying villages, schools, hospitals, apartment buildings, the ecology, separating people from their limbs, from their eyesight, spilling their intestines, traumatizing children for the rest of their days...destroying a life the Serbians may never know again—on day 33 William Jefferson Clinton, cautioning against judging the bombing policy prematurely, saw fit to declare: "This may seem like a long time. [But] I don't think that this air campaign has been going on a particularly long time."[11] And then the man continued it for another 45 days.

Clinton's vice president, Albert Gore, did not break new ground in moral leadership in 1999 when he played a leading role in putting great pressure on the South African government by threatening them with trade sanctions if they didn't cancel plans to produce or buy affordable generic AIDS drugs, which would cut into US companies' sales. South Africa, it should be noted, at the time had an estimated six million HIV-positive persons among its largely impoverished population. When Gore, who at the time had significant ties to the drug industry, was heckled for what he had done during a speech in New York, he declined to respond in substance, but instead called out: "I love this country. I love the First Amendment."[12]

Which brings us to the Bush administration: President George W., Vice-president Dick Cheney, Defense Secretary Donald Rumsfeld, Attorney General Alberto Gonzalez, and others of the imperial mafia, supporting, legalizing, covering up, and untroubled by, a hundred kinds of torture, brutality, and humiliation inflicted upon thousands of poor souls in Afghanistan, Iraq, and Guantánamo Base in Cuba; hundreds more taken by the CIA to other countries to be tortured.

Yes, American leaders are different from you and me.

No, the lesson here is not that power corrupts and dehumanizes.

Neither is it that US foreign policy is cruel because American leaders are cruel.

It's that these leaders are cruel because only those willing and able to be inordinately cruel and remorseless can hold positions of leadership in the foreign policy establishment; it might as well be written into the job description. People capable of expressing a full human measure of compassion and empathy toward faraway powerless strangers—let alone American soldiers—do not become president of the United States, or vice president, or secretary of state, or secretary of defense, or national security advisor, or attorney general, or secretary of the treasury. Nor do they particularly want to.

There's a sort of Peter Principle at work here. Laurence Peter wrote that in a hierarchy every employee tends to rise to his level of incompetence. Perhaps we can postulate that in a foreign policy establishment committed to imperialist domination by any means necessary, employees tend to rise to the level of cruelty they can't live with.

A few days after the bombing of Yugoslavia had ended, the *New York Times* published as its lead article in the Sunday Week in Review a piece by Michael Wines, which declared that "Human rights had been elevated to a military priority and a pre-eminent Western value.... The war only underscored the deep ideological divide between an idealistic New World bent on ending inhumanity and an Old World equally fatalistic about unending conflict.... there is also a yawning gap between the West and much of the world on the value of a single life."

And so on. A paean to the innate goodness of the West, an ethos unfortunately not shared by much of the rest of the world, who, Wines lamented, "just don't buy into Western notions of rights and responsibilities."[13] The *Times* fed us this morality tale after "the West" had just completed the most ferocious sustained bombing of a nation in the history of the planet, a small portion of whose dreadful consequences are referred to above.

During the American bombing of Iraq in 1991, the previous record for sustained ferociousness, a civilian air raid shelter was destroyed by a depleted-uranium projectile, incinerating to charred blackness many hundreds of people, a great number of them women and children. White House spokesman Marlin Fitzwater, reiterating US military statements that the shelter had been a command-and-control center, said: "We don't know why civilians were at that location, but we do know that Saddam Hussein does not share our value for the sanctity of human life."[14]

Similarly, during the Vietnam War, President Johnson and other government officials assured us that Asians don't have the same high regard for human life as Americans do. We were told this, of course, as American bombs, napalm, Agent Orange, and helicopter gunships were disintegrating the Vietnamese and their highly valued lives.

And at the same time, on a day in February 1966, David Lawrence, the editor of *US News & World Report*, was moved to put the following words to paper: "What the United States is doing in Vietnam is the most significant example of philanthropy extended by one people to another that we have witnessed in our times."[15]

I sent Mr. Lawrence a copy of a well-done pamphlet entitled *American Atrocities in Vietnam*, which gave graphic detail of its subject. To this I attached a note which first repeated Lawrence's quotation with his name below it, then added: "*One* of us is crazy.", followed by *my* name.

Lawrence responded with a full page letter, at the heart of which was: "I think a careful reading of it [the pamphlet] will prove the point I was trying to make—namely that primitive peoples with savagery in their hearts have to be helped to understand the true basis of a civilized existence."

The American mind—as exemplified by that of Michael Wines and David Lawrence—is, politically, so deeply formed that to liberate it would involve uncommon, and as yet perhaps undiscovered, philosophical and surgical skill. The great majority of Americans, even the most cynical—who need no convincing that the words that come out of a politician's mouth are a blend of mis-, dis- and non-information, and should always carry a veracity health warning—appear to lose their critical faculties when confronted by "our boys who are risking their lives". If love is blind, patriotism has lost all five senses.

To the extent that the cynicism of these Americans—and their counterparts in the media—is directed toward their government's habitual foreign adventures, it's to question whether the administration's stated interpretation of a situation is valid, whether the stated goals are worthwhile, and whether the stated goals can be achieved—but *not* to question the government's *motivation*. It is assumed *a priori* that their leaders *mean well* by the foreign people involved—no matter how much death, destruction and suffering their policies objectively result in.

Congressman Otis Pike (R-NY) headed a committee in 1975 which uncovered a number of dark covert actions of US foreign policy, many of which were leaked to the public, while others remained secret. In an interview he stated that any member of Congress could see the entire report if he agreed not to reveal anything that was in it. "But not many want to read it," he added.

"Why?" asked his interviewer.

"Oh, they think it is better not to know," Pike replied. "There are too many things that embarrass Americans in that report. You see, this country went through an awful trauma with Watergate. But even then, all they were asked to believe was that their president had been a bad person. In this new situation they are asked much more; they are asked to believe that their country has been evil. And nobody wants to believe that."[16]

This can be compared to going to a counselor because your child is behaving strangely, and being told, "You have a problem of incest in your family." People can't hear that. They go to a different counselor. They grab at any other explanation. It's too painful.

An American education

In *The History of the Peloponnesian War*, Thucydides, speaking of the practice of plundering villages, the main source of a warrior's livelihood, tells us that "no disgrace was yet attached to such an achievement, but rather credit".

Almost all of us grew up in an environment in which we learned that thou shalt not murder, rape, rob, probably not pay off a public official or cheat on your taxes—but not that there was anything wrong with toppling foreign governments, quashing revolutions, or dropping powerful bombs on foreign people, if it somehow served America's "national security".

Let us look at some of our teachers. During the bombing of Yugoslavia, the esteemed (= famous) CBS News reporter, Dan Rather, declared: "I'm an American, and I'm an American reporter. And yes, when there's combat involving Americans, you can criticize me if you must, damn me if you must, but I'm always pulling for us to win."[17] (During the Cold War, US journalists were quick to criticize their Soviet counterparts for speaking in behalf of the State.)

What does this mean? That he's going to support any war effort by the United States no matter the legal or moral justification? No matter the effect on democracy, freedom or self-determination? No matter the degree of horror produced? No matter *anything*? Many other American journalists have similarly paraded themselves as cheerleaders in modern times in the midst of one of the Pentagon's frequent marches down the warpath, serving a function "more akin to stenography than journalism".[18] During these wars, much of the media, led by CNN, appear to have had a serious missile fetish, enough so to suggest a need for counseling.

The president of National Public Radio (NPR), Kevin Klose, is the former head of all the major, worldwide US government broadcast propaganda outlets, including Voice of America, Radio

Free Europe, Radio Liberty, and the anti-Castro Radio Marti, which broadcasts into Cuba from Florida. NPR, it can be said, has never met an American war it didn't like. It was inspired to describe the war against Yugoslavia as Clinton's "most significant foreign policy success."[19]

And Robert Coonrod—from 1997-2004 the head of the congressionally-created Corporation for Public Broadcasting, which funds over 1,000 public television and radio stations nationwide—has a résumé remarkably similar to that of Klose, from Voice of America to Radio Marti.

Is it any wonder that during America's wars NPR has one military officer after another on the air offering commentary but virtually never anyone unambiguously opposed to the war? Moreover, is it any wonder that countless Americans, bearing psyches no less malleable than those of other members of the species, are only dimly conscious of the fact that they even have the *right* to be unequivocally against a war effort and to question the government's real intentions for carrying it out, without thinking of themselves as (horror of horrors) "unpatriotic"? Propaganda is to a democracy what violence is to a dictatorship.

In Spain, in the 16th century, the best minds were busy at work devising rationalizations for the cruelty its conquistadors were inflicting upon the Indians of the New World. It was decided, and commonly accepted, that the Indians were "natural slaves", created by God to serve the conquistadors.

Twentieth-century America took this a step further. The best and the brightest have assured the public that United States interventions—albeit rather violent at times—are not only in the natural order of things, but they're actually for the *good* of the natives.

The media and the public do in fact relish catching politicians' lies, but these are typically the small lies—lies about money, sex, drug use, and other peccadillos, and the ritual doubletalk of campaignspeak. A certain Mr. A. Hitler, originally of Austria, though often castigated, actually arrived at a number of very perceptive insights into how the world worked. One of them was this:

> The great masses of the people in the very bottom of their hearts tend to be corrupted rather than consciously and purposely evil...therefore, in view of the primitive simplicity of their minds, they more easily fall a victim to a big lie than to a little one, since they themselves lie in little things, but would be ashamed of lies that were too big.[20]

The big lies tend to elude exposure. How many Americans, for example, doubt the official rationale for dropping the A-bomb on Hiroshima and Nagasaki—to obviate the need for a land invasion of Japan, thus saving thousands of American lives? However, it's been known for years that the Japanese had been trying for many months to surrender and that the US had consistently ignored these overtures. The bombs were dropped, not to intimidate the Japanese, but to put the fear of the American god into the Russians. The dropping of the A-bomb, it has been said, was not the last shot of World War II, but the first shot of the Cold War.[21]

Altruistic America

The "humanitarian" bombing of Yugoslavia in 1999, which even many on the left swallowed without gagging, or the "liberation" of Iraq in 2003, which most on the left saw through, but most Americans did not at first, are two recent examples of the idea of United States "altruism", which has been a recurrent feature of America's love affair with itself. From 1918 to 1920, the United States was a major part of a Western invasion of the infant Soviet Union, an invasion that endeavored to "strangle at its birth", as Winston Churchill put it, the Russian Revolution, which had effectively removed one-sixth of the world's land surface from private capitalist development. A nation still recovering from a horrendous world war, in extreme chaos from a fundamental social revolution, and in the throes of a famine that was to leave many millions dead, was mercilessly devastated yet further by the invaders, without any provocation, aiming to put the "White Russians" in power in place of the Red ones.

When the smoke had cleared, the US Army Chief of Staff put out a report on the undertaking which said: "This expedition affords one of the finest examples in history of honorable, unselfish dealings...to be helpful to a people struggling to achieve a new liberty."[22]

Seventy years later, the Chairman of the Joint Chiefs of Staff, General Colin Powell, was moved to tell an audience in California that the United States has "so many friends" in the Pacific because of "our values, our economic system, and our altruism".[23] He made these remarks shortly after directing the slaughter by bombing of a multitude of Panamanian innocents.

In his inauguration speech of January 2005, which lasted 21 minutes, President George W. Bush used the word "liberty" 15 times and the word "freedom" 27 times; that's one or the other word casually dropped exactly once every 30 seconds, as he assured the world that America's interventions were fueled only by the deeply-felt desire to bring these blessings to one country after another.

Author Garry Wills has commented on this American benevolence toward foreigners: "We believe we can literally 'kill them with kindness', moving our guns forward in a seizure of demented charity. It is when America is in her most altruistic mood that other nations better get behind their bunkers."

What is it, then, that I mean to say here—that the US government does not care a *whit* about human life, human rights, humanity, and all those other wonderful human things?

No, I mean to say that doing the right thing is not a *principle* of American foreign policy, not an ideal or a goal of policy in and of itself. If it happens that doing the right thing coincides with, or is irrelevant to, Washington's overriding international ambitions, American officials have no problem walking the high moral ground. But this is rarely the case. A study of the many US interventions detailed in the "Interventions" chapter, shows clearly that the engine of American foreign policy has typically been fueled not by a devotion to any kind of morality, nor even simple decency, but rather by the necessity to serve other masters, which can be broken down to three imperatives:

1)   the care and feeding of American corporations: making the world open and hospitable for neo-liberal globalization; enhancing the financial statements of defense contractors who have contributed generously to members of Congress and residents of the White House;

2)   preventing the rise of any society that might serve as a successful example of an alternative to the capitalist model;

3)   expanding the empire: establishing political, economic and military hegemony over as much of the globe as possible to facilitate the first two imperatives, and to prevent the ascendancy of any regional power that might challenge American supremacy.

To American policymakers, these ends have justified the means, and all means have been available.[24]

In the wake of the 1973 military coup in Chile, which overthrew the socialist government of Salvador Allende, the Assistant Secretary of State for Inter-American Affairs, Jack Kubisch, was hard pressed to counter charges that the United States had been involved. "It was not in our interest to have the military take over in Chile," he insisted. "It would have been better had Allende served his entire term, taking the nation and the

Chilean people into complete and total ruin. Only then would the full discrediting of socialism have taken place. Only then would people have gotten the message that socialism doesn't work. What has happened has confused this lesson."[25]

Though based on a falsehood made up for the occasion—that Allende's polices were leading Chile to ruin—Kubisch's remark inadvertently expressed his government's strong fealty to the second imperative stated above.

Enemies without number, threats without end

During the Cold War, US foreign policy was carried out under the waving banner of fighting a moral crusade against what cold warriors persuaded the American people, most of the world, and perhaps themselves, was the existence of a malevolent International Communist Conspiracy. But it was always a fraud; there was never any such animal as the International Communist Conspiracy. There were, as there still are, people living in misery, rising up in protest against their condition, against an oppressive government, a government likely supported by the United States. To Washington, this was proof that the Soviet Union (or Cuba or Nicaragua, etc., functioning as Moscow's surrogate), or China, was again acting as the proverbial "outside agitator".

In the final analysis, this must be wondered: What kind of omnipresent, omnipotent, monolithic, evil international conspiracy bent on world domination would allow its empire to completely fall apart, like the classic house of cards, without bringing any military force to bear upon its satellites to prevent their escaping? And without an invasion from abroad holding a knife to the empire's throat?

It is now well known how during the Cold War the actual level of Soviet military and economic strength was magnified by the CIA, the Defense Department, the White House, et al., how data and events were falsified to exaggerate the Russian threat, how worst-case scenarios were put forth as if they were probable and imminent, even when they failed to meet the demands of plausibility.[26] One of the most enduring Soviet-threat stories— the alleged justification for the birth of NATO—was the coming Red invasion of Western Europe. If, by 1999, anyone still swore by this fairy tale, they could have read a report in *The Guardian* of London on newly declassified British government documents from 1968. Among the documents was one based on an analysis by the Foreign Office joint intelligence committee, which the newspaper summarized as follows:

> The Soviet Union had no intention of launching a military attack on the West at the height of the cold war, British military and intelligence chiefs privately believed, in stark contrast to what Western politicians and military leaders were saying in public about the "Soviet threat".
>
> "The Soviet Union will not deliberately start general war or even limited war in Europe," a briefing for the British chiefs of staff—marked Top Secret, UK Eyes Only, and headed The Threat: Soviet Aims and Intentions—declared in June 1968.
>
> "Soviet foreign policy had been cautious and realistic", the department argued, and despite the Vietnam war, the Russians and their allies had "continued to make contacts in all fields with the West and to maintain a limited but increasing political dialogue with Nato powers".[27]

After the Cold War, Washington spinmeisters could no longer cry "The Russians are coming, and they're ten feet tall!" as a pretext for intervention, so they have had to regularly come up with new enemies. America cherishes its enemies. Without enemies, it appears to be a nation without moral purpose and direction. The various managers of the National Security State need enemies to protect their jobs, to justify their swollen budgets, to aggrandize their work, to give themselves a mission in the aftermath of the Soviet Union, to send truckloads of taxpayer money to the corporations for whom the managers will go to work after leaving government service. And they understand the need for enemies only too well, even painfully. Presented here is US Col. Dennis Long, speaking in 1992, shortly after the end of the Cold War, when he was director of "total armor force readiness" at Fort Knox:

> For 50 years, we equipped our football team, practiced five days a week and never played a game. We had a clear enemy with demonstrable qualities, and we had scouted them out. [Now] we will have to practice day in and day out without knowing anything about the other team. We won't have his playbook, we won't know where the stadium is, or how many guys he will have on the field. That is very distressing to the military establishment, especially when you are trying to justify the existence of your organization and your systems.[28]

The United States had postponed such a distressing situation for as long as it could. A series of Soviet requests during the Cold War to establish a direct dialogue with senior NATO officials were rejected as "inappropriate and potentially divisive". Longstanding and repeated Soviet offers to dissolve the Warsaw Pact if the West would do the same with NATO were ignored.[29] After one such offer was spurned, the *Los Angeles Times* commented that the offer "increases the difficulty faced by U.S. policy-makers in persuading Western public opinion to continue expensive and often unpopular military programs."[30]

In 1991, Colin Powell touched upon the irony of the profound world changes in cautioning his fellow military professionals: "We must not...hope that it [the changes] will disappear and let us return to comforting thoughts about a resolute and evil enemy."[31]

But the thoughts are indeed comforting to the military

professionals and their civilian counterparts. So since the end of the Cold War, one month the new resolute and evil enemy has been North Korea, the next month the big threat is Libya, then China, or Iraq, or Iran, or Sudan, or Syria, or Afghanistan, or Serbia, or that old reliable demon, Cuba—countries each led by the newest Hitler, or at least a madman or mad dog; a degree of demonizing fit more for a theocratic society than a democratic one.

And in place of the International Communist Conspiracy, Washington has told the American people, on one day or another, that they're threatened by drug trafficking, or military or industrial spying, or the proliferation of "weapons of mass destruction", or organized crime, or, the latest flavor of the month, terrorism.

Moreover, in August 1999, a National Security Council global strategy paper for the next century declared that "the nation is facing its biggest espionage threat in history."[32]

A remarkable statement. What ever happened to the KGB? Any Americans now past the age of 30 had it drilled into their heads from the cradle on that there was a perpetual Soviet dagger aimed at their collective heart in the hand of the spy next door. Thousands lost their jobs and careers because of their alleged association to this threat, hundreds were imprisoned or deported, two were executed. Surely Senator Joe McCarthy and J. Edgar Hoover are turning over in their graves.

The whole aim of practical politics is to keep the populace alarmed (and hence clamorous to be led to safety) by an endless series of hobgoblins, most of them imaginary.

H.L. Mencken, 1920[33]

Our government has kept us in a perpetual state of fear— kept us in a continuous stampede of patriotic fervor— with the cry of grave national emergency. Always there has been some terrible evil at home or some monstrous foreign power that was going to gobble us up if we did not blindly rally behind it by furnishing the exorbitant funds demanded. Yet, in retrospect, these disasters seem never to have happened, seem never to have been quite real.

General Douglas MacArthur, 1957[34]

September 11, 2001

In light of what happened on this infamous date it may appear to some that the threats to the United States claimed by Washington officials were not in fact exaggerated, but rather were very real. But it is not the intention of the above text to imply that there never was or never will be a serious terrorist attack inside the United States. Given the constant belligerence and destructiveness of US foreign policy, retaliation has to be expected, at one time or another, at one place or another, in one form or another. (Chapter one deals with precisely this cause and effect.) But with all the scare talk issued by American administrations, what exactly has taken place in the real world? According to the State Department, in the six-year period of 1998-2003 the number of actual terrorist attacks by region was as follows:

Latin America 692, Asia 468, Western Europe 222, Middle East 208, Africa 174, Eurasia 93, North America 6.[35]

For more than forty years the "imminent threat" of a Soviet invasion of Western Europe or nuclear attack upon the United States was drummed into the American consciousness. Nothing of the sort ever happened of course. Nothing of the sort was ever seriously contemplated by the Soviets of course, for obvious reasons of self-preservation if nothing else. Then, with the demise of the Soviet Union, as elucidated above, multiple new "threats" to American security were declared by officials, and echoed by the media, to heighten the sense of danger and validate the replacement of the American republic by the national security state.

The attack of September 11 does not justify a half century of cynical propaganda.

After the attack it was Christmas every day for the national security managers. All their wish lists were fulfilled, and then some. In short order they massively increased the military budget; imposed sharp cutbacks in social spending; promoted obscenely extensive tax breaks for the wealthiest individuals and corporations; launched efforts to cut back on environmental legislation; unilaterally abrogated a leading arms control treaty; announced plans which would extend the reach of The American Empire, under the rubric of an "anti-terrorism crusade", to Afghanistan, Iraq, Iran, Somalia, North Korea, Syria, Sudan, and elsewhere; created a new Office of Homeland Security; greatly increased surveillance and prosecutory powers over the American people, including license to enter their homes virtually at will; rescinded virtually all legal rights for over a thousand people who were incarcerated for weeks or months, even years, without being charged with a crime; created an atmosphere in which many critics of the bombing and invasion of Afghanistan and Iraq suffered professional punishment and were called upon to prove their loyalty; and so it went.

What has taken place in the United States since the attack is a state of affairs much desired by the political and corporate elite. Indeed, it lends credence to the proposition that the purpose of all the fear mongering was what critics had always charged: to facilitate fulfilling wish lists.

Cold War continuum

Though the putative "communist threat" has disappeared, the taxpayers still fill tractor-trailers to the bursting with cash and send them off to what had once been known as the War Department, then humorously renamed the Defense Department.... That department's research into yet more futuristic weapons of the chemical dust and better ways to kill people en masse proceeds unabated, with nary a glance back at the body fragments littering the triumphant fields.... Belief in an afterlife has been rekindled by the Clinton and Bush administrations new missile defense system, after universal certainty that Star Wars was dead and buried.... NATO has also risen from the should-be- dead, more almighty than ever.... Many hundreds of US military installations, serving a vast panoply of specialized warfaring needs, still dot the global map, including many new ones in the territory of the former Soviet Union and Eastern Europe.... Even as you read this, American armed forces and special operations forces are being deployed in well over 100 countries in every part of the world.... Washington is supplying many of these nations with sizeable amounts of highly lethal military equipment, and training their armed forces and police in the brutal arts, regardless of how brutal they already are.... American nuclear bombs are still stored in a number of European countries, if not elsewhere...And American officials retain their unshakable belief that they have a god-given right to do whatever they want, wherever they want, to whomever they want, for as long as they want.

In other words, whatever the diplomats and policymakers at the time thought they were doing, the Cold War skeptics have been vindicated—it was not about containing an evil, expansionist, communist Soviet Union after all; it was about American imperialism, with "communist" merely the name given to those who stood in its way.

American foreign-policy makers are exquisitely attuned to the rise of a government, or a movement on the verge of taking power, that will not lie down and happily become an American client state, that will not look upon the free market or the privatization of the world known as "globalization" as the *summum bonum*, that will not change its laws to favor foreign investment, that will not be unconcerned about the effects of foreign investment upon the welfare of its own people, that will not produce primarily for export, that will not allow asbestos, banned pesticides, and other products restricted in the developed world to be dumped onto their people, that will not easily tolerate the International Monetary Fund, the World Bank, or the World Trade Organization inflicting a scorched-earth policy upon the country's social services and standard of living, that will not allow an American or NATO military installation upon its soil...To the highly-sensitive nostrils of Washington foreign-policy veterans, Yugoslavia in the 1990s smelled a bit too much like one of these governments.

Given the proper pretext, such bad examples have to be reduced to basket cases; or, where feasible, simply overthrown, like Albania and Bulgaria in the early 1990s; failing that, life has to be made impossible for these renegades, as with Cuba, still.

And this was the foundation—the *sine qua non*—of American foreign policy for the entire twentieth century, both before and after the existence of the Soviet Union, from the Philippines, Panama and the Dominican Republic in the first decade of the century, to El Salvador, Nicaragua, and Yugoslavia in the last decade.

Can we in fact say that the Cold War has actually ended? If the Cold War is defined as a worldwide struggle between the United States and the Soviet Union for the hearts and minds of the Third World (for whatever motives), then certainly it is over. But if the Cold War is seen not as an East-West struggle, but rather a "North-South" struggle, as an American effort—as mentioned above—to prevent the rise of any society that might serve as a successful example of an alternative to the capitalist model, and to prevent the rise of any regional power that might challenge American supremacy, then that particular map with the pins stuck in it still hangs on the wall in the Pentagon's War Room. (Said a

Defense Department planning paper in 1992: "Our first objective is to prevent the re-emergence of a new rival...we must maintain the mechanisms for deterring potential competitors from even *aspiring* to a larger regional or global role."[36] [emphasis added])

The current manifestation of this continuum, by whatever name, can be viewed as yet another chapter in the never-ending saga of the war of the rich upon the poor. And with the Soviet presence and influence gone, American interventions are more trouble-free than ever. (Consider that US friendliness toward Iraq and Yugoslavia lasted exactly as long as the Soviet Union and its bloc existed.)

There's a word for such a continuum of policy. Empire. The American Empire. An appellation that does not roll easily off an American tongue. No American has any difficulty believing in the existence and driving passion for expansion, power, glory, and wealth of the Roman Empire, the Ottoman Empire, the Austro- Hungarian Empire, or the British Empire. It's right there in their schoolbooks. But to the American mind, to American schoolbooks, and to the American media, "The American Empire" is an oxymoron. However, the invasion of Afghanistan and Iraq, the open threats made to several other countries, and a hundred instances of shameless arrogance emanating from the Bush administration has begun to make the label of "empire" more plausible to the media; some Americans are becoming rather proud of the idea.

The Madman philosophy

In March 1998, an internal 1995 study, "Essentials of Post-Cold War Deterrence", by the US Strategic Command, the headquarters responsible for the US strategic nuclear arsenal, was brought to light. The study stated:

> Because of the value that comes from the ambiguity of what

the US may do to an adversary if the acts we seek to deter are carried out, it hurts to portray ourselves as too fully rational and cool-headed. The fact that some elements may appear to be potentially 'out of control' can be beneficial to creating and reinforcing fears and doubts within the minds of an adversary's decision makers. This essential sense of fear is the working force of deterrence. That the US may become irrational and vindictive if its vital interests are attacked should be a part of the national persona we project to all adversaries.[37]

The author of these words would have the world believe that the United States has only been pretending to be "out of control" or "irrational and vindictive". However, it can be argued—based on the objective facts of what Washington has inflicted upon the world, as described in this book—that for more than half a century American foreign policy has, in actuality, been clinically mad.

On the other hand, the desire for world hegemony, per se, is not necessarily irrational, whatever else one may think of it morally or otherwise. Author Michael Parenti has pointed out that US foreign policy "may seem stupid because the rationales offered in its support often sound unconvincing, leaving us with the impression that policymakers are confused or out of touch. But just because the public does not understand what they are doing does not mean that national security leaders are themselves befuddled. That they are fabricators does not mean they are fools."[38]

A Truth Commission

Since the early 1990s the people of South Africa, Argentina, Guatemala, Chile and El Salvador have held official Truth Commissions to look squarely in the eyes of the crimes committed by their governments. There will never be any such official body to investigate and document the wide body of Washington's crimes, although several unofficial citizens' commissions have done so over the years for specific interventions, such as in Vietnam, Panama, Afghanistan, and Iraq; their findings were of course totally ignored by the establishment media (whose ideology is a belief that it doesn't have any ideology).

In the absence of an official Truth Commission in the United States, this book is offered up as testimony.

Washington, DC
May 2005

PART I

Ours and Theirs: Washington's Love/Hate Relationship With Terrorists and Human-Rights Violators

Chapter 1

Why Do Terrorists Keep Picking on the United States?

The notion that terrorist acts against the United States can be explained by envy and irrational hatred, and not by what the United States does to the world—i.e., US foreign policy—has been written on the face of the Bush administration ever since the attacks of September 11, 2001.

The fires were still burning at Ground Zero in New York when Secretary of State Colin Powell declared: "Once again, we see terrorism, we see terrorists, people who don't believe in democracy."[1]

President Bush picked up on that theme and ran with it. He's been its leading proponent with his repeated insistence, in one wording or another, that terrorists are people who hate America and all that it stands for, its democracy, its freedom, its wealth, its secular government. (Ironically, the president and his first Attorney General, John Ashcroft, probably hate America's secular government as much as anyone.)

Here is the president more than a year after September 11: "The threats we face are global terrorist attacks. That's the threat. And the more you love freedom, the more likely it is you'll be attacked."[2]

The American Council of Trustees and Alumni, a conservative watchdog group founded by Lynne Cheney, wife of the vice- president, announced in November 2001 the formation of the Defense of Civilization Fund, declaring that "It was not only America that was attacked on September 11, but civilization. We were attacked not for our vices, but for our virtues."[3]

In September 2002, the White House released the "National Security Strategy", purported to be chiefly the handiwork of

Condoleezza Rice, which speaks of the "rogue states" which "sponsor terrorism around the globe; and reject basic human values and hate the United States and everything for which it stands."

In July of the following year, we could hear the spokesman for Homeland Security, Brian Roehrkasse, declare: "Terrorists hate our freedoms. They want to change our ways."[4]

And in his January 2005 inauguration address, the president spoke of the threat to the United States: "We have seen our vulnerability—and we have seen its deepest source. For as long as whole regions of the world simmer in resentment and tyranny, prone to ideologies that feed hatred and excuse murder, violence will gather." Not a single word in his talk about anything the United States has ever done to contribute to this resentment and hatred. It's just there in the anti-American terrorists, perhaps in their genes.

To all of this, Thomas Friedman the renowned foreign policy analyst of the New York Times would say *amen*. Terrorists, he wrote in 1998 after two US embassies in Africa had been attacked, "have no specific ideological program or demands. Rather, they are driven by a generalized hatred of the US, Israel and other supposed enemies of Islam."[5]

This *idée fixe*—that the rise of anti-American terrorism owes nothing to American policies—in effect postulates an America that is always the aggrieved innocent in a treacherous world, a benign United States government peacefully going about its business but being "provoked" into taking extreme measures to defend its people, its freedom and its democracy. It follows from this idea that there's no good reason to modify US foreign policy, no choice but to battle to the death this irrational international force out there that hates the United States with an abiding passion.

Thus it was that Afghanistan and Iraq were bombed and invaded with seemingly little concern in Washington that this could well create many new anti-American terrorists. And indeed, following the first strike on Afghanistan in October 2001 there were literally scores of terrorist attacks against American institutions in the Middle East, South Asia and the Pacific, more than a dozen in Pakistan alone: military, civilian, Christian, and other targets associated with the United States, including the October 2002 bombings in Bali, Indonesia, which destroyed two nightclubs and killed more than 200 people, almost all of them Americans and their Australian and British allies. The following year brought the heavy bombing of the US-managed Marriott Hotel in Jakarta, Indonesia, the site of diplomatic receptions and 4th of July celebrations held by the American Embassy; all this in addition to the thousands of attacks in Iraq against US occupation.

Even when a terrorist attack is not aimed directly at Americans, the reason the target has been chosen can be because the country it takes place in has been cooperating with the United States in its so-called "War on Terrorism". Witness the horrendous attacks of recent years in Madrid, Turkey and Saudi Arabia.

A US State Department report on worldwide terrorist attacks—"Patterns of Global Terrorism"—showed that the year 2003 had more "significant terrorist incidents" than at any time since the department began issuing statistics in 1985, even though the figures did not include attacks on US troops by insurgents in Iraq, which the Bush administration explicitly labels as "terrorist".[6] When the 2004 report showed an even higher number of incidents, the State Department announced that it was going to stop publishing the annual statistics.[7]

Terrorists in their own words

The word "terrorism" has been so overused in recent years that it's now commonly used simply to stigmatize any individual or group one doesn't like, for almost any kind of behavior involving force. But the word's *raison d'être* has traditionally been to convey a political meaning, something along the lines of: the deliberate use of violence against civilians and property to intimidate or coerce a government or the population in furtherance of a political objective.

Terrorism is fundamentally propaganda, a very bloody form of making the world hear one's jeremiad.

It follows that if the perpetrators of a terrorist act declare what their objective was, their statement should carry credibility, no matter what one thinks of the objective or the method used to achieve it. Let us look at some of their actual declarations.

The terrorists responsible for the bombing of the World Trade Center in 1993 sent a letter to the *New York Times* which stated, in part: "We declare our responsibility for the explosion on the mentioned building. This action was done in response for the American political, economical, and military support to Israel the state of terrorism and to the rest of the dictator countries in the region."[8]

Richard Reid, who tried to ignite a bomb in his shoe while aboard an American Airline flight to Miami in December 2001, told police that his planned suicide attack was an attempt to strike a blow against the US campaign in Afghanistan and the Western economy. In an e-mail sent to his mother, which he intended her to read after his death, Reid wrote that it was his duty "to help remove the oppressive American forces from the Muslims land."[9]

After the bombings in Bali, one of the leading suspects, who was later convicted, told police that the bombings were "revenge" for "what Americans have done to Muslims." He said that he wanted to "kill as many Americans as possible" because "America oppresses the Muslims".[10]

In November 2002, a taped message from Osama bin Laden began: "The road to safety begins by ending the aggression. Reciprocal treatment is part of justice. The [terrorist] incidents that have taken place...are only reactions and reciprocal actions."[11]

That same month, when Mir Aimal Kasi (or Kansi), who killed several people outside of CIA headquarters in 1993, was on death row, he declared: "What I did was a retaliation against the US government" for American policy in the Middle East and its support of Israel.[12]

In June 2004, Islamic militants in Saudi Arabia beheaded an employee of the leading US defense contractor, Lockheed Martin, maker of the Apache helicopter, on which the victim, Paul Johnson, Jr. had long worked. His kidnappers said he was singled out for that reason. "The infidel got his fair treatment.... Let him taste something of what Muslims have long tasted from Apache helicopter fire and missiles."[13]

Finally, we have another audio message from Osama bin Laden, in April 2004, containing the following excerpts:

> The greatest rule of safety is justice, and stopping injustice and aggression.... What happened on 11 September and 11 March [the Madrid train bombings] is your commodity that was returned to you.... we would like to inform you that labeling us and our acts as terrorism is also a description of you and of your acts.... Our acts are reaction to your own acts, which are represented by the destruction and killing of our kinfolk in Afghanistan, Iraq and Palestine.... Which religion considers your killed ones innocent and our killed ones worthless? And which principle considers your blood real blood and our blood water? Reciprocal treatment is fair and the one who starts injustice bears greater blame.... The killing of the Russians was after their invasion of Afghanistan and Chechnya; the killing of Europeans was after their invasion of Iraq and Afghanistan; and the killing of Americans on the day of New York was after their support of the Jews in Palestine and their invasion of the Arabian Peninsula.[14]

Difficulty of maintaining the simplistic *idée fixe*

It should be noted that when Mir Aimal Kasi was executed, the State Department warned that this could result in attacks against Americans around the world.[15] It did not warn that the attacks would result from foreigners hating or envying American democracy, freedom, wealth, or secular government.

In the days following the start of the American bombing of Afghanistan there were numerous warnings from US government officials about being prepared for retaliatory acts, and during the war in Iraq, the State Department announced: "Tensions remaining from the recent events in Iraq may increase the potential threat to US citizens and interests abroad, including by terrorist groups."[16]

Similarly, in June 2002, after a car bomb exploded outside the US Consulate in Karachi, killing or injuring more than 60 people, the *Washington Post* reported that "US officials said the attack was likely the work of extremists angry at both the United States and Pakistan's president, Gen. Pervez Musharraf, for siding with the United States after September 11 and abandoning support for Afghanistan's ruling Taliban."[17]

George W. and others of his administration may or may not believe what they tell the world about the motivations behind anti-American terrorism, but, as in the examples just given, some officials, at least in effect, have questioned the party line for years. A Department of Defense study in 1997 concluded: "Historical data show a strong correlation between US involvement in international situations and an increase in terrorist attacks against the United States."[18]

Former US president Jimmy Carter told the *New York Times* in a 1989 interview:

> We sent Marines into Lebanon and you only have to go
> to Lebanon, to Syria or to Jordan to witness first-hand the

intense hatred among many people for the United States because we bombed and shelled and unmercifully killed totally innocent villagers—women and children and farmers and housewives—in those villages around Beirut.... As a result of that...we became kind of a Satan in the minds of those who are deeply resentful. That is what precipitated the taking of our hostages and that is what has precipitated some of the terrorist attacks.[19]

Colin Powell has also revealed that he knows better. Writing of this same 1983 Lebanon debacle in his memoir, he foregoes clichés about terrorists hating democracy: "The U.S.S. *New Jersey* started hurling 16-inch shells into the mountains above Beirut, in World War II style, as if we were softening up the beaches on some Pacific atoll prior to an invasion. What we tend to overlook in such situations is that other people will react much as we would."[20]

The ensuing terrorist attack against US Marine barracks in Lebanon took the lives of 241 American military personnel.

Hostile foreign policy, a list

The bombardment of Beirut in 1983 and 1984 is but one of many examples of American violence or other outrage against the Middle East and/or Muslims since the 1980s. The record includes:

- the support of corrupt and tyrannical Middle East governments, from the Shah of Iran to the Saudis

- the support for Russia and China against their Muslim populations

- the shooting down of two Libyan planes in 1981

- the bombing of Libya in 1986

- the bombing and sinking of an Iranian ship in 1987

- the shooting down of an Iranian passenger plane in 1988

- the shooting down of two more Libyan planes in 1989
- the massive bombing of the Iraqi people in 1991
- the continuing bombings and horrific sanctions against Iraq from 1991 to 2003
- the bombing of Afghanistan and Sudan in 1998
- the habitual support of Israel despite the routine devastation and torture it inflicts upon the Palestinian people
- the habitual condemnation of Palestinian resistance to this
- the abduction of "suspected terrorists" from Muslim countries, such as Malaysia, Pakistan, Lebanon and Albania, who are then taken to places like Egypt and Saudi Arabia, where they are tortured
- the large military and hi-tech presence in Islam's holiest land, Saudi Arabia, and elsewhere in the Persian Gulf region
- the devastation and occupation of Afghanistan beginning in 2001 and of Iraq beginning in 2003

"How do I respond when I see that in some Islamic countries there is vitriolic hatred for America?" asked George W. "I'll tell you how I respond: I'm amazed. I'm amazed that there's such misunderstanding of what our country is about that people would hate us. I am—like most Americans, I just can't believe it because I know how good we are."[21]

It's not just people in the Middle East who have good reason for hating what the US government does. The United States has created huge numbers of potential terrorists all over Latin America during a half century of American actions far worse than what it's done in the Middle East. If Latin Americans shared the belief of radical Muslims that they will go directly to paradise for martyring themselves in the act of killing the great Satan enemy, by now we might have had decades of repeated terrorist horror coming from south of the border.

As it is, there have been numerous non-suicidal terrorist attacks against Americans and their buildings in Latin America over the years.

To what extent do the American people really believe the official disconnect between what the US does in the world and anti-American terrorism? One indication that the public is somewhat skeptical came in the days immediately following the commencement of the bombing of Iraq on March 20, 2003. The airlines later announced that there had been a sharp increase in cancellations of flights and a sharp decrease in future flight reservations in those few days.[22]

How the Muslim world sees the United States

In June, 2003 the Pew Research Center released the results of polling in 20 Muslim countries and the Palestinian territories that brought into question the official thesis that support for anti-American terrorism goes hand in hand with hatred of American society. The polling revealed that people interviewed had much more "confidence" in Osama bin Laden than in George W. Bush. However, "the survey suggested little correlation between support for bin Laden and hostility to American ideas and cultural products. People who expressed a favorable opinion of bin Laden were just as likely to appreciate American technology and cultural products as people opposed to bin Laden. Pro- and anti- bin Laden respondents also differed little in their views on the workability of Western-style democracy in the Arab world."[23]

After another year of US occupation of Iraq and torture scandals, polling results unsurprisingly offered Washington no more support for its claims. A June, 2004 Zogby International survey of men and women in Saudi Arabia, Egypt, Jordan,

Lebanon, Morocco and the United Arab Emirates produced results such as the following, reported the *Washington Post*:

> Those polled said their opinions were shaped by U.S. policies, rather than by values or culture. When asked: 'What is the first thought when you hear "America?" respondents overwhelmingly said: 'Unfair foreign policy.' And when asked what the United States could do to improve its image in the Arab world, the most frequently provided answers were 'Stop supporting Israel' and 'Change your Middle East policy'.... Most Arabs polled said they believe that the Iraq war has caused more terrorism and brought about less democracy, and that the Iraqi people are far worse off today than they were while living under Hussein's rule. The majority also said they believe the United States invaded Iraq for oil, to protect Israel and to weaken the Muslim world.[24]

The Pentagon's own advisory panel, the Defense Science Board, corroborated some of the above, reporting in November 2004: "Today we reflexively compare Muslim 'masses' to those oppressed under Soviet rule. This is a strategic mistake. There is no yearning-to-be-liberated-by-the-U.S. groundswell among Muslim societies—except to be liberated perhaps from what they see as apostate tyrannies that the U.S. so determinedly promotes and defends.... Muslims do not 'hate our freedom,' but rather they hate our policies...when American public diplomacy talks about bringing democracy to Islamic societies, this is seen as no more than self-serving hypocrisy.... [Muslims believe] American occupation of Afghanistan and Iraq has not led to democracy there, but only more chaos and suffering."[25]

Lastly, we have Michael Scheuer, a 22-year veteran of the CIA, where he was a senior terrorism analyst. In his 2004 book, *Imperial Hubris: Why The West is Losing the War on Terror* (written under the name "Anonymous"), and elsewhere, he makes the following observations:

None of bin Laden's stated reasons for waging war on the United States "have anything to do with our freedom, liberty, and democracy, but everything to do with U.S. policies and actions in the Muslim world," notably unlimited support for Israel's repression of the Palestinians and the destruction of Iraq.[26]..."As long as unchanged U.S. policies motivate Muslims to become insurgents," the United States will have to "kill many thousands of these fighters in what is a barely started war."[27]..."This mind-set holds that America does not need to reevaluate its policies, let alone change them; it merely needs to better explain the wholesomeness of its views and the purity of its purposes to the uncomprehending Islamic world. What could be more American in the early 21st century, after all, than to re- identify a *casus belli* *as* a communication problem, and then call on Madison Avenue to package and hawk a remedy called "Democracy- Secularism-and-Capitalism-are-good-for-Muslims" to an Islamic world that has, to date, violently refused to purchase?"[28]

The Iraqi resistance

The official Washington mentality about the motivations of individuals they call terrorists has also been manifested in US occupation policy in Iraq. Secretary of War Donald Rumsfeld has declared that there are five groups opposing US forces—looters, criminals, remnants of Saddam Hussein's government, foreign terrorists and those influenced by Iran.[29] An American official in Iraq maintained that many of the people shooting at US troops are "poor young Iraqis" who have been paid between $20 and $100 to stage hit-and-run attacks on US soldiers. "They're not dedicated fighters," he said. "They're people who wanted to take a few potshots."[30]

With such language do American officials avoid dealing with the idea that any part of the resistance is composed of Iraqi citizens who are simply demonstrating their resentment about being bombed, invaded, occupied, tortured, slain, and subjected to daily humiliations.

Some officials convinced themselves that it was largely the most loyal followers of Saddam Hussein and his two sons who were behind the daily attacks on Americans, and that with the capture or killing of the evil family, resistance would die out; tens of millions of dollars were offered as reward for information leading to this joyful prospect. Thus it was that the killing of the sons elated military personnel. US Army trucks with loudspeakers drove through small towns and villages to broadcast a message about the death of Hussein's sons. "Coalition forces have won a great victory over the Baath Party and the Saddam Hussein regime by killing Uday and Qusay Hussein in Mosul," said the message broadcast in Arabic. "The Baath Party has no power in Iraq. Renounce the Baath Party or you are in great danger." It called on all officials of Hussein's government to turn themselves in.[31]

What followed was several days of some of the deadliest attacks against American personnel since the guerrilla war began. Unfazed, American officials in Washington and Iraq continued to suggest that the elimination of Saddam himself would surely write *finis* to anti-American actions. His capture, in December 2003, of course did no such thing.

Another way in which the political origins of anti-American terrorism are obscured is by the common practice of blaming poverty or repression by Middle Eastern governments (as opposed to US support for such governments) for the creation of such terrorists. Defenders of US foreign policy cite this also as a way of showing how enlightened they are. Here's Condoleezza Rice as National Security Advisor:

[The Middle East] is a region where hopelessness provides a

fertile ground for ideologies that convince promising youths to aspire not to a university education, a career or family, but to blowing themselves up, taking as many innocent lives with them as possible. We need to address the source of the problem.[32]

There are those on the left who speak in a similar fashion, apparently unconscious of what they're obfuscating. Their analysis confuses terrorism with revolution. But, in any case, why would a person suffering from hopelessness become a suicide bomber instead of merely committing suicide, if not for a political reason?

September 11 Commission

On June 16, 2004, the National Commission on Terrorist Attacks Upon the United States (investigating the events of September 11, 2001), issued a report which stated that Khalid Sheik Mohammed, regarded as the mastermind of the attacks, wanted to personally commandeer one aircraft and use it as a platform to denounce US policies in the Middle East. Instead of crashing it in a suicide attack, the report says, Mohammed planned to kill every adult male passenger on the plane, contact the media while airborne, and land at a US airport. There he would deliver his speech before releasing all the women and children.[33]

The question once again arises: Why was Mohammed planning on denouncing US policies in the Middle East? Why wasn't he instead planning to denounce America's democracy, freedom, wealth and secular government, or its music, films or clothing?

A while ago, I heard a union person on the radio proposing what he called "a radical solution to poverty—pay people enough to live on." Well, I'd like to propose a radical solution to anti- American terrorism—stop giving terrorists the motivation to attack America. As long as the United States insists that anti-American terrorists have no good or rational reason for retaliation against the United States for anything the US has ever done to their countries, as long as the Bush administration feverishly experiments with one program after another to improve America's image in the Muslim world instead of putting and end to a foreign policy of bloody and oppressive interventions, the "War on Terrorism" is as doomed to failure as the war on drugs has been.

Chapter 2

America's Gift to the World: the Afghan Terrorist Alumni

Osama bin Laden—alleged to have been the mastermind behind the September 11, 2001 terrorist attacks in the United States and the bombing of two US embassies in Africa in 1998—was not always on Washington's hate list. He, and many other Islamic fundamentalists, were supremely useful during the 1980s in Washington's war which quashed the last chance the Afghan people had for desperately needed social and economic reform and a secular society. Because of their battle against the government and its Soviet military allies in Afghanistan, the fundamentalists—the moujahedeen (Muslim holy warriors)—were *good* terrorists. They were *our* terrorists. After the success of their *jihad*, these forces roamed afar, carrying out grisly actions in numerous corners of the world, metamorphosing into really *bad* terrorists.

Forcing the Soviet Union to withdraw its military forces from Afghanistan truly went to the heads of the moujahedeen. They thought they were invincible and had a god-given mission. *Allah Akbar*! They seemed to place little weight upon the fact that it had been the United States, bringing its military, political, and financial weight to bear, that had been the *sine qua non* of the victory.

In 1992, after 12 years of battle, the various factions of the moujahedeen could claim Afghanistan as all their own, albeit now fighting each other. The war had been a rallying point for Muslim zealots from throughout the world—an Islamic Abraham Lincoln Brigade—and laid the groundwork for their future collaboration and support. Tens of thousands of veterans of the war—young men from every Muslim nation, battle-hardened and armed—dispersed to many lands to carry out other *jihads* against the infidels and to inflame and train a new generation of militant Islamists and terrorists, ready to drink the cup of martyrdom; a virtual Islamic Foreign Legion.

In the midst of a wave of assault weapons—a "Kalashnikov culture,"—left over from the Afghanistan wars, Pakistan Prime Minister Benazir Bhutto complained in 1996 that her country had gotten stuck with this air of frenzy as a direct result of cooperation with the United States in forcing Soviet troops from Afghanistan. "We are left on our own to cope with the remnants of the Afghan war, which include arms smuggling...drugs and... [religious] zealots who were leaders at the time of the Afghan war."[1]

"Your government participated in creating a monster," complained an Algerian sociologist to a *Los Angeles Times* correspondent in Algiers. "Now it has turned against you and the world—16,000 Arabs were trained in Afghanistan, made into a veritable killing machine."[2] His figure may be low inasmuch as there were an estimated 15,000 veterans of the Afghanistan war— or "Afghans" as they came to be known all over, whether from Afghanistan or not—in Saudi Arabia alone in 1996.[3]

Professor of Middle East Studies, Eqbal Ahmad, has observed:

> The propaganda in the West suggests that violence and holy war are inherent in Islam. The reality is that as a worldwide movement, *Jihad* International, Inc. is a recent phenomenon.... Without significant exception during the 20th century, *jihad* was used in a national, secular and political context until, that is, the advent of the anti-Soviet war in Afghanistan.[4]

Following are some of the highlights of the bloodletting of the "Afghans"; the list is confined to the 1990s, although their international jihad has continued into the new century.

In the United States

Mir Aimal Kansi (AKA Kasi)—the Pakistani who slew two CIA employees and wounded two other CIA employees and an employee of a CIA contractor outside CIA headquarters in Virginia in 1993—came of age in the Pakistani province that borders Afghanistan, which was used as a key staging area for the moujahedeen. His father and other relatives had ties to the CIA-Pakistani intelligence operations of the war. Kansi, those who knew him said, was "one of the children of the C.I.A.'s jihad."[5]

Most of those involved in the 1993 bombing of the World Trade Center in New York—which killed six people, wounded more than 1,000, and caused half a billion dollars in damage—were veterans of the Afghan war.[6]

In October, 1995, 10 men were convicted for a plot to bomb New York targets, including the UN building, an FBI office, and the Lincoln and Holland tunnels. The spiritual leader of the group, and one of the defendants, was Sheik Omar Abdul Rahman, who had worked with the moujahedeen in the war in Afghanistan. He had obtained a US visa in 1990 from a CIA undercover agent[7], leading to speculation that at that time he (still) had CIA links. At least one of the other defendants—who came mainly from Egypt and Sudan—had fought in Afghanistan.

Three men were convicted in New York in 1996 of plotting to bomb 12 US jumbo jets and 4,000 passengers out of the sky over the Pacific Ocean. Ramzi Ahmed Yousef, the alleged mastermind of the World Trade Center bombing, who had been a fugitive, was one of the three defendants. He had been trained in explosives by the moujahedeen. Investigators found in his computer a manifesto pledging terror to punish Americans for their government's support of Israel.[8]

Elsewhere

Ramzi Ahmed Yousef was also convicted in the Philippines in 1994, in absentia, of bombing a Philippine Airlines jet, killing one passenger. He reportedly was involved in training activities with the radical Muslim Abu Sayyaf Organization of the Philippines.[9]

March 1995, Karachi, Pakistan: Two US diplomats were killed and a third wounded in an assault upon the car they were driving in. The FBI, which arrived in Pakistan to investigate the crime, announced that it was treating the attack as a possible retaliation for the arrest of Ramzi Ahmed Yousef the previous month in Pakistan by US and Pakistani agents and his extradition to the United States.[10]

In November 1995, five Americans and two Indians died when a pickup truck stuffed with explosives detonated outside a US Army building in Riyadh, Saudi Arabia. Three of the four Saudis who confessed to the attack admitted to having received firearms and explosives training in Afghanistan and to having fought in combat there. The following June, 19 US airmen died in the bombing of their housing complex in Dhahran, Saudi Arabia. The same groups claimed credit for both attacks.[11]

In summer 1995, France underwent a series of eight bomb attacks beginning with a blast in a train station which killed eight and wounded 160. "Almost all of the leaders of the people we have arrested for terrorism have passed by Afghanistan or Pakistan," said a French law enforcement official.[12]

The Chechnyan guerrillas, who have bedeviled the Russians for years with their insurrection to create a Muslim society, have had their ranks swelled by Middle East and African "Afghans", as well as their own people who received military instruction in Afghanistan.[13]

Russian officials estimate that 4,000 to 5,000 Muslim militants from Tajikistan alone passed through camps in northern

Afghanistan, then returned to the former Soviet Central Asian republic in 1993 to do battle against the secular government.[14] Another former Soviet republic, Azerbaijan, has experienced a similar fate.[15]

In western provinces of China, Afghan veterans have armed and trained Chinese Muslims and fought alongside them against the Chinese authorities.[16]

Since 1992, Egypt has been swept by a wave of anti-government terrorism in which graduates of the military training camps in Afghanistan and Pakistan have played a major role. They are believed to have also been behind the attempted assassination of President Hosni Mubarak while he was visiting Ethiopia.[17]

In August 1994, three "Afghans" robbed a hotel in Morocco, killing tourists in an effort to destabilize Morocco's vital tourism industry.[18]

Throughout much of the 1990s, Kashmiris and other nationals trained in Afghanistan, have been fighting against India in the mountains of Kashmir, waging "holy war" for secession from New Delhi.[19]

Since Algeria's cancellation of the 1992 election, Algerian veterans of the Afghanistan conflict have played a key role in the rise of the Armed Islamic Group, responsible for many thousands of gory murders in their crusade for an Islamic state.[20]

In Bosnia, beginning in 1992, Afghans fought ferociously alongside the predominantly Muslim Bosnian army for two years, attacking Serbian positions to liberate Muslim villages.[21] One of those who confessed to the November 1995 bombing in Saudi Arabia, referred to above, said that he had fought with the Bosnian Muslims.[22]

In a 1999 interview, Libyan leader Moammar Qaddafi told a London-based Arabic newspaper that his government had crushed an Islamic militant movement of "Afghans". "They returned desperate and destructive," he said, "and adopted killing and explosives as their profession, according to the training they received from the American intelligence."[23]

And more of the same in other places, from the men Ronald Reagan fancied as "freedom fighters".

"This is an insane instance of the chickens coming home to roost," said a US diplomat in Pakistan in 1996. "You can't plug billions of dollars into an anti-Communist jihad, accept participation from all over the world and ignore the consequences. But we did. Our objectives weren't peace and grooviness in Afghanistan. Our objective was killing Commies and getting the Russians out."[24]

Yet more chickens will come home to roost as a result of the American occupation of Afghanistan beginning in 2001 and Iraq beginning in 2003. Thousands more "Afghans" and "Iraqis," from all over the Middle East and South Asia, have acquired skills of urban warfare under American occupation—car bombing, suicide bombing, all manner of improvised explosive devices, assassination, kidnapping, and the use of rocket-propelled grenades and other weapons. Americans and all those who work with them in much of the world are in greater peril than ever.

Chapter 3

Assassinations

I don't want to wipe out everyone.... Just my enemies.

Michael Corleone, "The Godfather, Part II"

On June 26, 1993, President William Clinton went before the American people and announced that the United States had fired several missiles against Iraq that day. It turned out that the missiles killed 8 people and injured many more. The attack, said the president, was in retaliation for an Iraqi plot to assassinate former president George Bush who was due to visit Kuwait. (This alleged plot remains no more than that...alleged.[1]) Clinton announced that the US attack "was essential to send a message to those who engage in state-sponsored terrorism and to affirm the expectation of civilized behavior among nations."[2]

Following is a list of prominent foreign individuals whose assassination (or planning for same) the United States has been involved in since the end of the Second World War. (CIA humorists have at times referred to this type of operation as "suicide involuntarily administered", to be carried out by the Agency's "Health Alteration Committee".)

1949	Kim Koo, Korean opposition leader
1950s	CIA/Neo-Nazi hit list of more than 200 political figures in West Germany to be "put out of the way" in the event of a Soviet invasion
1950s	Zhou Enlai, Prime minister of China, several attempts on his life
1950s, 1962	Sukarno, President of Indonesia
1951	Kim Il Sung, Premier of North Korea

1953	Mohammed Mossadegh, Prime Minister of Iran
1950s (mid)	Claro M. Recto, Philippines opposition leader
1955	Jawaharlal Nehru, Prime Minister of India
1957	Gamal Abdul Nasser, President of Egypt
1959/63/69	Norodom Sihanouk, leader of Cambodia
1960	Brig. Gen. Abdul Karim Kassem, leader of Iraq
1950s-70s	José Figueres, President of Costa Rica, two attempts on his life
1961	Francois "Papa Doc" Duvalier, leader of Haiti
1961	Patrice Lumumba, Prime Minister of the Congo
1961	Gen. Rafael Trujillo, leader of Dominican Republic
1963	Ngo Dinh Diem, President of South Vietnam
1960s-70s	Fidel Castro, President of Cuba, many attempts and plots on his life
1960s	Raúl Castro, high official in government of Cuba
1965	Francisco Caamaño, Dominican Republic opposition leader
1965-6	Charles de Gaulle, President of France
1967	Che Guevara, Cuban leader
1970	Salvador Allende, President of Chile
1970	Gen. Rene Schneider, Commander-in-Chief of Army, Chile
1970s, 1981	General Omar Torrijos, leader of Panama
1972	General Manuel Noriega, Chief of Panama Intelligence
1975	Mobutu Sese Seko, President of Zaire

1976	Michael Manley, Prime Minister of Jamaica
1980-1986	Moammar Qaddafi, leader of Libya, several plots and attempts upon his life
1982	Ayatollah Khomeini, leader of Iran
1983	Gen. Ahmed Dlimi, Moroccan Army commander
1983	Miguel d'Escoto, Foreign Minister of Nicaragua
1984	The nine *comandantes* of the National Directorate of Nicaragua
1985	Sheikh Mohammed Hussein Fadlallah, Lebanese Shiite leader
1991	Saddam Hussein, leader of Iraq
1993	Mohamed Farah Aideed, prominent clan leader of Somalia
1998, 2001-2	Osama bin Laden, leading Islamic militant
1999	Slobodan Milosevic, President of Yugoslavia
2002	Gulbuddin Hekmatyar, Afghan Islamic leader and warlord
2003	Saddam Hussein and his two sons, Qusay and Uday, and his half-brother, Barzan Ibrahim Hassan al-Tikriti; all had been senior government officials

In case they run short of assassins

In 1975, a US Navy psychologist, Lt. Com. Thomas Narut, revealed that his naval work included establishing how to induce servicemen who may not be naturally inclined to kill, to do so under certain conditions. He referred to these men using the words "hitmen" and "assassin". Narut added that convicted murderers as well had been released from military prisons to become assassins.

The training of the carefully-selected recruits ranged from
dehumanization of the enemy, to acclimating them emotionally
through special films showing people being killed and injured in
violent ways.[3] The disclosure by Narut was pure happenstance.
We can only speculate about what programs are taking place or
being planned today in that five-sided building in Virginia.

Blasphemy American style

The Western world was shocked when Iran condemned British
author Salmon Rushdie to death in 1989 because of one of his
books, which the ayatollahs called "blasphemous". But the United
States has also condemned blasphemers to death—Castro, Allende,
Sukarno and a host of others mentioned above who didn't believe
in the holy objectives of American foreign policy.

Aberrations?

The senate committee known as the Church committee, in its
Assassination Report in 1975, said: "The committee does not
believe that the acts [of assassination] which it has examined
represent the real American character. They do not reflect the
ideals which have given the people of this country and the world
hope for a better, fuller, fairer life. We regard the assassination
plots as aberrations."[4]

At the time the committee wrote this, it knew of about a dozen
CIA assassination plots and still could call them all aberrations.
Would members of Congress today, knowing of the more than 50
incidents listed above, call them all aberrations?

Could they explain how these "aberrations" have continued
through each of the eleven presidencies, from Truman through
George W. Bush?

For some years following the Church committee's report,

American presidents made it a point to issue public statements on assassination, perhaps trying to convince the world that "We don't really mean it".

1976: Gerald Ford signed a presidential order which stated: "No employee of the United States shall engage in, or conspire to engage in, political assassination."

1978: Jimmy Carter also issued an executive order prohibiting assassinations.

1981, Dec. 4: Ronald Reagan issued an executive order with language almost identical to that of Ford's.

But on Nov. 13, 1984, Reagan, consumed with fighting the "International Communist Conspiracy" on several fronts, canceled his executive order, creating what was actually called by the press, a "license to kill"[5]—a license to kill anyone deemed a "terrorist".

On April 10, 1985, Reagan canceled the "license to kill" because the previous month, the CIA had paid some people in Beirut to kill a certain sheikh Fadlallah, who was not to Washington's liking; a car bomb had been used and 80 people were killed, the sheikh not being among their number.

August 11, 1985: The "license to kill" was reinstated because of a hijacking of a TWA plane in June.

May 12, 1986: A new executive order was signed without the controversial language, apparently in deference to congressional objections.[6]

Oct. 13, 1989: George H.W. Bush added a new twist. He issued a "memorandum of law" that would allow "accidental" killing if it was a byproduct of legal action: "A decision by the President to employ overt military force...would not constitute assassination if U.S. forces were employed against the combatant forces of another nation, a guerrilla force, or a terrorist or other organization whose actions pose a threat to the security of the United States."[7]

In a classified 1998 intelligence finding, President Clinton authorized the CIA to use covert lethal force against Osama bin Laden and his deputies.[8]

Having declared after September 11, 2001 that Osama bin Laden was wanted "dead or alive," President George W. Bush issued another intelligence finding, this one giving the CIA permission to use lethal force against a wider class of al-Qaeda personnel.[9]

Reagan and his successors have clearly not been acting out of any ethical or legal principle for or against assassination. It's all been *realpolitik* and public relations, and the actual American policy in the field over the years has never varied to speak of, whatever the "official" message of the day coming out of the White House was.

The Doolittle Report

A 1954 White House commission to study the CIA's covert activities included in its report the following now-famous passage, which is relevant to this discussion of assassination. It may be what psychologists call "projection".

> It is now clear that we are facing an implacable enemy whose avowed objective is world domination by whatever means and at whatever cost. There are no rules in such a game. Hitherto acceptable norms of human conduct do not apply. If the United States is to survive, long-standing American concepts of "fair play" must be reconsidered. We must develop effective espionage and counterespionage services and must learn to subvert, sabotage and destroy our enemies by more clever, more sophisticated, and more effective methods than those used against us. It may become necessary that the American people be made acquainted with, understand and support this fundamentally repugnant philosophy.[10]

Does it work both ways?

If the United States could bomb Iraqi intelligence headquarters—-
which was their target in the bombing referred to above—because
of an alleged assassination plot against an American leader, and
cite self-defense under the UN charter as Washington did (a
claim at least as questionable as the alleged plot), think of the
opportunities opened to countries like Panama, Libya, and Cuba
to name but a few. Cuba could claim the right to bomb CIA
headquarters because of CIA attempts on the life of Fidel Castro.
It's safe to say though, that neither the White House nor American
courts would accept this legal argument; nor would they be able to
see behind the Irony Curtain.

Chapter 4

Excerpts from US Army and CIA training manuals

CIA, "A Study of Assassination", written early 1950s:[1]

For secret assassinations...the contrived accident is the most effective technique. When successfully executed, it causes little excitement and is only casually investigated. The most efficient accident...is a fall of 75 feet or more onto a hard surface. Elevator shafts, stairwells, unscreened windows and bridges will serve.... The act may be executed by sudden, vigorous grabbing of the ankles, tipping the subject over the edge. If the assassin immediately sets up an outcry, playing the 'horrified witness', no alibi or surreptitious withdrawal is necessary."

"Drugs can be very effective. If the assassin is trained as a doctor or nurse and the subject is under medical care, this is an easy and sure method. An overdose of morphine administered as a sedative will cause death without disturbance and is difficult to detect. The size of the dose will depend upon whether the subject has been using narcotics regularly. If not, two grains will suffice. If the subject drinks heavily, morphine or a similar narcotic can be injected at the passing out stage, and the cause of death will often be held to be acute alcoholism."

"Edge weapons: Any legally obtained edge device may be successfully employed. A certain minimum of anatomical knowledge is needed for reliability. Puncture wounds of the body cavity may not be reliable unless the heart is reached. The heart is protected by the rib cage and is not always easy to locate.... Absolute reliability is obtained by severing the spinal cord in the cervical region. This can be done with the point of a knife or a light blow of an axe or hatchet. Another reliable method is the severing of both jugular and carotid vessels on both sides of the windpipe."

"Conference room technique: [Assassin] #1 Enters room quickly but quietly. #2 Stands in doorway. #2 Opens fire on first subject to react. Swings across group toward center of mass. Times burst to empty magazine at end of swing. #1 Covers group to prevent individual dangerous reactions; if necessary, fires individual bursts of 3 rounds. #2 Finishes burst. Commands 'Shift'. Drops back through door. Replaces empty magazine. Covers corridor. #1 On command 'Shift', opens fire on opposite side of target. Swings one burst across group. Leaves propaganda [to implicate the opposition]."

US Army, "Terrorism and the Urban Guerilla", 1960s[2]

"Measures of Controlling the Population and Resources:

1. ID Cards. An effective system of identification is fundamental to the program...

2. Registration. A program of registering families is used to supplement the system of ID cards. This is the system of inventorying all families by house, making a list of all members of the family who live in the house along with the family's resources. One can also note the presence of insurgent tendencies and affiliations among the population.

3. Control by block. The purpose of block-by-block control is to detect the individuals who are supporting or sympathizing with the insurgents and the type of support they are providing.

4. Police patrols. Their purpose is to detect sources of insurgent support, sympathizers, and routes used by the insurgent forces for intelligence, logistics, and routine activities...

Curfew: The purpose is to permit the authorities to identify violators and take actions based on the premise that anyone who violates the curfew is an insurgent or sympathizes with the insurgents until he can prove the contrary.

Checkpoints. It is of little use to establish a program of passes and ID cards unless there is a system of verifying these official papers. Therefore, establishing checkpoints in all travel routes is necessary once the use of passes has started."

US Army, "Handling of Sources", 1960s[3]

"The CI [counterintelligence] agent should cause the arrest of the employee's [paid government informant] parents, imprison the employee or give him a beating as part of the placement plan of said employee in the guerrilla organization." [It's not clear whether these things were to be done to force the person to be an informer or to give him credibility as such.]

"The employee's value could be increased by means of arrests, executions or pacification, taking care not to expose the employee as the information source."

"To assure the promotion of an employee...eliminate a potential rival among the guerrillas."

"[Employees are required because] the government is not able to depend only on the information provided voluntarily by faithful citizens or information obtained involuntarily from insurgents ho have been captured."

The official Defense Department view of these manuals was that the objectionable material in them had simply fallen through the cracks. The DOD stated: "There was no evidence that there was a deliberate attempt to violate Army or Defense Department policies in the preparation or use of these manuals." However, the office of Rep. Joseph Kennedy (D-MA), which had followed the issue closely, said that at the School of the Americas, where the manuals had been used, at least two officers had raised questions about the objectionable material with their superiors in the early 1980s, but had been rebuffed.[4]

CIA, "KUBARK Counterintelligence Interrogation-July 1963"[5]

"The effectiveness of most of the non-coercive techniques depends on their unsettling effect. The interrogation situation is in itself disturbing to most people encountering it for the first time. The aim is to enhance this effect...[and to create] a traumatic or sub-traumatic experience which explodes, as it were, the world that is familiar to the subject as well as his image of himself within that world."

"Usually his own clothes are taken away because familiar clothing reinforces identity and thus the capacity for resistance."

"The following are the principal coercive techniques of interrogation: arrest, detention, deprivation of sensory stimuli through solitary confinement or similar methods, threats and fear, debility, pain, heightened suggestibility and hypnosis, narcosis, and induced regression."

CIA, "Human Resource Exploitation Training Manual-1983"[6]

"Control—The capacity to cause or change certain types of human behavior by implying or using physical or psychological means to induce compliance. Compliance may be voluntary or involuntary."

"Subject is brought into the facility blindfolded and handcuffed and should remain so during the entire processing.... Subject is completely stripped and told to take a shower. Blindfold remains in place while showering and guard watches throughout. Subject is given a thorough medical examination, including all body cavities"

"Allowing a subject to receive carefully selected letters from home can help create an effect desired by the 'questioner'; for example, the subject may get the idea that his relatives are under duress or suffering. A suggestion at the proper time that his cooperation or confession can help protect the innocent may be effective."

"Bedding should be minimal—cot and blanket—no mattress. {The idea is to prevent the subject from relaxing and recovering from shock.) There should be no built-in toilet facilities. The subject should have to ask to relieve himself. Then he should either be given a bucket or escorted by a guard to the latrine. The guard stays at his side the entire time he is in the latrine."

"Deprivation of sensory stimuli induces stress and anxiety. The more complete the deprivation, the more rapidly and deeply the subject is affected."

"The purpose of all coercive techniques is to induce psychological regression in the subject by bringing a superior outside force to bear on his will to resist. Regression is basically a loss of autonomy."

CIA, "Freedom Fighters' Manual", 1984[7]

A 16-page "comic book" for Nicaraguans; its more than 40 illustrations showed the reader how s/he could "liberate Nicaragua from oppression and misery" of "the Marxist tyranny" by "a series of useful sabotage techniques". Amongst these were:

Stop up toilets with sponges...pull down power cables...put dirt into gas tanks...put nails on roads and highways...cut and perforate the upholstery of vehicles...cut down trees over highways... telephone to make false hotel reservations and false alarms of fires and crimes...hoard and steal food from the government...leave lights and water taps on...steal mail from mailboxes...go to work late...call in sick...short circuit electricity...break light bulbs...rip up books...spread rumors...threaten supervisors and officials over the phone ...

CIA, "Psychological Operations in Guerrilla Warfare", 1984[8]

A manual designed for the US-backed Contra forces (the guerrillas) fighting in Nicaragua against the leftist Sandinista government. It advised:

"Kidnap all officials or agents of the Sandinista government and place them in 'public places'."

"Shame, ridicule and humiliate the 'personal symbols' of the government of repression in the presence of the people and foster popular participation through guerrillas within the multitude, shouting slogans and jeers."

"If a guerrilla fires at an individual, make the town see that he was an enemy of the people" and "that if that citizen had managed to escape, he would have alerted the enemy that is near the town or city, and they could carry out acts of reprisal such as rapes, pillage, destruction, captures, etc....Make the population see that it was the repressive system of the regime that...really killed the informer, and that the weapon fired was one recovered in combat against the Sandinista regime."

"It is possible to neutralize carefully selected and planned targets, such as court judges, mesta judges [justices of the peace], police and State Security officials, CDS [Sandinista Defense Committees] chiefs, etc." [As writer Holly Sklar has noted: "A hit list that starts with court judges and ends with *etcetera* is a mighty broad license for murder."]

"The notification of the police, denouncing a target who does not want to join the guerrillas, can be carried out easily...through a letter with false statements of citizens who are not implicated in the movement."

"If possible, professional criminals will be hired to carry out specific selected 'jobs'."

"Specific tasks will be assigned to others, in order to create a 'martyr' for the cause, taking the demonstrators to a confrontation with the authorities, in order to bring about uprisings or shootings, which will cause the death of one or more persons, who would become the martyrs, a situation that should be made use of immediately against the regime, in order to create greater conflicts."

"Shock Troops. These men should be equipped with weapons (knives, razors, chains, clubs, bludgeons) and should march slightly behind the innocent and gullible participants."

Throughout, the manual reads like what the Western world was always taught was the way communists scheme and indoctrinate.

In 1986, the World Court found that in producing and disseminating this manual, the United States "encouraged the commission...of acts contrary to general principles of humanitarian law," including the Geneva Conventions of 1949.[9]

Chapter 5

Torture

The first jolt was so bad I just wanted to die."

—Gloria Esperanza Reyes, speaking of her torture in Honduras, where electric wires were attached to her breasts and vagina.

"They always asked to be killed. Torture is worse than death."

—José Barrera, Honduran torturer.[1]

Turkey, July 14, 1999, the police break into the home of a Kurdish family and announce they want to take the two daughters—Medine, 14, and her younger sister Devran—in for questioning. "I headed for the bedroom to get dressed," said Devran later, "but Medine...went straight to the window and jumped."

Medine's mother explained: "My daughter, you see, preferred death to being tortured once again."[2]

"Torture might last a short time, but the person will never be the same."

Amnesty International report[3]

"No exceptional circumstances whatsoever, whether a state of war or a threat of war, internal political instability or any other public emergency, may be invoked as a justification for torture."

The Convention Against Torture and Other Cruel, Inhuman or Degrading Treatment or Punishment, 1987[4]

P hysical abuse or other degrading treatment was rejected, not only because it is wrong, but because it has historically proven to be ineffective."—Richard Stolz, Deputy Director of Operations of the Central Intelligence Agency, 1988.[5]

The CIA likes to say things like this because they think it sounds like good plausible denial. But who can believe that torture does not loosen up tongues, that for such purpose it is not exceedingly effective? Richard Stolz and the CIA would have us believe that Medine, in the above example, if denied the opportunity to kill herself, would not talk under torture.

Torture's effectiveness extends yet further, for its purpose is frequently not so much to elicit information as it is to punish, to coerce the victims from any further dissident activity by gouging out the idealism from their very being, and as a warning to their comrades.

For these ends, the CIA has co-existed with torture for decades. (Turkey, it must be remembered, is one of Washington's very closest strategic allies; for Honduras, see below.) Sleeping with friendly torturers has been a closely guarded secret at the Agency, and for that reason the actual painful details have been difficult to come by over the years. But here is some of the record that has made its way to the light of day:

Greece

During the late 1940s, the CIA was instrumental in the creation of a new internal security agency, KYP. Before long, KYP was carrying out all the endearing practices of secret police everywhere, including systematic torture. It was most active during the military junta, 1967-74, a period of routine horrific torture. Amnesty International later reported that "American policy on the torture question as expressed in official statements and official testimony has been to deny it where possible and minimize it where denial was not possible. This policy flowed naturally from general support for the military regime."[6]

James Becket, an American attorney sent to Greece by Amnesty, wrote in 1969 that some torturers told prisoners that some of their equipment had come as US military aid. One item was a special "thick white double cable" whip that was "scientific, making their work easier"; another was the head screw, known as an "iron wreath", which was progressively tightened around the head or ears.[7] American support, reported Becket, was vital to the torturers:

> Hundreds of prisoners have listened to the little speech given by Inspector Basil Lambrou, who sits behind his desk which displays the red, white, and blue clasped-hand symbol of American aid. He tries to show the prisoner the absolute futility of resistance: "You make yourself ridiculous by thinking you can do anything. The world is divided in two. There are the communists on that side and on this side the free world. The Russians and the Americans, no one else. What are we? Americans. Behind me there is the government, behind the government is NATO, behind NATO is the U.S. You can't fight us, we are Americans."[8]

Iran

The notorious Iranian security service, SAVAK, which employed torture routinely, was created under the guidance of the CIA and Israel in the 1950s.[9] According to a former CIA analyst on Iran, Jesse J. Leaf, SAVAK was instructed in torture techniques by the Agency.[10] After the 1979 revolution, the Iranians found CIA film made for SAVAK on how to torture women.[11]

Germany

In the 1950s, in Munich, the CIA tortured suspected infiltrators of Soviet émigré organizations in Western Europe, which the Agency was using in anti-Soviet operations. Amongst the techniques employed by the CIA were such esoteric torture methods as applying turpentine to a man's testicles or sealing someone in a room and playing Indonesian music at deafening levels until he cracked.[12] This information probably surfaced because it's weird-sounding to the point of being amusing; there was likely more of regular torture methods not fit for conversation.

Vietnam

The Green Berets taught its members who were slated for duty in Vietnam in the 1960s how to use torture as part of an interrogation.[13] The notorious Operation Phoenix, set up by the CIA to wipe out the Vietcong infrastructure, subjected suspects to torture such as electric shock to the genitals of both men and women, and the insertion into the ear of a six-inch dowel, which was tapped through the brain until the victim died; suspects were also thrown out of airborne helicopters to persuade the more important suspects to talk, although this should probably be categorized as murder of the ones thrown out, and a form of torture for those not.[14] In violation of the Geneva Convention, the US turned prisoners over to their South Vietnamese allies in full knowledge that they would be tortured, American military personnel often being present during the torture.[15]

Bolivia

In 1967, anti-Castro Cubans, working with the CIA to find Che Guevara, set up houses of interrogation where Bolivians suspected of aiding Che's guerrilla army were brought for questioning and sometimes tortured. When the Bolivian interior minister learned of the torture, he was furious and demanded that the CIA put a stop to it.[16]

Uruguay

In the late 1960s, Dan Mitrione, an employee of the US Office of Public Safety (part of Agency for International Development), which trained and armed foreign police forces, was stationed in Montevideo, Uruguay. Torturing political prisoners in Uruguay had existed before Mitrione's arrival. However, in a surprising interview given to a leading Brazilian newspaper, *Jornal do Brasil* in 1970, the former Uruguayan Chief of Police Intelligence, Alejandro Otero, declared that US advisers, and Mitrione in particular, had instituted torture as a more routine measure; to the means of inflicting pain, they had added scientific refinement; and to that a psychology to create despair, such as playing a tape in the next room of women and children screaming and telling the prisoner that it was his family being tortured.[17]

The newspaper interview greatly upset American officials in South America and Washington. The director of OPS in Washington tried to explain it all away by asserting: "The three Brazilian reporters in Montevideo all denied filing that story. We found out later that it was slipped into the paper by someone in the composing room at the *Jornal do Brasil*."[18]

Mitrione built a soundproofed room in the cellar of his house in Montevideo, in which he assembled Uruguayan police officers to observe a demonstration of torture techniques. Four beggars were rounded up to be the subjects upon whom Mitrione demonstrated the effects of different voltages on different parts of the body. The four of them died.

"The precise pain, in the precise place, in the precise amount, for the desired effect," was Mitrione's motto.

"When you get what you want, and I always get it, "he said, "it may be good to prolong the session a little to apply another softening-up. Not to extract information now, but only as a political measure, to create a healthy fear of meddling in subversive activities."[19]

And in 1981, a former Uruguayan intelligence officer declared that US manuals were being used to teach techniques of torture to his country's military. He said that most of the officers who trained him had attended classes run by the United States in Panama. Among other niceties, the manuals listed 35 nerve points where electrodes could be applied.[20]

Brazil

Before the Office of Public Safety assigned Dan Mitrione to Uruguay, he had been stationed in Brazil. There, he and other Americans worked with OPS, AID and CIA in supplying Brazilian security forces with the equipment and training to facilitate the torture of prisoners. The Americans also advised on how much electric shock could be administered without killing the person, if his or her death might prove awkward.[21]

Guatemala

From the 1960s through the 1980s, Guatemalan security forces, notably the Army unit called G-2, routinely tortured "subversives". One method was electric shock to the genital area, using military field telephones hooked up to small generators, equipment and instructions for use supplied by Uncle Sam. The US and its clients in various countries were becoming rather adept at this technique. The CIA advised, armed, and equipped the G-2, which maintained a web of torture centers, whose methods reportedly included chopping off limbs and singeing flesh, in addition to electric shocks. The Army unit even had its own crematorium, presumably to dispose of any incriminating evidence. The CIA thoroughly infiltrated the G-2, with at least three G-2 chiefs of the 1980s and early 90s, as well as many lower-level officers, being on the Agency's payroll.[22]

Also benefiting from the Agency's generosity was General Hector Gramajo Morales (see chapter 9), who was Defense Minister during the armed forces' 1989 abduction of Sister Dianna Ortiz, an American nun. She was burned with cigarettes, raped repeatedly, and lowered into a pit full of corpses. Typically, torturers exult in demonstrating the power they hold over their victims—one of them put a large knife or machete into Ortiz's hand, put his own hands on top of hers, and forced her to stab another female prisoner. Ortiz thinks she may have killed the woman. A fair-skinned man, whom the others referred to as "Alejandro", and as their "boss", seemed to be in charge, she said. He spoke Spanish with an American accent and cursed in English. Later, Ortiz adds, when this man realized she was American, he ordered the torture stopped. Clearly, if his motivation had been humanitarian, and not simply trying to avoid a possible political flap, he would have stopped it regardless of her nationality.[23]

In 1996, in the United States, Ortiz received a number of documents from the State Department in response to a Freedom of Information Act request. Only one, dated 1990, contained a significant reference to Alejandro. It read as follows:

> VERY IMPORTANT: We need to close the loop on the issue of the "North American" named by Ortiz as being involved in the case...The EMBASSY IS VERY SENSITIVE ON THIS ISSUE, but it is an issue we will have to respond to publicly ...[24]

The next two pages were completely redacted.

El Salvador

During the counter-insurgency period of the 1980s, there was widespread torture practiced by the various Salvadoran security forces, all of whom had close working relations with the CIA and/or the US military. In January 1982, the *New York Times* published an interview with a deserter from the Salvadoran Army who described a class where severe methods of torture were demonstrated on teenage prisoners. He stated that eight US military advisers, apparently Green Berets, were present. Watching "will make you feel more like a man," a Salvadoran officer apprised the army recruits, adding that they should "not feel pity of anyone" but only "hate for those who are enemies of our country."[25]

Another Salvadoran, a former member of the National Guard, later testified in a 1986 British television documentary: "I belonged to a squad of twelve. We devoted ourselves to torture, and to finding people whom we were told were guerrillas. I was trained in Panama for nine months by the [unintelligible] of the United States for anti-guerrilla warfare. Part of the time we were instructed about torture."[26]

Honduras

During the 1980s, the CIA gave indispensable support to the infamous Battalion 316, which kidnapped, tortured and killed hundreds of citizens, using shock and suffocation devices for interrogation, amongst other techniques. The CIA supplied torture equipment, torture manuals, and in both Honduras and the US, taught battalion members methods of psychological and physical torture. On at least one occasion, a CIA officer took part in interrogating a torture victim. The Agency also funded Argentine counter-insurgency experts to provide further training for the Hondurans. At the time, Argentina was famous for its

"Dirty War", an appalling record of torture, baby kidnappings, and disappearances. Argentine and CIA instructors worked side by side training Battalion 316. US support for the battalion continued even after its director, Gen. Gustavo Alvarez Martinez, told the US ambassador, John Negroponte, that he intended to use the Argentine methods of eliminating subversives. In 1983, the Reagan administration awarded Alvarez the Legion of Merit "for encouraging the success of democratic processes in Honduras". At the same time, the administration was misleading Congress and the American public by denying or minimizing the battalion's atrocities.[27] Negroponte was later appointed by George W. Bush to be the US Ambassador to the United Nations and then Director of National Intelligence.

Panama

During the occupation of Panama following the invasion of December 1989, some American soldiers engaged in torture of soldiers of the Panama Defense Forces. In one case, a metal cable was inserted into an open wound, producing intense pain. In another reported case, a PDF soldier was hung up by one arm on which he already had an injury to the elbow, which had been stitched up.[28]

Iraq, Afghanistan, Guantánamo Bay, Cuba

The period following the September 11, 2001 attacks on New York and the Pentagon gave the United States all the justification and license it needed to torture at will under the cover of "fighting terrorism", while the best legal minds at the White House and the Justice Department put their heads together and decided that it was all lawful, and, anyhow, wasn't really torture. Here in capsule form are some of the acts carried out by American military forces, their contract employees, and the CIA against detainees in one or another edifice of the sprawling global prison complex maintained by the United States in occupied Iraq, occupied Afghanistan, and occupied Cuba; the same, and probably worse (because more hidden), has taken place daily in other secret CIA prisons around the world. The details are derived from major news organizations, the International Red Cross, human-rights organizations, and US Army reports which made it to the open after photos of abuses appeared in the American media.[29]

For the great majority of these acts, multiple similar instances have been reported. It should be noted that the US State Department's annual human-rights reports about the rest of the world routinely denounce some of these acts, such as sleep deprivation.

Standing or kneeling or forced into contorted, painful positions for hours...in leg shackles and handcuffs with eyes, ears, and mouths covered and wearing mittens in tropical heat...stripping detainees naked, leading them around with a dog leash...depriving them of sleep, subjecting them to a 24-hour bombardment of bright lights or blaring noise, hooding them, exposing them to extremes of heat or cold...death in custody with bag over his head, hands tied behind back...

Guards staged races of detainees in short leg shackles, violently punishing them if they fell...withholding painkillers and other medications from the injured...sensory deprivation...male detainees made to wear female underwear..."water boarding", in which a prisoner is strapped to an inclined board, head down, towel over his face, water poured on the towel to simulate drowning... made to lie naked on a sheet of ice...

Fake blood smeared on Muslim men before they intended to pray, told that it was menstrual blood...one female soldier sat on his lap, another rubbed her breasts against his back and massaged his chest and a third squatted near his crotch. He head-butted the woman behind him, knocking her off him. All three ran out and a team of soldiers stormed in and beat him... kicked by female officers...

The Iraqi general "was put headfirst into a sleeping bag, wrapped with electrical cord and knocked down before the soldiers sat and stood on him. The cause of death was determined to be suffocation."

Chained to the ceiling, shackled so tightly that the blood flow stops...shackled to the floor in fetal positions for more than 24 hours at a time, left without food and water, and allowed to defecate on themselves, a detainee found almost unconscious on the floor, with a pile of hair next to him; he had apparently been literally pulling his own hair out throughout the night...

Wrapping a prisoner in an Israeli flag...kept naked and hooded and kicked to keep them awake for days on end...use of unmuzzled, growling dogs to frighten, in at least one instance actually biting and severely injuring a detainee..."burn marks on their backs"...detainee left at an Iraqi hospital, comatose, with massive head trauma, burns on the bottoms of his feet caused by electrocution, bruises on his arms...at least 37 detainees have died during interrogations...

The death of two captives in Afghanistan: one from "blunt force injuries to lower extremities complicating coronary artery disease"; an autopsy showed that his legs were so damaged that amputation would have been necessary; the other captive suffered from a blood clot in the lung that was exacerbated by a "blunt force injury".

Kicks to the groin and legs, shoving or slamming detainees into walls and tables, forcing water in their mouths until they could not breathe...He had his hands handcuffed behind him and was suspended by his wrists in an effort to coerce his cooperation. "His arms were so badly stretched I was surprised they didn't pop out of their sockets."...

Female American soldier, cigarette dangling from her mouth, giving a jaunty thumbs-up sign and pointing at the genitals of a young Iraqi, naked except for a sandbag over his head, as he is forced to masturbate while being photographed and videotaped. She stands arm in arm with male soldier, both are grinning and giving the thumbs-up behind a cluster of about seven naked Iraqis, piled on top of each other in a pyramid.

Punched a detainee in the chest so hard he almost went into cardiac arrest...a prisoner placed in an isolation cell with little or no clothes, no toilet or running water, no ventilation or window, for as much as three days...forcing naked male detainees to wear women's underwear...standing a naked detainee on an electrified metal drum with a sandbag on his head, wires attached to his fingers, toes, and penis to simulate electric torture...

The report by General Taguba found that between October and December of 2003 there were numerous instances of "sadistic, blatant, and wanton criminal abuses" at Abu Ghraib prison in Iraq. The report listed: breaking chemical lights and pouring the phosphoric liquid on detainees; pouring cold water on naked detainees; beating detainees with a broom handle and a chair; threatening male detainees with rape; allowing a military police guard to stitch the wound of a detainee who was injured after being slammed against the wall in his cell; sodomizing a detainee with a chemical light and perhaps a broom stick...

A 14-year-old Iraqi with a broken arm being hurled to the ground and then mocked by US soldiers as the boy wept and wet himself...a male soldier having sex with a female detainee... 18 days naked alone in a cell, often with his hands and feet bound together, frequently beaten..."He locked his arm under mine and holding the back of my head he beat my head against the doors of the cells"...his hands and feet were pushed through the metal bars of the cell door and then tied together. "There was a stereo inside the cell and it played music with a sound so loud I couldn't sleep.

I stayed like that for 23 hours."

Six weeks after his release, he says he has lost the will to live. He is too ashamed to be seen by his friends and family and has not seen or spoken to his fiancée. The wedding is off. "I was a man before, but my manhood was taken away. Since this happened to me, I consider myself dead. My life feels over."

Jamadi died an hour after his arrival at Abu Ghraib in early November, 2003; he had been beaten while in CIA custody and then hung by his wrists, with his arms crossed across his back. US Army guards at the prison then packed his body in ice and posed with the corpse in mocking photographs.

Iraqi prisoners were forced to crawl through broken glass and wear women's sanitary products...two drunken interrogators took a female Iraqi prisoner from her cell in the middle of the night and stripped her naked to the waist...an Iraqi woman in her 70s was harnessed and ridden like a donkey...detainees were pressed to denounce Islam, or force-fed pork and liquor...

"We believe she was raped and that she was pregnant by a US guard. After her release from Abu Ghraib, I went to her house. The neighbours said her family had moved away. I believe she has been killed." Honor killings are not unusual in Islamic society.

"They forced us to walk like dogs on our hands and knees... And we had to bark like a dog, and if we didn't do that they started hitting us hard on our face and chest with no mercy."...."Do you believe in anything?" the soldier asked. "I said to him, 'I believe in Allah.' So he said, 'But I believe in torture and I will torture you'."

Taken out and tied to a post, rubber bullets were fired at them; made to kneel in the sun until they collapsed..."They tied my hands to my feet behind my back. My left hand to my right foot and my right hand to my left foot. I was lying face down and they were beating me like this"...inmates kept in wire cages with concrete floors and no protection from the elements.

"They actually said: 'You have no rights here'. After a while, we stopped asking for human rights—we wanted animal rights."... crosses shaved into their scalp or body hair...dislocated his arms, beat his leg with a bat, crushed his nose, and put an unloaded gun in his mouth and pulled the trigger...Six Kuwaiti prisoners said they were severely beaten, given electric shocks and sodomized by US forces in Afghanistan...

A CIA officer ordered guards to strip naked an uncooperative young Afghan detainee, chain him to the concrete floor and leave him there overnight without blankets. He was dragged around on the concrete floor, bruising and scraping his skin, before putting him in his cell. By morning he had frozen to death.

The Afghan detainee had been captured in Pakistan along with a group of other Afghans. His connection to al Qaeda or the value of his intelligence was never established before he died. "He was probably associated with people who were associated with al Qaeda," one US government official said.

No release from the stress, increased by uncertainty over whether they will ever be released...Guards telling prisoners repeatedly: "You will never go home."..."In my cell I was shouting: 'Please come and take me. Please kill me. I am Osama bin Laden, I was in the plane that hit the World Trade Centre.' I wished for death at that time. I wanted to be dead 1,000 times. I asked my God to take my soul."...numerous suicide attempts...

No family contact. No charges. No lawyers. No appeals.

The brazenness with which the servicemen and women conducted themselves, snapping photographs and flashing the "thumbs-up" sign as they abused prisoners, suggests they felt they had nothing to hide from their superiors.[30] After the photos became public and a "scandal" broke out, the GIs insisted that they had been encouraged by military intelligence officers and other higher-ranking officers to "soften up" prisoners for interrogation purposes, to "take the gloves off", but in the end none of their superiors were indicted and only a handful of the lower-ranking servicemembers were. The military judge in a court-martial of some of the servicemembers refused defense attorneys' requests to consider the role of officers in the trial.[31] Neither have any civilian officials in the Pentagon or White House, instrumental in formulating and condoning policies on torture, faced any charges.

As further indication that the American military was not terribly upset about the use of torture, two US defense contractors being sued over allegations of abuse at Abu Ghraib prison were awarded valuable new contracts by the Pentagon, despite demands from American human rights groups that they should be barred from any new government work. Three employees of the firms, CACI International and Titan, had been separately accused of abusive behavior, including rape and the use of dogs.[32]

President George W. Bush, 2004: "The world is better off without Saddam Hussein in power. The world is better off because he sits in a prison cell. Because we acted, torture rooms are closed, rape rooms no longer exist."[33]

Brian Whitman, spokesman for the US Department of Defense, 2005: "The United States treats all detainees in their custody with dignity and respect."[34]

At home

At the US Navy's schools in San Diego and Maine during the 1960s and 1970s, students were supposedly learning about methods of "survival, evasion, resistance and escape" which they could use if they were ever a prisoner of war. There was in the course something of survival in a desert, where students were forced to eat lizards, but the naval officers and cadets were also subjected to beatings, jarring judo flips, "tiger cages"—hooded and placed in a 16-cubic-foot box for 22 hours with a coffee can for their excrement—and a torture device called the "water board": the subject strapped to an inclined board, head downward, a towel placed over his face, and cold water poured over the towel; he would choke, gag, retch and gurgle as he experienced the sensation of drowning. A former student, Navy pilot Lt. Wendell Richard Young, claimed that his back was broken during the course and that students were tortured into spitting, urinating and defecating on the American flag, masturbating before guards, and, on one occasion, engaging in sex with an instructor.[35]

In 1992, a civilian oversight board revealed that over a 13-year period (1973-1986), Chicago police officers and commanders engaged in "systematic" torture and abuse of suspects, including electric shock to penises, testicles and other areas; beatings, suffocation (plastic bags secured over the heads, stopping the flow of oxygen; some subjects passed out, and when they recovered, the bag was placed over their head again); guns stuck in prisoners' mouths and triggers pulled; prisoners hung from hooks by handcuffs attached to their wrists and beaten on the bottoms of their feet and on their testicles; as well as much psychological torture. Some were released after being tortured and were never charged. More than 40 cases were collected. According to one of their attorneys, "All of the victims were black or Latino, so far as we've seen, and the people who were doing the torturing were white officers."[36]

A Human Rights Watch investigation in 1995 of more than 20 US prisons and jails in New York, California, Florida and Tennessee, and a close look at prison litigation for a ten-year period, showed "extensive abuses of the U.N.'s minimum standards for the treatment of prisoners...amounting to torture"...a handcuffed prisoner forced into a tub of 145-degree water...prisoners dying after receiving repeated jolts of electricity from stun guns or stun belts (50,000 volt shock for 8 seconds)...prisoners held in outdoor cages, rain or shine...prisoners held in total isolation from other human beings for long periods of time with sensory deprivation ...[37]

Amnesty International has released reports such as "Torture, Ill Treatment and Excessive Force by Police in Los Angeles, California" (1992), and "Police Brutality and Excessive Force in the New York City Police Department" (1996), as well as later reports dealing with Chicago and other cities. Amnesty states that US police forces have been guilty of "violating international human rights standards through a pattern of unchecked excessive force amounting to torture or other cruel, inhuman and degrading treatment".[38]

Amnesty has also published "The Pain Merchants" (2003), which deals with the practice of American companies exporting millions of dollars worth of equipment known to be used for torture, such as electro-shock devices, leg-irons, shackles, and restraints. Sales have been made to a dozen countries where the US State Department says the use of torture is "persistent".

Lest any of the above give the impression that the United States government is not disturbed by the practice of torture, it should be pointed out that Congress passed a bill in 1996 allowing, for the first time, an American citizen to sue a foreign government in a US court for having been tortured in that foreign country. There was, however, one small limitation imposed. The only countries that can be sued under this law are Washington's officially-designated enemies (ODE), those categorized as "state sponsors of terrorism".[39]

For other countries, the situation may be like the case in the early 1990s of Scott Nelson, an American who sued Saudi Arabia in a US court for torture. A Circuit Court of Appeals ruled that he had a right to sue, but the State Department helped the Saudis to get the case reversed in the Supreme Court.[40]

In 2002, 17 former US prisoners of war who say they were tortured during the 1991 Persian Gulf War filed a claim against Iraq. The following year, when Iraq failed to appear in court, the former servicemen won a default judgment of $959 million, against Iraq's $1.7 billion in assets frozen by the US government. When that judgment was overturned by the Court of Appeals, the servicemen appealed their case to the Supreme Court. By this time, however, the United States had occupied Iraq as the de facto government. Thus it was that the Bush administration intervened in the lawsuit, saying that the money was needed to rebuild Iraq. The Supreme Court declined to hear the case.[41]

Chapter 6

The Unsavories

During the 1980s, there were a number of disclosures of past and present CIA involvement with torturers, death-squaders, drug traffickers, and other types not fit for American schoolbooks, particularly men from Latin America. At some unrecorded moment, a government spinhead came up with the term "unsavory persons", implying that the government was as repulsed by these types as much as any decent American citizen ought to be.

The media obediently picked up on it. With each new revelation of the CIA's connection to human rights violations in the company of some despicable people abroad, who were on the Agency payroll, Americans were told—and told officially—that the CIA had no choice but to associate with "unsavory" persons if it wished to obtain certain important information in foreign countries; information, of course, vital to America's "national security". A new whitewash cliché had been born, still very much alive.

Even when the media is critical of the CIA for working with unsavories, there's no indication that the relationship has ever been anything more than paying for information while holding one's nose.

But it should be clearly understood that these unsavories have not been simply informants.

To the CIA and the US military these men are America's allies on the same side of a civil conflict.

US propaganda insists that the side these men are fighting on is the side of freedom and democracy.

We champion their cause, for it is our cause as well.

We select certain of them to attend American military schools and we bestow graduation certificates upon them.

We wine and dine them in the US, we give them gifts, we set them up with prostitutes.

We train them and give them their weapons and uniforms.

We teach them methods of bomb-making, methods of assassination, and methods of interrogation (read torture).

We provide them with information about individuals from the CIA's mammoth international databases. Some of these individuals then wind up tortured and/or murdered.

We cover up their atrocities.

We facilitate and cover up their drug trafficking.

We socialize with them. They are our friends. They have often betrayed their own country for us.

The money paid to unsavories is of course available to them to finance their vile purposes. When someone like Qaddafi of Libya did this, it was called "supporting terrorism".

CIA payments and other support to these unsavories necessarily bring more than information—they bring influence and control. When one looks at the anti-democratic and cruelty levels of the recipients, one has to wonder what the CIA's influence was. And at the same time one has to ask the following question: If the United States must take sides in a foreign civil war, why must it repeatedly be on the same side as the unsavories?

Other unsavory skeletons in Washington's closet

In the post-World War II period, US foreign policy embraced many other unsavories—"former" Nazis (including war criminals like Klaus Barbie), Italian fascists, Japanese enemy armed forces, Japanese scientists who had carried out terrible experiments on prisoners, including Americans; and thousands of others who had collaborated with these individuals during the war. In many parts of Europe and Asia, collaborators with the enemy were publicly disgraced, imprisoned, and/or executed by the post-war governments or citizens' groups. But in China, Italy, Greece, the Philippines, Korea, Albania, West Germany, Iran, Soviet Union, Vietnam and elsewhere, many of the fascists and collaborators who eluded punishment became American allies in setting up new governments, trying to overthrow governments, fighting civil wars, suppressing the left, gathering intelligence, and in manipulating electoral politics; indeed, many of them eluded punishment *because* they became American allies.[1]

As late as 1988, there were a number of genuine pro-Nazi, anti-Semitic types from Eastern and Central Europe in the Republican Party's National Republican Heritage Groups Council. Several of these worthies were leaders of the George Bush presidential campaign's ethnic outreach arm, the Coalition of American Nationalities, despite the fact that their checkered past was not a big secret. One of them, Laszlo Pasztor (or Pastor) had served in the pro-Nazi Hungarian government's embassy in Berlin during the war. This had been revealed in a 1971 page-one story in the *Washington* Post.[2] When this past was again brought up in September 1988, the Republicans were obliged to dump Pasztor and four others of his ilk from Bush's campaign.[3]

When lying down with unsavories has such a long heritage, for Washington to pretend that it's no more than a temporary marriage of convenience to an (unfortunately) unattractive bride, is an exercise that fails to rise above simplistic propaganda. What has attracted the two sides to each other over the years has been a shared class-consciousness, manifesting itself in an abhorrence of progressive movements, or something called "communism", or most anything or anyone seen as a threat to a mutually-desired status quo. The lowly, crude Guatemalan lieutenant relishes hanging around the American stage door more than gazing upon his country's Indian peasants. His Yankee drinking buddy is convinced it's an act of duty to help the lieutenant get rid of them.

Chapter 7

Training New Unsavories

I have seen no evidence in my 24 years in Congress of one
instance where because of American military involvement
with another military that the Americans have stopped that
foreign army from carrying out atrocities against their own
people. No evidence, none.

— Senator Tom Harkin (D-Iowa), 1999[1]

School of the Americas

The School of the Americas (SOA), an Army school at
Fort Benning, Georgia, has been beleaguered for years by
protesters because so many of its graduates have been involved
in very serious human- rights abuses in Latin America, often
involving torture and murder. SOA insists that it teaches its
students to respect human rights and democracy. To examine this
claim we must note that wars between nations in Latin America
are extremely rare. The question which thus arises is: Who are
these military men being trained to fight if not the army of another
country? Who but their own citizens?

Over the years, SOA has trained tens of thousands of
Latin American military and police in subjects such as counter-
insurgency, infantry tactics, military intelligence, anti-narcotics
operations, and commando operations. The students have also
been taught to hate and fear something called "communism", later
something called "terrorism", with little, if any, distinction made
between the two, thus establishing the ideological justification
to suppress their own people, to stifle dissent, to cut off at the
knees anything bearing a likeness to a movement for social

change which—although the military men might not think in such terms—might interfere with Washington's global agenda.

Those who have been on the receiving end of anti-communist punishment would have a difficult time recognizing themselves from this piece of philosophy from an SOA class: "Democracy and communism clash with the firm determination of the Western countries to conserve their own traditional way of life."[2] This reads as if dissidents came from some faraway land, with alien values, and no grievances that could be comprehended as legitimate by the "Western" mind.

In September 1996, under continual insistence from religious and grassroots groups, the Pentagon released seven Spanish-language training manuals used at the SOA until 1991. A *New York Times* editorial declared:

> Americans can now read for themselves some of the noxious lessons the United States Army taught to thousands of Latin American military and police officers at the School of the Americas during the 1980s. A training manual recently released by the Pentagon recommended interrogation techniques like torture, execution, blackmail and arresting the relatives of those being questioned.[3]

SOA graduates have led a number of military coups—so many that the *Washington Post* reported in 1968 that the school was "known throughout Latin America as the 'escuela de golpes' or coup school".[4] The most recent SOA-linked coup was the 2002 short-lived overthrow of Hugo Chavez in Venezuela. Amongst the plotters were two SOA grads: Army Commander in Chief Efrain Vasquez and General Ramirez Poveda.[5]

The school's alumni are also responsible for the murders of thousands of people, particularly in the 1980s, such as the Uraba massacre in Colombia; the El Mozote massacre, the assassination of Archbishop Oscar Romero, the rape and murder of four US churchwomen, and the Jesuit massacre in El Salvador; the La

Cantuta massacre in Peru; the torture and murder of a UN worker in Chile; and hundreds of other human-rights abuses.

In the village of El Mozote, El Salvador, in December 1981, from 700 to 1,000 persons were reported killed, mostly the elderly, women and children, in extremely cruel and gruesome ways.[6] Ten of the twelve soldiers cited for the massacre were SOA graduates. In the slaying of six Jesuit priests and two others in November 1989, the UN Truth Commission revealed that 19 of the 26 Salvadoran officers involved had been trained at the SOA.[7]

For decades SOA grads have been involved in the chain of command of virtually every major human rights atrocity in Latin America. The School of the Americas Watch has compiled a large amount of relevant information, which can be accessed on their website.

The SOA has always claimed that it doesn't teach its students how to torture or how to commit other human-rights abuses. When the truth was revealed by the release of the training manuals, the SOA claimed that it had changed its ways. But only one of 42 courses in the 1996 course catalogue—"Democratic Sustainment"—centers on issues of democracy and human rights. In 1997, only 13 students took this course, compared with 118 who took "Military Intelligence". The "mandatory human-rights component" of other courses comprises only a very small portion of the total course hours. Former SOA human-rights instructor Charles Call has reported that human- rights training is not taken seriously at the school, comprising an insignificant amount of students' overall training.[8]

Access

Why, in the face of decades of terrible publicity, increasingly more militant protests and civil disobedience at the base in Georgia, thousands of arrests, and sharply decreasing Congressional support, has the Pentagon clung to the School of the Americas? What is it that's so vital to the military brass? The answer may lie in this: The school and its students, along with a never-ending supply of US military equipment to countries in Latin America, are part of a package that serves the US foreign policy agenda in a special way. The package is called "access". Along with the equipment come American technicians, instructors, replacement parts, and more. Here is the testimony before Congress of General Norman Schwarzkopf, Commander in Chief, U.S. Central Command (CENTCOM), in 1990.

> Security assistance leads directly to access, and without access afforded by our friends we cannot project U.S. military forces into [an] area and stay there for any appreciable length of time.... [If] our military assistance programs diminish, our influence will erode and we will come to the point where we will have little or no ability to control the use of the weapons or the escalation of hostilities.... The second pillar of our strategy is presence. It is the symbol of America's continued interest in and commitment to stability in the region.... The third pillar of CENTCOM's strategy is combined [military] exercises. They demonstrate our resolve and commitment to the region. They foster increased cooperation, and they enhance our ability to work with our friends in a coalition environment."[9]

Thus it is that military aid, military exercises, Naval port visits, etc.—like the School of the Americas—means repeated opportunities to foster close ties, even camaraderie, between American officers and foreign military personnel; and, at the same time, the opportunity to build up files of information on many thousands of these foreigners, as well as acquiring language skills, maps, and photos of the area. In sum total: personal connections, personal information, country databases—indispensable assets in time of coup, counter-coup, revolution, counter-revolution, or invasion.

US military presence has, in effect, served the purpose of "casing the joint"; it also facilitates selecting candidates, not just Latin Americans for SOA, but thousands of military and police personnel from other continents who come to the US for training at scores of other military schools; the process of access replenishes itself. It is not unusual for the military-to-military contacts to thrive even while diplomatic relations between Washington and the students' government are rather cool (in the late 1990s, e.g., Algeria, Syria and Lebanon)   another indication of the priority given to the contacts.[10]

The military equipment sales that access leads to are highly valued as well.

The New Improved School of the Americas

When Congress came close to ending funding for the school in fall 1999, the Defense Department finally saw the writing on the wall. It announced that it was planning on making major changes to the school—less strictly military focus and more academic; civilian students as well as military; teaching democratic principles, etc.; changing the name to the Center for Inter- American Security Cooperation (later changed to Western Hemisphere Institute for Security Cooperation or WHINSEC).

The question remains: Why keep the school at all? Are there not enough academic schools here and in Latin America that meet such a need? Americans don't have free university education. Why should the United States provide it for foreigners?

The answer appears to be the factor that the changes wouldn't affect—access; perhaps new, improved access, inasmuch as in addition to military students, there will be further access to present and future political and civilian leaders as students.[11]

In any event, there will still be the numerous other military training facilities for foreigners in the US, in addition to the extensive training the Pentagon carries out abroad.

SOA/WHINSEC now claims that all their applicants must undergo a stringent vetting process, declaring: "Specifically, Chiefs of Missions should ensure that all nominees for training or travel grants, military or civilian, in country or in the U.S., are scrutinized for records of human rights abuses, corruption, or criminal activities that would render them ineligible or inappropriate for U.S. training programs."

School of the Americas Watch, in Washington, DC, has questioned this. The activist group claims that the screening process for applicants to WHINSEC is mostly cosmetic. They offer the following examples:

In a well known and high profile case, Col. Francisco del Cid Diaz was investigated by the 1992 UN-mandated El Salvadoran Truth Commission as having bound, beaten, and shot 16 residents from the Los Hojas cooperative of the *Asociacion Nacional de Indigenas*. Yet Col. del Cid Diaz attended WHINSEC in 2003.

While a Captain, Filmann Urzagaste Rodriguez, was one of those responsible for the kidnap and torture of Waldo Albarracin, then the director of the Popular Assembly for Human Rights in Bolivia. The now-Major Urzagaste took a 49-week officer training course at WHINSEC in 2002.

Three Colombian police officers—Captain Dario Sierro Chapeta, Lieutenant Colonel Francisco Patino Fonseca, and Captain Luis Benavides—were under investigation for personal use of counter-narcotics funds at the same time they attended WHINSEC in 2002-03.[12]

Office of Public Safety schools

From the early 1960s until the mid 1970s, the US Office of Public Safety (part of AID), operated The International Police Academy, at first in Panama, then in Washington. It did for foreign police officers what the SOA did for the military. OPS provided training abroad for more than a million policemen in the Third World, ten thousand of whom were selected to come to Washington for advanced training. There may well have been more serious human-rights abusers amongst the OPS police students than amongst the SOA military graduates because of the former's closer and more frequent contact with the populace. Moreover, most of the classes were held abroad, where the instructors could feel less constrained than in Washington or Georgia about lecturing in a very militant manner on "the communist menace" and the use of any means necessary to combat it. Amongst the means sometimes taught was torture. (See "Torture" chapter, sections on Latin America.)

OPS provided the police with weapons, ammunition, radios, patrol cars, tear gas, gas masks, batons, and other crowd control devices; a class on Assassination Weapons—"A discussion of various weapons which may be used by the assassin" is how OPS put it; and instruction on the design, manufacture and employment of bombs and incendiary devices, taught at the "bomb school" in Los Fresnos, Texas. The official OPS explanation for the bomb courses was that policemen needed such training in order to deal with bombs placed by terrorists. There was, however, no instruction in destroying bombs, only in making them.[13]

When Congress abolished the Public Safety Program in 1975 in response to rising criticism of this dark side of American foreign policy, the Drug Enforcement Administration, with help from the FBI and the Defense Department, quietly stepped in and continued the program.[14] In various reincarnations, the program has continued, just as the School of the Americas made it to the 21st century.[15]

Brazil

The *Escola Superior de Guerra* (Higher War College*)*, founded
in Rio de Janeiro in 1949, allowed the United States to foster
relationships with Brazilian officers similar to those with SOA
students, while passing on a similar political mentality. Latin
America historian Thomas E. Skidmore has observed:

> Under the U.S.-Brazilian military agreements of the early
> 1950s, the U.S. Army received exclusive rights to render
> assistance in the organization and operation of the college,
> which had been modeled on the National War College in
> Washington. In view of the fact that the Brazilian War College
> became a rallying point for leading military opponents of
> civilian populist politicians, it would be worth examining
> the extent to which the strongly anti-Communist ideology—
> bordering on an anti-political attitude—was reinforced (or
> moderated?) by their frequent contacts with United States
> officers.[16]

There was, moreover, the ongoing US Military Assistance
Program, which US Ambassador to Brazil, Lincoln Gordon,
described in a March 1964 cable to the State Department as a
"major vehicle for establishing close relationships with personnel
of the armed forces" and "a highly important factor in influencing
[the Brazilian] military to be pro-US."[17]

Just weeks after this cable was sent, the Brazilian military
overthrew a populist government which was on Washington's
hate/hit list.

Chapter 8

War Criminals:
Theirs and Ours

I suppose if I had lost the war, I would have been tried as a war criminal. Fortunately, we were on the winning side.
US General Curtis LeMay, commander of the 1945
Tokyo fire bombing operation.[1]

On December 3, 1996, the US Justice Department issued a list of 16 Japanese citizens who would be barred from entering the United States because of "war crimes" committed during the Second World War. Among those denied entry were some who were alleged to have been members of the infamous "Unit 731", which, said the Justice Department, "conducted inhumane and frequently lethal pseudo- medical experiments—on thousands of...prisoners and civilians," including mass dissections of living humans.[2] Oddly enough, after the war the man in charge of the Unit 731 program—whose test subjects included captured American soldiers—General Shiro Ishii, along with a number of his colleagues, had been granted immunity and freedom in exchange for providing the United States with details about their experiments, and were promised that their crimes would not be revealed to the world. The justification for this policy, advanced by American scientists and military officials, was, of course, the proverbial, ubiquitous "national security".[3]

Apart from the hypocrisy of the Justice Department including Unit 731 members on such a list while protecting its leaders, we are faced with the fact that any number of countries would be justified in issuing a list of Americans barred from entry because of "war crimes" and "crimes against humanity". Such a list, of those still alive in 2005, might include:

William Clinton, president, for his merciless bombing of the people of Yugoslavia for 78 days and nights in 1999, taking the lives of many hundreds of civilians, and producing one of the greatest ecological catastrophes in history; for his relentless continuation of the sanctions and rocket attacks upon the people of Iraq; and for his illegal and lethal bombings of Somalia, Bosnia, Sudan, and Afghanistan.

General Wesley Clark, Supreme Allied Commander in Europe, for his direction of the NATO bombing of Yugoslavia with an almost sadistic fanaticism..."He would rise out of his seat and slap the table. 'I've got to get the maximum violence out of this campaign—now!'"[4]

George H. W. Bush, president, for the death of more than a million innocent Iraqi citizens, the result of his 40 days of bombing in 1991, the deliberate ruination of the public water supply, the widespread use of depleted uranium weapons which has brought continuing suffering to many thousands of American servicemen and to many more Iraqis, and for the institution of draconian sanctions against Iraq, which lasted 12 years.
For his unconscionable bombing of Panama in 1989, producing widespread death, destruction and homelessness, for no discernible reason that would stand up in a court of law or a court of public opinion.

General Colin Powell, Chairman of the Joint Chiefs of Staff, for his prominent role in the attacks on Panama and Iraq, the latter including destruction of nuclear reactors as well as plants making biological and chemical agents. Hardly more than a month had passed since the United Nations, under whose mandate the United

States was supposedly operating in Iraq, had passed a resolution reaffirming its "prohibition of military attacks on nuclear facilities" in the Middle East.[5] In the wake of the destruction, Powell gloated: "The two operating reactors they had are both gone, they're down, they're finished."[6] He was just as cavalier about the lives of the people of Iraq. In response to a question concerning the number of Iraqis killed in the war, the good general replied: "It's really not a number I'm terribly interested in."[7]

For his part in the cover up of war crimes in Vietnam by troops of the same brigade that carried out the My Lai massacre.[8]

General Norman Schwarzkopf, Commander in Chief, U.S. Central Command, for his military leadership of the Iraqi carnage in 1991; for continuing the carnage two days after the cease-fire; for continuing it against Iraqis trying to surrender.

Elliott Abrams, assistant secretary of state under Reagan; a tireless campaigner and propagandist for the vilest of dictatorships, death squads, and torturers in Central America and Pinochet's Chile; a spinmeister for the ages, who wrestled facts into ideological submission. "When history is written," he declared, "the Contras will be folk heroes," he wrote of the terrorists who carried out multiple atrocities against the people of Nicaragua.[9]

Caspar Weinberger, Secretary of Defense for seven years under Reagan, for his official and actual responsibility for the numerous crimes against humanity perpetrated by the United States in Central America and the Caribbean, and for the bombing of Libya in 1986.

Lt. Col. Oliver North, assigned to Reagan's National Security Council, for being a prime mover behind the Contras of Nicaragua, and for his involvement in the planning of the completely illegal invasion of Grenada, which took the lives of hundreds of innocent civilians.

Henry Kissinger (who has successfully combined three careers: scholar, Nobel peace laureate, and war criminal), National Security Adviser under Nixon and Secretary of State under Nixon and Ford, for his Machiavellian, amoral, immoral roles in the US interventions into Angola, Chile, East Timor, Vietnam, and Cambodia, which brought unspeakable horror and misery to the peoples of those lands.

Gerald Ford, president, for giving his approval to Indonesia to use American arms to brutally suppress the people of East Timor, thus setting in motion a quarter-century-long genocide.

Robert McNamara, Secretary of Defense under presidents Kennedy and Johnson, a prime architect of, and major bearer of responsibility for, the slaughter in Indochina, from its early days to its extraordinary escalations; and for the violent suppression of popular movements in Peru.

General William Westmoreland, Army Chief of Staff, for the numerous war crimes under his command in Vietnam. In 1971, Telford Taylor, the chief US prosecutor at the post-World War II Nuremberg Tribunal, cited the "Yamashita" case as grounds for indicting Westmoreland. Following the war, a US Army Commission had sentenced Japanese General Tomayuki Yamashita to be hanged for atrocities committed by his troops in the Philippines. The Commission held that as the senior commander, Yamashita was responsible for not stopping the atrocities. The same ruling could of course apply to General Powell and General Schwarzkopf. Yamashita, in his defense, presented considerable evidence that he had lacked the communications to adequately control his troops; yet he was still hanged. Taylor pointed out that with helicopters and modern communications, Westmoreland and his commanders didn't have this problem.[10]

And the Bush administration, some of them are still at it, even as you read this: George W. Bush, president, Richard Cheney, vice president, Donald Rumsfeld, Secretary of Defense, Paul Wolfowitz, Deputy Secretary of Defense, Colin Powell, Secretary of State, Condoleezza Rice, National Security Advisor, for the awful horrors and grave suffering they deliberately brought down upon the heads of the people of Iraq and Afghanistan, who had done them no harm; for the unending lying they engaged in, in an attempt to enlist American and world support for these atrocities.

The crime of bombing

As mentioned in the "Bombings" chapter, the bombing of cities from airplanes goes not only unpunished but virtually unaccused. This is a legacy of World War II. The Nuremberg and Tokyo judgments are silent on the subject of aerial bombardment. Since both sides had played a terrible game of urban destruction—the Allies far more successfully—there was no basis for criminal charges against the Germans or Japanese, and in fact no such charges were brought. But as Telford Taylor has asked: "Is there any significant difference between killing a babe-in-arms by a bomb dropped from a high-flying aircraft, or by an infantryman's point-blank gunfire?...The aviator's act [is described] as more 'impersonal' than the ground soldier's. This may be psychologically valid, but surely is not morally satisfactory."[11]

No one ever thinks they're guilty of anything...they're all just good ol' patriots

"Asked whether he wants to apologize for the suffering he caused, he looks genuinely confused, has the interpreter repeat the question, and answers 'No'....'I want you to know that everything I did, I did for my country.'"

Journalist Nate Thayer interviewing a dying Pol Pot, 1997[12]

"I tell you how I feel. I would like to be remembered as a man who served his country, who served Chile throughout his entire life on this earth. And what he did was always done thinking about the welfare of Chile."

General Augusto Pinochet, under house arrest in England, 1998[13] (While Pinochet was being held, George H.W. Bush, the Pope, and the Dalai Lama all called for his release.)

How to deal with the unthinkable

At the close of World War II, the International Military Tribunal for the Far East held a trial in Tokyo of former Japanese Prime Minister Hideki Tojo. His lawyer asked why Tojo's crimes were any worse than dropping the A-bomb on Hiroshima and Nagasaki. At that moment, the prosecution interrupted the Japanese translation and ordered the removal of the remarks in the official trial record and in the press.[14]

Another unthinkable

The Convention on the Prevention and Punishment of the Crime of Genocide ("Genocide Convention"), adopted by the United Nations General Assembly in 1948: "The Contracting Parties confirm that genocide, whether committed in time of peace or in time of war, is a crime under international law which they undertake to prevent and to punish." The Convention then goes on to define genocide as certain acts, listed therein, "committed with intent to destroy, in whole or in part, a national, ethnical, racial or religious group, as such."

Missing from this list is perhaps the most significant manifestation of genocide in modern times: the extermination of people because of their political ideology. The Nazis became notorious for their slaughter of Jews and Gypsies, but German fascism, as in Italy, Spain, Greece, Chile, Indonesia, and elsewhere, was firstly and primarily directed against socialists and communists, regardless of any other characteristic. (Hitler, in any event, largely equated Jews and communists.)

As can be seen in the chapter on "Interventions" and in other chapters—from China and the Philippines in the 1940s to Colombia and Yugoslavia in the 1990s, the United States has long been practicing this *politicide*. However, the CEOs of The World's Only Superpower can rest easily. There will be no international convention against it, and no American official will ever have to answer to a court for it.

Yugoslavia—another war-crimes trial that will never be

Beginning about two weeks after the US-inspired and led NATO bombing of Yugoslavia began in March, 1999, international-law professionals from Canada, the United Kingdom, Greece, and the American Association of Jurists began to file complaints with the International Criminal Tribunal for the Former Yugoslavia in The Hague, Netherlands, charging leaders of NATO countries and officials of NATO itself with crimes similar to those for which the Tribunal had issued indictments shortly before against Serbian leaders. Amongst the charges filed by the law professionals were: "grave violations of international humanitarian law", including "willful killing, willfully causing great suffering and serious injury to body and health, employment of poisonous weapons and other weapons to cause unnecessary suffering, wanton destruction of cities, towns and villages, unlawful attacks on civilian objects, devastation not necessitated by military objectives, attacks on undefended buildings and dwellings, destruction and willful damage done to institutions dedicated to religion, charity and education, the arts and sciences."

The Canadian suit named 68 leaders, including William Clinton, Madeleine Albright, William Cohen, Tony Blair, Canadian Prime Minister Jean Chretien, and NATO officials Javier Solana, Wesley Clark, and Jamie Shea. The complaint also alleged "open violation" of the United Nations Charter, the NATO treaty itself, the Geneva Conventions, and the Principles of International Law Recognized by the International Military Tribunal at Nuremberg.

The complaint was submitted along with a considerable amount of evidence to support the charges. The evidence makes the key point that it was NATO's bombing campaign which had given rise to the bulk of the deaths in Yugoslavia, provoked most of the Serbian atrocities, created an environmental disaster, and left a dangerous legacy of unexploded depleted uranium and cluster bombs.

In June, some of the complainants met in The Hague with the court's chief prosecutor, Louise Arbour of Canada. Although she cordially received their brief in person, along with three thick volumes of evidence documenting the alleged war crimes, nothing of substance came of the meeting, despite repeated follow-up submissions and letters by the plaintiffs. In November, Arbour's successor, Carla Del Ponte of Switzerland, also met with some of the complainants and received extensive evidence.

The complainants' brief in November pointed out that the prosecution of those named by them was "not only a requirement of law, it is a requirement of justice to the victims and of deterrence to powerful countries such as those in NATO who, in their military might and in their control over the media, are lacking in any other natural restraint such as might deter less powerful countries." Charging the war's victors, not only its losers, it was argued, would be a watershed in international criminal law.

In one of the letters to Arbour, Michael Mandel, a professor of law in Toronto and the initiator of the Canadian suit, stated:

> Unfortunately, as you know, many doubts have already been raised about the impartiality of your Tribunal. In the early days of the conflict, after a formal and, in our view, justified complaint against NATO leaders had been laid before it by members of the Faculty of Law of Belgrade University, you appeared at a press conference with one of the accused, British Foreign Secretary Robin Cook, who made a great show of handing you a dossier of Serbian war crimes. In early May, you appeared at another press conference with US Secretary of State Madeleine Albright, by that time herself the subject of two formal complaints of war crimes over the targeting of civilians in Yugoslavia. Albright publicly announced at that time that the US was the major provider of funds for the Tribunal and that it had pledged even more money to it.[15]

Arbour herself made little attempt to hide the pro-NATO bias she wore beneath her robe. She trusted NATO to be its own police, judge, jury, and prison guard. In a year in which General Pinochet was still under arrest, which was giving an inspiring lift to the cause of international law and justice, the International Criminal Tribunal for the Former Yugoslavia, under Arbour's leadership, ruled that for the Great Powers it would be business as usual, particularly the Great Power that was most vulnerable to prosecution, and which, coincidentally, paid most of her salary. Here are her own words:

> I am obviously not commenting on any allegations of violations of international humanitarian law supposedly perpetrated by nationals of NATO countries. I accept the

assurances given by NATO leaders that they intend to conduct
their operations in the Federal Republic of Yugoslavia
in full compliance with international humanitarian law. I
have reminded many of them, when the occasion presented
itself, of their obligation to conduct fair and open-minded
investigations of any possible deviance from that policy, and
of the obligation of commanders to prevent and punish, if
required.[16]

NATO Press Briefing, May 16, 1999:
Question: Does NATO recognize Judge Arbour's jurisdiction over
their activities?
Jamie Shea: I think we have to distinguish between the theoretical
and the practical. I believe that when Justice Arbour starts her
investigation [of the Serbs], she will because we will allow her
to.... NATO countries are those that have provided the finance to
set up the Tribunal, we are amongst the majority financiers.

The Tribunal—created in 1993, with the US as the father, the
Security Council as the mother, and Madeleine Albright as the
midwife—also relies on the military assets of the NATO powers
to track down and arrest the suspects it tries for war crimes.

There appeared to be no more happening with the complaint
under Del Ponte than under Arbour, but in late December, in an
interview with *The Observer* of London, Del Ponte was asked if
she was prepared to press charges against NATO personnel. She
replied: "If I am not willing to do that, I am not in the right place.
I must give up my mission."

The Tribunal then announced that it had completed a study of
possible NATO crimes, which Del Ponte was examining, and that
the study was an appropriate response to public concerns about
NATO's tactics. "It is very important for this tribunal to assert its
authority over any and all authorities to the armed conflict within
the former Yugoslavia."

Was this a sign from heaven that the new millennium was going to be one of more equal justice? Could this really be?

No, it couldn't. From official quarters, military and civilian, of the United States and Canada, came disbelief, shock, anger, denials..."appalling"..."unjustified". Del Ponte got the message. Her office quickly issued a statement: "NATO is not under investigation by the Office of the Prosecutor of the International Criminal Tribunal for the former Yugoslavia. There is no formal inquiry into the actions of NATO during the conflict in Kosovo."[17] And there wouldn't be, it was unnecessary to add.

But the claim against NATO—heretofore largely ignored by the American media—was now out in the open. It was suddenly receiving a fair amount of publicity, and supporters of the bombing were put on the defensive. The most common argument made in NATO's defense, and against war-crime charges, was that the death and devastation inflicted upon the civilian sector was "accidental". This claim, however, must be questioned in light of certain reports. For example, the commander of NATO's air war, Lt. Gen. Michael Short, declared at one point during the bombing:

> If you wake up in the morning and you have no power to your house and no gas to your stove and the bridge you take to work is down and will be lying in the Danube for the next 20 years, I think you begin to ask, "Hey, Slobo [Serbian president Slobodan Milosevic], what's this all about? How much more of this do we have to withstand?"[18]

General Short, said the *New York Times*, "hopes that the distress of the Yugoslav public will undermine support for the authorities in Belgrade."[19]

At another point, NATO spokesman Jamie Shea declared: "If President Milosevic really wants all of his population to have water and electricity all he has to do is accept NATO's five conditions and we will stop this campaign."[20]

After the April NATO bombing of a Belgrade office building—which housed political parties, TV and radio stations, 100 private companies, and more—the *Washington Post* reported:

> Over the past few days, U.S. officials have been quoted as expressing the hope that members of Serbia's economic elite will begin to turn against Milosevic once they understand how much they are likely to lose by continuing to resist NATO demands.[21]

Before missiles were fired into this building, NATO planners spelled out the risks: "Casualty Estimate 50-100 Government/ Party employees. Unintended Civ Casualty Est: 250—Apts in expected blast radius."[22] The planners were saying that about 250 civilians living in nearby apartment buildings might be killed in the bombing, in addition to the government and political party employees.

What do we have here? We have grown men telling each other: We'll do A, and we think that B may well be the result. But even if B does in fact result, we're saying beforehand—as we'll insist afterward—that it was *unintended*.

The International Criminal Court

Following World War II there was an urgent need for a permanent international criminal court to prosecute those accused of war crimes, crimes against humanity, and genocide, but the Cold War intervened. Finally, in 1998 in Rome, the nations of the world drafted the charter of The International Criminal Court. American negotiators, however, insisted on provisions in the charter that would, in essence, give the United States veto power over any prosecution through its seat on the Security Council. The American request was rejected, and primarily for this reason the US refused to join 120 other nations who supported the charter. The ICC is an instrument Washington can't control sufficiently to keep it from prosecuting American military and government officials. Senior US officials have explicitly admitted that this danger is the reason for their aversion to the proposed new court,[23] although most commonly US government spokespersons speak of "frivolous lawsuits". They know they have no legal or moral argument to explain why the United States and its officials should be exempt from international law and justice, so they insist that all such indictments would be "frivolous" or "politically motivated"; i.e., without sufficient merit to take seriously and undertaken purely out of some perverse anti-Americanism. Their real concern of course is not that charges of war crimes will be made against American civilian and military officials "frivolously", but that they will be made "seriously" and that there are indeed quite a few American officials who would qualify.

But this is clearly not the problem with the International Criminal Tribunal for the Former Yugoslavia. It's Washington's kind of international court, a court for the New World Order.

The key human right promoted abroad by the United States is the right to shop. Washington tries to sell the notion that respect for human rights arises organically from free-market economics.

Chapter 9

Haven for Terrorists

America has a message for the nations of the world. If you harbor terrorists, you are terrorists. If you train or arm a terrorist, you are a terrorist. If you feed a terrorist or fund a terrorist, you're a terrorist, and you will be held accountable by the United States and our friends.

George W. Bush, November 22, 2001

In 1998, the State Department issued its annual human-rights report, listing Cuba amongst those nations alleged to "sponsor terrorism". Curious about this, I called up the State Department and was connected to what they called "The Terrorism Desk", where a gentleman named Joe Reap told me that Cuba was included because "They harbor terrorists."

"So does the United States," I replied. "The Cuban exiles in Miami have committed hundreds of terrorist acts, in the US and abroad."

Mr. Reap exploded. "Sir," he cried in a rising voice, "that is a fatuous remark and I will not listen to such nonsense!" And he hung up.

Unrepentant trouble-maker that I am, the following year, May 4, 1999 to be exact, when the new human-rights report was issued (does the word "self-righteous" ring a bell with the folks at the State Department?), I again called 202-647-8682, and again 'twas Joe Reap who answered. I doubt he knew that I was the same caller as the year before but, in any event, we went through the same dance steps. When I repeated my comment about the Cuban terrorists being harbored in Miami, he became instantly indignant and said that they were not terrorists.

"But the FBI has labeled some of them just that," I said.

"Then take it up with the FBI," said Joe.

"But we're discussing a State Department report," I pointed out.

His voice rising..."I will not listen to people call this government a terrorist sponsor!" Phone slammed down. The intervening year had not mellowed ol' Joe any more than it had me.

It's always fascinating to observe how a True Believer reacts to a sudden, unexpected and unanswerable threat to his fundamental Ideological underpinnings.

The Cuban exiles living in the United States are in fact one of the longest lasting and most prolific terrorist groups in the world, and they're still at it. During 1997 they carried out a spate of hotel bombings in Havana, directed from Miami.[1] In 2000, four of them were arrested in Panama where they had gone to assassinate Fidel Castro when he was speaking before a crowd of students. If their bombs had gone off there's no telling how many of the students would have lost their lives in addition to Castro. These four men had on their record such activities as blowing up a plane, which killed 73 people; the assassination of Orlando Letelier in Washington, DC (see below); shooting a UN diplomat dead in NY in front of his 12-year-old son; and much more. They were charged in Panama with crimes less than attempted murder and were pardoned after four years by the Panamanian president who was a close ally of President Bush. It's safe to say that Washington influenced her decision. When these four super-terrorists—the most notorious of whom was Luis Posada Carriles—were released, there was not a word of condemnation from the American government. They are all now living safely in the United States,[2] as is Posada's accomplice in the blowing up of the plane in 1976, Orlando Bosch. (In 1983, the city of Miami staged "Orlando Bosch Day".)[3]

Leading anti-Castro members of Congress, Reps. Lincoln

Diaz-Balart and Ileana Ros-Lehtinen, with the backing of Florida Governor Jeb Bush, have written letters on behalf of exile militants held in US prisons for acts of political violence. Some of the prisoners were released in 2001, including Jose Dionisio Suarez Esquivel and Virgilio Paz Romero, both convicted for the notorious 1976 car bomb-murder in Washington of Chilean diplomat Orlando Letelier, former associate of Salvador Allende. Once released, instead of being deported like other non-citizen criminals, they were allowed to settle into the good life in Miami.[4]

So safe and secure do Cuban anti-Castro terrorists feel in the United States that in June 2004 several of them from the Florida-based Comandos F4 organization appeared in a one-hour program on Miami television. Dressed in fatigues they spoke openly of their preparation for an armed attack against Cuba and assassination of Fidel Castro. A former Venezuelan army captain was also present in full uniform to discuss the help Comandos F4 were giving to his efforts to bring down the Hugo Chavez government by force.[5]

Hijacking is generally regarded as a grave international crime, but although there have been numerous air and boat hijackings over the years from Cuba to the US, at gunpoint, knifepoint, and/ or with the use of physical force, including at least one murder, it's difficult to find more than a single instance where the United States brought criminal charges against the hijackers. (In most cases the United States refused to even return the plane or boat.) In August 1996, three Cubans who hijacked a plane to Florida at knifepoint were indicted and brought to trial. In Florida. This is like trying someone for gambling in a Nevada court. Even though the kidnapped pilot was brought back from Cuba to testify against the men, the defense simply told the jurors that the man was lying, and the jury deliberated less than an hour before acquitting the defendants.[6]

Cubans are not the only foreign terrorists or serious human-rights violators who have enjoyed safe haven in the United States in recent decades. Like the Cubans, the others listed below are fervent anti-communists, or in some other way are compatible with past or present US foreign-policy objectives. (For sources not indicated, see this note.[7])

There's former Guatemalan Defense Minister Hector Gramajo Morales. In 1995, a US court ordered Gramajo to pay $47.5 million in damages to eight Guatemalans and a US citizen for his responsibility in the torture of an American (Sister Dianna Ortiz—see "Torture" chapter) and the massacre of family members of the Guatemalans (among thousands of other Indians whose death he was responsible for). Gramajo had been served a court summons in 1991 as he graduated from the Kennedy School of Government at Harvard, where he had studied on a scholarship provided by the US government. The judge stated that "The evidence suggests that Gramajo devised and directed the implementation of an indiscriminate campaign of terror against civilians." It was only following the court judgment that the Defense Department withdrew Gramajo's invitation to speak at a military seminar.[8] Gramajo subsequently returned to Guatemala, without having paid any of the court judgment. In speaking of his previous residence in Guatemala, he said that he had carried out what he described as "a more humanitarian" means of dealing with perceived dissenters. "We instituted civil affairs [in 1982] which provides development for 70 percent of the population, while we kill 30 percent. Before, the strategy was to kill 100 percent."[9]

Florida is the retirement home of choice for serious human-rights violators seeking to depart from the scene of their crimes. Former general, José Guillermo Garcia, head of El Salvador's armed forces in the 1980s, when military-linked death squads killed thousands of people suspected of being "subversives", has lived in Florida since the early 1990s.

Garcia's successor, Gen. Carlos Eugenio Vides Casanova,

who also served as the head of the much-feared National Guard, is now a resident of the sunshine state too. According to the U.N. Truth Commission for El Salvador, Vides covered up and protected those who raped and murdered three American nuns and a lay worker in 1980. He was physically present on at least two occasions when Dr. Juan Romagoza Arce was tortured; in the end, the injuries inflicted on Arce left him unable to perform surgery.

During the time that Garcia and Vides have lived in the United States, US Immigration has denied asylum status to many refugees from El Salvador even though they've claimed they were in fear of being tortured or losing their lives if sent back.

In 2002, a Florida court ruled in favor of three Salvadoran torture victims who had sued Garcia and Vides, awarding them $54 million. This was reversed in 2005 by a Federal Appeals Court, which ruled that the plaintiffs had waited more than 10 years, or beyond a statute of limitations, to bring legal action.

Another Salvadoran, Alvaro Saravia, has been living in the United States since at least 1987, in California and Florida. A former Captain in the Salvadoran Air Force, he worked closely with the late Roberto D'Aubuisson, the infamous death squad leader who was officially condemned by the Truth Commission for ordering the assassination of Archbishop Oscar Romero. Romero, a momentous figure in the struggle for human rights in El Salvador, for whom the Vatican started a beatification process in 2005, was shot in 1980 while saying mass. Saravia was sued by a relative of Romero for the death. In September 2004, a US court held Saravia responsible for the murder and ordered him to pay $10 million. Amnesty International and other groups have denounced Saravia's presence in the United States.

Col. Nicolas Carranza, now living in Memphis, was Vice-Minister of Defense of El Salvador during 1979-1981, a period of rampant human rights abuses, forced disappearances, arbitrary detention and murder. Carranza exercised command and control over the three units of the security forces—the National Guard, National Police, and Treasury Police—responsible for most of the attacks on civilians. He was also head of the Treasury Police for a period beginning in 1983. The Center for Justice and Accountability (CJA) of San Francisco, has filed a suit against Carranza on behalf of several Salvadorans for the torture they endured and for the murder of their family members. The trial is scheduled for September 2005.

Numerous Haitian human-rights violators have resided in the United States in recent years, unmolested by the authorities. Their hands and reputations are bloody from carrying out the repression of the Duvalier dynasty, or the overthrow of the democratically elected Father Jean-Bertrand Aristide in 1991, or the return to repression after the coup. Among their number are:

Luckner Cambronne, Haiti's minister of the interior and defense under Francois "Papa Doc" Duvalier and advisor to his son and successor, Jean Claude "Baby Doc" Duvalier.

Army Lt. Col. Paul Samuel Jeremie. After Baby Doc was forced to abdicate in 1986, Jeremie was convicted of torturing Duvalier opponents and sentenced to 15 years in prison. He escaped in 1988.

General Prosper Avril, another Haitian dictator, responsible for the torture of opposition activists, whom he then displayed, bloodied, on television. Forced out by angry mobs in 1990, he was flown to Florida by the US government, where he might have lived happily ever after except that some of his former torture victims brought suit against him. At one point in the process, he failed to make a court appearance and thus defaulted. He fled to several countries trying to find haven. Meanwhile, in 1994, a US federal judge awarded $41 million to six Haitians living in the US.

We also have leading Haitian death-squad leader, Emmanuel Constant, former head of FRAPH, the paramilitary group of thugs which spread deep fear amongst the Haitian people with its regular murders, torture, public beatings, arson raids on poor neighborhoods, and mutilation by machete in the aftermath of the coup against Aristide. He was on the CIA payroll in Haiti and has lived and worked openly in New York since 1995. The US government tried at first to deport Constant, but suspended its efforts and released him from detention after he threatened on the "60 Minutes" news program to expose information about the CIA's role in the formation of FRAPH. The State Department subsequently refused a Haitian extradition request for Constant.

Other Haitians of this ilk residing in the United States include Major General Jean-Claude Duperval, and Ernst Prud'homme, a high-ranking member of the Bureau du Information et Coordination, a notoriously violent propaganda unit.

Armando Fernández Larios, a member of a Chilean military squad responsible for the torture and execution of at least 72 political prisoners in the month following the 1973 coup (known as the "Caravan of Death"), is now residing in the United States. Fernández has publicly acknowledged his service as a member of the military squad, as well as his role as an agent of Chile's notorious secret police, the DINA, during the Pinochet regime. He struck a plea bargain with US government prosecutors, pleading guilty to being an "accessory after the fact" in the DINA- sponsored 1976 Washington, DC bombing murder of former Chilean dissident official, Orlando Letelier, the only assassination of a foreign diplomat in Washington in United States history. After serving a five-month federal prison term, Fernández moved to Florida. The Chilean government reportedly would like Fernández extradited from the US, but his lawyer in Miami has said that the 1987 plea-agreement between his client and the Department of Justice stipulated that Fernández would never be returned to Chile. Department of Justice officials have declined to comment on the degree of Fernández's protection under the terms of the agreement, which is under court seal.[10] In 2003, a US court awarded $4 million to the relatives of one of Fernández's Chilean victims.

Michael Tinley of Chile played an even more significant role in the Letelier assassination. He served some time in a US prison and is now in the Federal Witness Protection Program. So if you see him, you don't know him.

Argentine Admiral Jorgé Enrico, who was associated with *La Escuela Mecanica* in Buenos Aires, the infamous torture center of "The Dirty War" period (1976-83), now freely enjoys Hawaii when he wishes.

At least two former members of the Honduran army's Battalion 316 (see "Torture" chapter), a CIA-trained intelligence unit that murdered hundreds of suspected leftists in the 1980s, are also known to be living undisturbed in South Florida.

Kebassa Negawa of Ethiopia was a defendant in an Atlanta case for torture. When he lost the case and his wages began to be garnished, he disappeared.

Mohamed Ali Samantar was Somali Minister of Defense from 1980 to 1986 and Prime Minister 1987 to 1990, during which period the military and security agencies carried out widespread atrocities against suspected opponents of the military dictatorship. Human rights reports implicate the military in the systematic use of extrajudicial killings, torture, rape, and arbitrary and prolonged detention. Samantar now lives in Fairfax, Virginia and in 2004 was sued by CJA on behalf of six Somalis who were the victims of these policies.

Also a resident is Sintong Panjaitan, an Indonesian general responsible for the 1991 Santa Cruz massacre in East Timor that took hundreds of lives.

General Mansour Moharari, an Iranian who was in charge of prisons under the Shah, and thus no stranger to the practice of torture, has lived in the US for many years despite a price being put on his head by the Iranian mullahs.

Twenty former South Vietnamese officers who have admitted to committing torture and other human rights violations during the Vietnam War are residing legally in California.[11]

Throughout the 1980s and into the 90s, numerous other Vietnamese carried out a violent terrorist campaign against their countrymen in California who were deemed not sufficiently anti- communist, sometimes merely for calling for resumption of contacts with Hanoi; others were attacked simply for questioning the terrorists' actions. Under names such as "Anti-Communist Viets Organization" and "Vietnamese Organization to Exterminate Communists and Restore the Nation", on hundreds of occasions they assaulted and murdered, burned down businesses and vehicles, forced Vietnamese newspapers to cease publishing, issued death threats, engaged in extortion and many other aspects of organized crime...all with virtual impunity, even with numerous witnesses to some murders. In the few cases where arrests were made, suspects were generally released or acquitted; the few who were convicted had their wrists slapped.[12] This clear pattern of law- enforcement neglect suggests some kind of understanding with higher-ups in Washington. If there was indeed a "see-no-evil" federal policy, the most likely explanation would be the powerful, lingering antipathy toward any Vietnamese with a presumed leaning toward Hanoi.

The above doesn't include all the dictators *cum* terrorists whom the United States was kind enough to fly to safe havens in third countries (enabling them to be reunited with their bank accounts), such as those from Haiti who are still alive: Gen. Raoul Cédras and President Jean-Claude "Baby Doc" Duvalier; as well as the nefarious Police Chief Joseph Michel Francois.

In 1998 President Clinton went before the United Nations to speak about terrorism. "What are our global obligations?" he asked. "To give terrorists no support, no sanctuary."[13]

Extradite or prosecute

The system of international criminal prosecution covering genocide, terrorism, war crimes and torture makes all governments responsible for the criminal prosecution of offenders. Under this basic principle of "universal enforcement," countries where alleged offenders are found are obligated to either extradite them for prosecution by a more directly affected government (e.g., the country where the offenses were committed, or the country of citizenship of the victims or the abusers), or to initiate prosecution themselves. The Pinochet arrest in the UK in 1998 was as an example of this.

The US government strongly supports this principle of "extradite or prosecute" in theory, and in fact invoked it in the 1990s in a proceeding before the International Court of Justice as the basis for seeking extradition from Libya of two men alleged to be responsible for the bombing of Pan Am flight 103. Washington also strongly supports the application of this principle to those indicted for war crimes by the International War Crimes Tribunals for former Yugoslavia and Rwanda. One of those indicted as a war criminal by the Rwanda tribunal was discovered in Texas, arrested, and bound over for criminal extradition by a federal court in that State.[14]

Yet, when it comes to the relics of the Cold War being given haven in the US, as listed above, Washington chooses to neither prosecute nor extradite, although Cuba, for one, has asked for the extradition of a number of individuals, including Luis Posada Carriles.

Zero tolerance for other havens

Presidential Decision Directive 39, signed by President Clinton in 1995, states:

> If we do not receive adequate cooperation from a state that
> harbors a terrorist whose extradition we are seeking, we shall
> take appropriate measures to induce cooperation. Return of
> suspects by force may be affected without the cooperation of
> the host government.[15]

So determined was the Clinton administration to punish
other states that compete with the US in harboring terrorists,
that in February 1999 it asserted the right to bomb government
facilities in such nations. "We may not just go in a strike against a
terrorist facility; we may choose to retaliate against the facilities
of the host country, if that host country is a knowing, cooperative
sanctuary," Richard Clarke, President Clinton's coordinator for
counter-terrorism, declared.[16]

I tried to reach Mr. Clarke at his White House office to ask
him what he thought of the proposition that Cuba could justifiably
designate the United States as a "knowing, cooperative sanctuary"
and bomb CIA headquarters or a Cuban exile office in Miami,
amongst other sites. However, I was told that he was "not available
to the general public to speak to". Pity. So I sent him a letter posing
these questions, but did not receive a reply.

Chapter 10

Supporting Pol Pot

T he Killing Fields...the borders sealed, the cities emptied at gunpoint, a forced march to the countryside...being a professional, knowing a foreign language, wearing eyeglasses, almost anything, might be cause enough for persecution, execution...or the overwork will kill you, or a beating, or the hunger, or disease. For whatever reason: shortage of food, creation of an agrarian society impervious to the economic world order, internal party power, security...well over a million dead at the hands of the Cambodian Communist Party, the Khmer Rouge, under Pol Pot, after ousting the US-supported regime of Lon Nol...the world is horrified, comparisons to the Nazi genocide mushroom, "worse than Hitler" is Pol Pot ...

Four years later, January 1979, Vietnam—responding to years of attacks by the Khmer Rouge against ethnic Vietnamese in Cambodia and cross-border raids into Vietnam itself—invaded what was now called Kampuchea, overthrew Pol Pot's government, and installed a government friendly to Vietnam. The Khmer Rouge forces retreated to the western end of Cambodia, by the border with Thailand, and later some set up camp in Thailand itself.

Washington's reaction was not any kind of elation that the Cambodian nightmare had come to an end, but rather undisguised displeasure that the hated Vietnamese were in control and credited with ousting the terrible Khmer Rouge. For years afterwards, the United States condemned Vietnam's actions as "illegal". A lingering bitterness by American cold warriors against the small nation which monumental US power could not defeat appears to be the only explanation for this attitude. Humiliation runs deep, particularly when you're the world's only superpower.

Thus it was that an American policy took root—to provide the

Khmer Rouge with food, financial aid, and military aid beginning soon after their ouster.[1] The aim, in conjunction with China and long-time American client state, Thailand, was to restore Pol Pot's troops to military capability as the only force which could make the Vietnamese withdraw their army, leading to the overthrow of the Cambodian government.

President Carter's National Security Adviser, Zbigniew Brzezinski, has stated that in the spring of 1979: "I encouraged the Chinese to support Pol Pot. I encouraged the Thai to help the [Khmer Rouge]. The question was how to help the Cambodian people. [sic] Pol Pot was an abomination. We could never support him. But China could."[2]

In November 1980, Ray Cline, former Deputy Director of the CIA, visited a Khmer Rouge enclave inside Cambodia in his capacity as senior foreign-policy adviser to President-elect Ronald Reagan. A Khmer Rouge press release said that Cline "was warmly greeted by thousands of villagers."[3] The Reagan administration was apparently preparing to continue the policy of opposition to the Vietnamese-supported Phnom Penh government.

Some of the relief organizations operating in Cambodia considered supporting the Khmer Rouge guerrillas inconsistent with their humanitarian goals, in addition to the fact that distributing aid to military personnel was impermissible for such organizations as UNICEF and the International Committee of the Red Cross. But as two American relief aid workers, Linda Mason and Roger Brown, later wrote: "Thailand, the country that hosted the relief operation, and the U.S. government, which funded the bulk of the relief operation, insisted that the Khmer Rouge be fed."[4]

In the 1979-81 period, the World Food Program, which was strongly under US influence, gave almost $12 million in food to the Thai Army to distribute to predominantly Khmer Rouge camps by the border.[5]

In 1982, trying to remove the smell from the Khmer Rouge,

the United States put together a coalition composed of the Khmer Rouge and two "non-communist" groups also opposed to the Cambodian government, one headed by former Cambodian ruler, Prince Sihanouk.

The coalition became the recipient of much aid from the US and China, mainly funneled through Thailand. The American aid, by the late 1980s, reached $5 million officially, with the CIA providing between $20 and $24 million behind Congress's back.[6] The aid was usually referred to as "non-lethal" or "humanitarian", but any aid freed up other money to purchase military equipment in the world's arms markets. Officially, Washington was not providing any of this aid to the Khmer Rouge, but it knew full well that Pol Pot's forces were likely to be the ultimate beneficiaries. As one US official put it: "Of course, if the coalition wins, the Khmer Rouge will eat the others alive".[7] In any event, the CIA and the Chinese were supplying arms directly as well to the Khmer Rouge.[8]

From 1985 on, there was a Federal law prohibiting the government from providing any money to Cambodia which would have the effect of helping the Khmer Rouge's fighting capacity, either directly or indirectly.[9] After reports appeared in 1990 that aid to the coalition was getting into the hands of the Khmer Rouge, the Bush administration announced an official halt to the program.[10] Whether this was a serious effort to comply with the law, or simply an effort at damage control is not known; nor is it clear how long the halt lasted, if indeed it had been halted at all. The following February, the administration acknowledged to Congress that there may have been "tactical military cooperation" between US-backed non-communist forces and the Khmer Rouge.[11]

The Khmer Rouge were meanwhile using this aid to regularly attack Cambodian villages, seed minefields, kill peasants, and make off with their rice and cattle. But they never seriously threatened the Phnom Penh government.

The United States also successfully defended the right of the Khmer Rouge to the United Nations Cambodian seat, although their government had ceased to exist in January 1979. They held the seat until 1993. Beginning in 1982, the seat ostensibly represented the coalition, but the chief UN representative, Thiounn Prasith, had been a senior representative of the Khmer Rouge and was a leading apologist for Pol Pot's horrendous crimes.[12]

During the late 1980s and the early 1990s, the United States pressed for the dismantling of the Cambodian government and the inclusion of the Khmer Rouge in an interim government and in elections[13], despite still-lingering revulsion against Pol Pot and his followers amongst the Cambodian people and the international community, and despite the fact that the Vietnamese withdrew virtually all their forces from Cambodia in September 1989.

> *The death of Khmer Rouge leader Pol Pot has again brought to international attention one of the most tragic chapters of inhumanity in the twentieth century.... senior Khmer Rouge, who exercised leadership from 1975 to 1979, are still at large and share responsibility for the monstrous human rights abuses committed during this period. We must not permit the death of the most notorious of the Khmer Rouge leaders to deter us from the equally important task of bringing these others to justice.*
>
> President William Clinton, April 16, 1998[14]

PART II

United States' Use of
Weapons of Mass Destruction

Chapter 11

Bombings

It is a scandal in contemporary international law, don't forget, that while "wanton destruction of towns, cities and villages" is a war crime of long standing, the bombing of cities from airplanes goes not only unpunished but virtually unaccused. Air bombardment is state terrorism, the terrorism of the rich. It has burned up and blasted apart more innocents in the past six decades than have all the antistate terrorists who ever lived. Something has benumbed our consciousness against this reality. In the United States we would not consider for the presidency a man who had once thrown a bomb into a crowded restaurant, but we are happy to elect a man who once dropped bombs from airplanes that destroyed not only restaurants but the buildings that contained them and the neighborhoods that surrounded them. I went to Iraq after the Gulf war and saw for myself what the bombs did; "wanton destruction" is just the term for it.

C. Douglas Lummis, political scientist[1]

The above was written in 1994, before the wanton destruction generated by the bombing of Yugoslavia, the latest in a long list of countries the United States has bombarded since the end of World War II, which is presented below.

There appears to be something about launching bombs or missiles from afar onto cities and people that appeals to American military and political leaders. In part it has to do with a conscious desire to not risk American lives in ground combat. And in part, perhaps not entirely conscious, it has to do with not wishing to look upon the gory remains of the victims, allowing American GIs and TV viewers at home to cling to their warm fuzzy feelings about themselves, their government, and their marvelous "family values".

Washington officials are careful to distinguish between the explosives the US drops from the sky and "weapons of mass destruction" (WMD), which only the officially-designated enemies (ODE) are depraved enough to use. The US government speaks sternly of WMD, defining them as nuclear, chemical and biological in nature, and "indiscriminate" (meaning their use can't be limited to military objectives), as opposed to the likes of American "precision" cruise missiles. This is indeed a shaky semantic leg to stand on, given the well-known extremely extensive damage to non-military targets, including numerous residences, schools and hospitals, even from American "smart" bombs, in almost all of the bombings listed below.

Moreover, Washington does not apply the term "weapons of mass destruction" to other weapons the US has regularly used, such as depleted uranium and cluster bombs, which can be, and often are, highly indiscriminate.

WMD are sometimes further defined as those whose effects linger in the environment, causing subsequent harm to people. This would certainly apply to cluster bombs, and depleted uranium weapons, the latter remaining dangerously radioactive after exploding. It would apply less to "conventional" bombs, but even with those there are unexploded bombs lying around, and the danger of damaged buildings later collapsing. But more importantly, it seems highly self-serving and specious, not to mention exceptionally difficult, to try to paint a human face on a Tomahawk Cruise missile whose payload of a thousand pounds of TNT crashes into the center of a densely-populated city, often with depleted uranium in its warhead.

A terrorist is someone who has a
bomb but doesn't have an air force

Korea and China 1950-53 (Korean War)
Guatemala 1954
Indonesia 1958
Cuba 1959-1961
Guatemala 1960
Congo 1964
Laos 1964-73
Vietnam 1961-73
Cambodia 1969-70
Guatemala 1967-69
Grenada 1983
Lebanon 1983, 1984 (both Lebanese and Syrian targets)
Libya 1986
El Salvador 1980s
Nicaragua 1980s
Iran 1987
Panama 1989
Iraq 1991 (Persian Gulf War)
Kuwait 1991
Somalia 1993
Bosnia 1994, 1995
Sudan 1998
Afghanistan 1998
Yugoslavia 1999
Yemen 2002
Iraq 1991-2003 (US/UK on regular basis)
Iraq 2003-05
Afghanistan 2001-05

Plus

Iran, April 2003—hit by US missiles during bombing of Iraq, killing at least one person[2]

Pakistan, 2002-03—bombed by US planes several times as part of combat against the Taliban and other opponents of the US occupation of Afghanistan[3]

China, 1999—its heavily bombed embassy in Belgrade is legally Chinese territory, and it appears rather certain that the bombing was no accident (see chapter 25)

France, 1986—After the French government refused the use of its air space to US warplanes headed for a bombing raid on Libya, the planes were forced to take another, longer route; when they reached Libya they bombed so close to the French embassy that the building was damaged and all communication links knocked out.[4]

Philadelphia, Pennsylvania, May 13, 1985—A bomb dropped by a police helicopter burned down an entire block, some 60 homes destroyed, 11 dead, including several small children. The police, the mayor's office, and the FBI were all involved in this effort to evict a black organization called MOVE from the house they lived in.

Them other guys are really shocking

> "We should expect conflicts in which adversaries, because of cultural affinities different from our own, will resort to forms and levels of violence shocking to our sensibilities."
>
> Department of Defense, 1999[5]

The Targets

It's become a commonplace to accuse the United States of choosing as its bombing targets only people of color, those of the Third World, or Muslims. But it must be remembered that one of the most sustained and ferocious American bombing campaigns was carried out against the people of the former Yugoslavia—white, European, Christians. The United States is an equal-opportunity bomber. The only qualifications for a country to become a target are: (1) It poses a sufficient obstacle to the desires of the American Empire; (2) It is virtually defenseless against aerial attack.

The survivors

A study by the American Medical Association: "Psychiatric disorders among survivors of the Oklahoma City bombing":

> Nearly half the bombing survivors studied had an active postdisaster psychiatric disorder, and full criteria for PTSD [post-traumatic stress disorder] were met by one third of the survivors. PTSD symptoms were nearly universal, especially symptoms of intrusive reexperience and hyperarousal.[6]

Martin Kelly, publisher of a nonviolence website:

> We never see the smoke and the fire, we never smell the blood, we never see the terror in the eyes of the children, whose nightmares will now feature screaming missiles from unseen terrorists, known only as Americans.

Chapter 12

Depleted Uranium

T he United States," wrote international environmental campaigner Dr. Helen Caldicott some years ago, "has conducted two nuclear wars. The first against Japan in 1945, the second in Kuwait and Iraq in 1991."

We can now add a few more: Yugoslavia in 1999, Afghanistan beginning in 2001[1], Iraq beginning in 2003.

Depleted uranium (DU) is a by-product of the production of enriched uranium fuel for nuclear reactors and weapons. It's used in the manufacture of armaments such as tank cartridges, bombs, rockets, and missiles.

Because DU is denser than steel, shells containing it are capable of drilling a hole through the strongest of tank armors or penetrating thick-walled bunkers under the ground. But depleted uranium has its drawbacks—it's radioactive, and like all heavy metals, uranium is chemically toxic. Upon impact with a target, some of the DU aerosolizes into a fine mist of particles, which can be inhaled or ingested and then trapped in the lung, the kidneys, or elsewhere in the body where it becomes an internal radiation source. The impact also produces DU shrapnel, and a chunk of radioactive metal can wind up imbedded in a person's insides. Moreover, DU debris left lying at the scene, in various states of smash-up, is subject to any mishap, and is continually radiating. One atomic scientist has asserted that DU particles thrown into the air by the armament's impact, or by resultant fires and explosion, can be carried downwind for 25 miles or more.[2]

These exposures to DU can lead to lung cancer, bone cancer, kidney disease, genetic defects, and other serious medical problems.

In the 1991 Gulf War, countless Iraqi and American soldiers

breathed in the deadly DU dust, the product of tens of thousands of DU rounds fired by US aircraft and tanks. A study by the Operation Desert Shield/Desert Storm Association revealed that out of 10,051 Gulf War veterans who had reported mysterious illnesses, 82 percent had entered captured enemy vehicles, the main targets of DU weapons. Virtually all did so in full innocence of even the existence of DU, let alone its danger.[3]

To add to the dangers posed by depleted uranium, if it gets into the food chain or water, the potential health problems can multiply.

In 1995, Iraqi health officials reported alarmingly high increases in rare and unknown diseases, primarily in children, and presented a study of this state of affairs to the United Nations. The increases occurred in leukemia, carcinoma, cancers of the lung and digestive system, late-term miscarriages, congenital diseases, and deformities in fetuses, such as anencephaly (absence of a brain), and fused fingers and toes, not unlike those found in the babies of Gulf War veterans. Dr. Siegwart Gunther, professor of infectious disease and epidemiology and president of the International Yellow Cross in Austria, ascribed these ailments to the extensive use of DU in Iraq.[4]

Dr. Gunther believed that the DU had also infiltrated the food chain, resulting in new diseases among newborns and infants that he was unable to diagnose. Symptoms included abnormal abdominal distention that may be related to kidney or liver dysfunction, a known effect of exposure to DU. "But we have no way of knowing, because there is no way to examine them thoroughly," he said. "These children usually die within three months. Because of the impossibility of treatment, they die of secondary infections."[5]

In January 2003, the European Parliament called for a moratorium on depleted uranium use after reports of an unusual number of leukemia deaths among Italian soldiers who served in Kosovo, the Yugoslav province where the United States had dropped a large quantity of bombs containing DU. Yet, only two months after the European Parliament's declaration, a whole new generation of young American soldiers were sent off to the Iraqi depleted-uranium killing fields, just as ignorant and innocent as those shipped there in 1991, just as lacking in protective equipment, firing their technical-wonder weapons, adding to the considerable mass of DU already in the environment and in the Iraqi people. A year later they began coming home with the usual long list of depressing symptoms: joint aches, ever present nausea, overpowering fatigue, pain when swallowing, daily headaches, constant numbness in the hands, rashes on the stomach...the worse was likely yet to come, including to their offspring.[6]

One does not have to be caught in a war to become a victim of depleted uranium. In Scotland in 1999, DU was linked to a leukemia cluster around the Ministry of Defense firing range at Dundrennan. Communities close to the range, where 7,000 shells containing depleted uranium were tested from 1983 on, reportedly showed the highest rate of childhood leukemia in the UK.[7]

In training exercises, DU has been dropped on the island of San Clemente off the southern California coast, and perhaps only on some future day will we realize what the effects were of what drifted across to the mainland by air and sea. That island is at least uninhabited, unlike the island of Vieques in Puerto Rico, where over 9,000 American citizens dwell. They had to endure some 60 years of aerial target practice and war games, ending in 2003, including the dropping of napalm, and in later years, depleted uranium shells. Puerto Rican activists have claimed that Vieques has become contaminated with radioactivity, which contributed to a cancer rate among the island's inhabitants that was twice the national average. Studies in fact showed that Vieques' cancer rate was by far the highest of any of Puerto Rico's 78 municipalities.[8] Moreover, the landscape is littered with bomb and shell casings, including some that the US Navy warns are still live; a container with three unexploded anti-tank rockets (presumably DU-tipped) was found in a civilian sector in 1997; and, amongst other mishaps, four years earlier five 500- pound bombs were dropped, and exploded, one-and-a-half miles from civilian homes.[9]

Similar DU testing was carried out by the US military for years in Okinawa, Germany and South Korea.

In the United States, the military-industrial complex has been busy for decades paying off members of Congress and state legislatures to allow the acquisition of large tracts of public land, primarily in western states, and permit end-runs around existing environmental and other laws, as well as pesky environmental activists. These hundreds of thousands of acres have been turned into depleted-uranium-weapons testing grounds in California, Nevada, New Mexico, Washington, and other states.

In New Mexico, open-air testing of DU has been going on in some parts for several decades. Los Alamos National Laboratory, White Sands Missile Range, New Mexico Institute of Mining and Technology in Socorro, Sandia National Laboratories in Albuquerque—these are some of the famous institutions that blast DU munitions into mountains and soil, contaminating the ground, water and air; at the same time using their not- inconsiderable influence to try to convince the state's citizens that—even though they admit the contamination—radiation levels are no more than the proverbial "background level", or within Environmental Protection Agency safety levels. As the old saying goes, just don't breathe the air or drink the water. And don't raise your babies anywhere nearby.

In Socorro, the residents did not know until 1986 that DU testing had been taking place since 1972 less than two miles from the town square, downwind from the proving grounds. Over the years, there were a few scattered surveys and anecdotal evidence of a high incidence of the congenital birth defect hydrocephalus (excess fluid in the brain), but the year 1999 saw an increasing movement of Socorro citizens demanding broad epidemiological and contamination surveys of the area.[10]

In April 1995, French general and military author Pierre-Marie Gallois observed, "If we equip these tanks with these sorts of munitions [DU], that means that chemical-nuclear war is morally allowable."[11] A decade later, the United Nations General Assembly unanimously approved a treaty which criminalizes the possession or use of "radioactive material" which may "cause death, serious bodily injury or substantial damage to property or to the environment". That would do as a description of depleted uranium. However, the International Convention for the Suppression of Acts of Nuclear Terrorism was not aimed at the United States; the world would not dare, and Washington would not allow it. The treaty does not cover official actions of a nation's armed forces; instead, it was aimed at "non-state actors", such as rebels or insurgents not supported by a state. In any event, the US, though a signatory, will probably not ratify it; thus the treaty will have no legal validity in the United States. That has been the fate of the dozen previous international conventions against terrorism, approved between 1963 and 1999, but which ran afoul of those in Congress who feel that the United States should not be party to international conventions because they either override domestic law or are perceived as being not in the national interest.

Chapter 13

Cluster Bombs

The Pentagon places them in the category of "combined effects munitions." The manufacturer describes them as an "all-purpose, air-delivered cluster weapons system." Human rights and anti-landmine activists say that cluster bombs are indiscriminate weapons of mass destruction, and they have been campaigning for years to get them placed explicitly on the Geneva Convention list of banned weapons.

Cluster bombs are ingeniously designed. After being dropped from a plane, the canister breaks open in midair at a predetermined altitude, typically scattering 200 or so "bomblets" the size of a soft drink can. The bomblets (or "sub-munitions" as they're often called) explode upon hitting the ground, each one shooting out hundreds of shards of jagged steel at high velocity, able to saturate an extremely large area. One description of cluster bombs says "they can spray incendiary material to start fires, chunks of molten metal that can pierce tanks and other armor, or shrapnel that can slice with ease through...human flesh and bone."[1]

When the shards of steel strike a person they can set off pressure waves within the body, causing horrific damage to soft tissue and organs. Even a single fragment can rupture the spleen, or cause the intestines to explode. Victims who survive may suffer from a variety of injuries including loss of limbs, ruptured eardrums, and blindness.[2]

The military values cluster bombs because of their wide dispersal; they can destroy the usefulness of broad targets such as airfields and surface-to-air missile sites.

In the past 40 years, the United States has unleashed hundreds of millions of bomblets upon the land and people of Laos, Cambodia, Vietnam, Iraq, Kuwait, Yugoslavia and Afghanistan.

According to the Defense Department, US warplanes dropped 1,100 cluster bombs upon Yugoslavia in 1999, each carrying 202 bomblets. Thus, 222,200 of these weapons were propelled across the country. With a stated failure rate of 5 percent (other reports claim rates of up to 30 percent), this means that about 11,110 cluster bomblets were left lying unexploded[3], ready to detonate on contact; in effect becoming landmines. One reason the United States opposes signing the International Treaty Banning the Use, Production, Stockpiling and Transfer of Anti-Personnel Landmines is because the treaty's definition of land mines is broad enough to cover cluster bombs. Under the treaty, an anti-personnel mine is one "designed to be exploded by the presence, proximity or contact of a person and that will incapacitate, injure or kill one or more persons." Human-rights activists argue that since manufacturers of cluster bombs concede that a certain failure rate is inevitable, the bombs can be included under the definition.[4] The treaty entered into force on March 1, 1999 without the United States being a signatory.

The proclivity of cluster bombs to turn into land mines is not the only reason there has been a campaign to ban the weapon. There is also the immediate danger they pose to civilians during attacks due to their inaccuracy and wide dispersal pattern; they are not precision-guided weapons. It is for such reasons that cluster bombs can be categorized as weapons of mass destruction.

Unexploded cluster bomblets are even more of a concern than regular landmines because children in particular are drawn to the colorful devices, which often have little parachutes attached. (On April 24, 1999, even before the bombing of Yugoslavia had come to an end, five young brothers playing with an unexploded bomblet were killed, and two cousins severely injured, near Doganovic in southern Kosovo.[5]) Landmines are usually laid down in more or less expected places, whereas unexploded cluster bomblets can wind up in the back yards of homes, school playgrounds, anywhere.

The laying down of landmines is often tracked or mapped, the fields marked; not so with unexploded cluster bomblets, making them a long-lasting threat to civilians, soldiers, peacekeepers, and even landmine-clearance experts. Moreover, landmines are designed to maim rather than kill, whereas cluster bombs, which contain more explosive power and metal fragmentation, are more likely to kill and to cause multiple casualties.

When the bombing of Yugoslavia ended in June 1999, many areas of villages were left virtually uninhabitable, in desperate need of explosive experts who could find and incapacitate all the volatile live remnants; in one cluster bomb incident at this time, two British peacekeeping soldiers and three Albanians lost their lives in a Kosovo village.[6]

The effects of the unexploded munitions from the bombing of Yugoslavia reached beyond that country's borders. Two months after the war's end, 161 explosive devices, including 97 bomblets, had been recovered by NATO minesweepers in the Adriatic Sea. The munitions caused deaths and injuries to Italian fishermen and cost others the majority of their year's profits. A fishing ban was imposed in the Adriatic to allow minesweepers to collect more of the devices. In addition, tourists abandoned the beaches along the Adriatic coast during the summertime for fear of encountering unexploded bombs.[7]

Here are the words of a Yugoslav orthopedist: "Neither I nor my colleagues have ever seen such horrific wounds as those caused by cluster bombs. They are wounds that lead to disabilities to a great extent. The limbs are so crushed that the only remaining option is amputation. It's awful, awful."[8]

Stories of equal gruesomeness, too numerous to mention, have come out of the other countries attacked by American cluster bombs. The stories will continue for a long time for unexploded ordnance—mainly cluster bombs—are still killing and maiming people in Laos a generation after the massive US carpet-bombing of 1965-73. It is estimated that up to 30 percent of the two million tons of bombs dropped by the United States in Laos failed to explode, and that 11,000 people have been killed or injured subsequently, of which more than 30 percent have been children. "More than half of the victims die almost immediately following the accident. If the victim survives, the explosion often causes severe wounding and trauma, especially to the upper half of the body."[9]

Vietnam and Cambodia harbor similar dangers. As does the Persian Gulf. A 2004 Human Rights Watch report estimated that some two million unexploded bomblets were left behind after the Gulf War of 1991. By February 2003, these had killed 1,600 civilians and injured more than 2,500 in Iraq and Kuwait. Despite one of the most extensive and expensive clearance operations in history following the war, there were still 2,400 cluster munition duds detected and destroyed in Kuwait in 2002, and a similar number in 2001.[10]

Chapter 14

United States Use of Chemical and Biological Weapons Abroad

Poison gas and germ weapons turn civilization on its head. Diseases are not fought, but carefully cultivated; doctors use their knowledge of the functions of the human body to devise ever more effective means of halting those functions; agriculturalists deliberately induce fungi and develop crop destroyers.... Modern nerve gases were originally designed to help mankind by killing beetles and lice: now, in the hands of the military, they are, literally, insecticides for people. Chemical and biological warfare, as one writer has put it, is "public health in reverse".[1]

Bahama Islands

From the late 1940s to sometime in the 1950s, a joint US-Canada- British team sprayed highly virulent organisms in this area of the Caribbean as part of a chemical and biological weapons (CBW) testing program. Thousands of animals died as a result of the tests. It is not known whether there were any human victims. Details of the test are still classified.[2]

Canada

In 1953, the US Army used air blowers atop trucks to disseminate potentially dangerous zinc cadmium sulfide (see chapter 15) through the city of Winnipeg as part of its chemical and biological weapons tests.[3]

China and Korea

In the early part of 1952, during the Korean War (1950-53), the Chinese claimed that the United States was dropping quantities of bacteria, insects, feathers, decaying animal and fish parts, and many other strange objects that carried disease, over Korea and northeast China. The Chinese government declared that there had been casualties and quick deaths from plague, anthrax and encephalitis, amongst other diseases. They took testimony from some 36 captured American airmen who had purportedly flown the planes with the deadly cargo, and published 25 of these accounts. Many of the men went into voluminous detail about the entire operation: the kinds of bombs and other containers dropped, the types of insects, the diseases they carried, etc. Photographs of the alleged germ bombs and insects were also published. Then, in August, an "International Scientific Committee" was appointed, composed of scientists from Sweden, France, Great Britain, Italy, Brazil and the Soviet Union. After a two-month investigation in China, the committee produced a report of some 600 pages, many photos, and the conclusion that: "The peoples of Korea and China have indeed been the objectives of bacteriological weapons. These have been employed by units of the U.S.A. armed forces, using a great variety of different methods for the purpose."

However, some of the American airmen's statements contained so much technical biological information and were so full of communist rhetoric—"imperialist, capitalist Wall Street war monger" and the like—that their personal authorship of the statements must be seriously questioned. Moreover, it was later learned that most of the airmen had confessed only after being subjected to great mental and physical duress, and at least one case of a beating. And some did not necessarily know what they were dropping in their supposed explosive or leaflet bombs. When the pilots came home after the war, they retracted their confessions, but that was under threat of court martial, even "charges of treason", said the US Attorney General, and other threatened punishments—in short, great mental duress.[4]

It should be noted that in December 1951, the US Secretary of Defense had ordered that "actual readiness be achieved in the earliest practicable time" for offensive use of biological weapons. Within weeks, the chief of staff of the Air Force reported that such capabilities "are rapidly materializing".[5]

Moreover, it was revealed in 1979 that the US Army had experimented within the United States with the use of turkey feathers to conduct biological warfare.[6]

Apart from the above, the United States dropped huge amounts of napalm on Korea, an average of 70,000 gallons daily in 1952.[7] (Napalm is a highly flammable explosive, in the form of jellied gasoline, that clings to victims and produces horrific burning.)

And during 1967-69, the US sprayed the dangerous herbicide Agent Orange (see Vietnam below) and other toxic defoliants over 23,607 acres of the southern boundary of the demilitarized zone between North and South Korea, in order to strip vegetation and discourage North Korean infiltration.[8]

Vietnam

For about a decade beginning in the early 1960s, the United States sprayed tens of thousands of tons of herbicides over three million acres of South Vietnam (as well as parts of Laos and Cambodia) to wipe out the foliage used as a cover by the enemy and to destroy crops. The herbicides, particularly the extensively-used Agent Orange, polluted Vietnam with some five hundred pounds of dioxin, a nearly indestructible pollutant that is regarded as one of the most toxic substances in the world; at least as toxic as nerve gas, and highly carcinogenic. Amongst other health effects associated with exposure to dioxin are metabolic disorders, immunological abnormalities, reproductive abnormalities, and neuro-psychiatric disorders.[9] Three ounces in the water supply is thought to be enough to wipe out the population of New York City.[10]

As many as two million people were affected by these poisons in Vietnam (in addition to many thousands of American soldiers). There have been reports of high levels of birth defects in areas which were saturated with Agent Orange, and the Vietnam government estimates that the various chemicals have contributed to birth defects in 500,000 children, although this has not been documented.[11] No compensation has ever been paid by the United States to the Vietnamese people or government for any damage to health.

In addition, the US Army employed CS, DM and CN gasses, which, Washington officials insisted, did not constitute "gas warfare". They designated these gasses as "riot control" agents. The Army pumped CS gas—a violent purgative that causes uncontrollable vomiting—into Vietnamese tunnels and caves, causing many Vietcong to choke to death on their own vomit in the confined spaces.[12] The North Vietnamese branch of the International Red Cross and other international sources reported numerous deaths amongst women and children from these gasses, as well as injuries such as destroyed eyeballs, blistered faces, and scorched and erupted skin.[13] US Deputy Secretary of Defense Cyrus Vance disclosed that cyanide and arsenic compounds were being used as well.[14] Other harmful chemicals employed by the US in Vietnam were napalm and Naphthalene flamethrowers.

Laos

In September 1970, American forces in Laos, acting under "Operation Tailwind", used aerosolized sarin nerve agent (referred to also as CBU-15 or GB) to prepare their entry in an attack upon a Laotian village base camp, with the object of killing a number of American military defectors who were reported to be there. The operation succeeded in killing in excess of 100 people, military and civilian, including at least two Americans. How many died before the attack from the gas and how many from the attack itself is not known.

Sarin, which was developed in Germany in the 1930s, can kill within minutes after inhalation of its vapor. A tiny drop of it on the skin will do the same; it may even penetrate ordinary clothing. It works by inhibiting an enzyme needed to control muscle movements. Without the enzyme, the body has no means of stopping the activation of muscles, and any physical horror is possible.

When the invading Americans were making their getaway, they were confronted by a superior force of North Vietnamese and communist Pathet Lao soldiers. The Americans called for help from the air. Very shortly, US planes were overhead dropping canisters of sarin upon the enemy. As the canisters exploded, a wet fog enveloped the enemy soldiers, who dropped to the ground, vomiting and convulsing. Some of the gas spread towards the Americans, not all of whom were adequately protected. Some began vomiting violently. Today, one of them suffers from creeping paralysis, which his doctor diagnoses as nerve-gas damage.[15]

This story was reported on June 7, 1998, on the TV program "NewsStand: CNN & Time", and featured the testimony of Admiral Thomas Moorer, who had been Chairman of the Joint Chiefs of Staff in 1970, as well as lesser military personnel, both on and off camera, who corroborated the incidents described above.

Then all hell broke loose. This was a story too much in conflict—painfully so—with American schoolbooks, Readers Digest, the flag, apple pie, and mom. It was damage-control time. The big guns were called out—Henry Kissinger, Colin Powell, Green Beret veterans, the journalistic elite, the Pentagon itself. The story was wrong, absurd, slanderous, they cried. CNN retracted, Moorer retracted, the show's producers were fired...lawsuits all over the place.[16]

Like the dissidents who became "non-persons" under Stalin, Operation Tailwind is now officially a "non-event".

Notwithstanding this, the program's producers, April Oliver and Jack Smith, put together a 78-page document supporting their side of the story, with actual testimony by military personnel confirming the use of the nerve agent.[17]

Panama

From the 1940s to the 1990s, the United States used various parts of Panama as a testing ground for all manner of chemical weapons, including mustard gas, VX nerve agent, sarin nerve agent, hydrogen cyanide, and other nerve agents, in such forms as mines, rockets, and shells; perhaps tens of thousands of chemical munitions in total. Some of the earlier tests used US troops as guinea pigs, with horrific results for some of the soldiers. When the US military vacated Panama at the end of 1999, it left behind many sites containing chemical and conventional weapons residue, including numerous chemical weapons dropped from planes which failed to detonate.[18]

The US military also conducted secret tests of Agent Orange and other toxic herbicides in Panama during the 1960s and 70s, potentially exposing many civilians and military personnel to these lethal chemicals. Hundreds of drums of dioxin-containing Agent Orange were shipped to Panama. Spraying was carried out in jungle areas and near popular outdoor sites in an effort to simulate the tropical battlefield conditions of Southeast Asia.[19] During the American invasion of Panama in December 1989 it was reported that the semi-mountainous village of Pacora, near Panama City, was bombed with a chemical substance by helicopters and aircraft from the US Southern Command in Panama. Residents complained to human rights organizations and the press that the substances burned their skin, producing intense stinging and diarrhea. The bombing may have been carried out to keep the villagers from offering any assistance to the Panamanian soldiers who were camped in the nearby mountains.[20]

What the long-term effects have been on the people of Panama of the chemical exposures referred to above are not known.

Cuba

1) In August 1962, a British freighter under Soviet lease, having damaged its propeller on a reef, crept into the harbor at San Juan, Puerto Rico for repairs. It was bound for a Soviet port with 80,000 bags of Cuban sugar. The ship was put into dry dock and 14,135 sacks of sugar were unloaded to a warehouse to facilitate the repairs. While in the warehouse, the sugar was contaminated by CIA agents with a substance that was allegedly harmless but unpalatable. When President Kennedy learned of the operation he was furious because it had taken place in US territory and if discovered could provide the Soviet Union with a propaganda field day and set a terrible precedent for chemical sabotage in the cold war. He directed that the sugar not be returned to the Russians, although what explanation was given to them is not publicly known.[21] Similar undertakings were apparently not canceled. A CIA official, who helped direct worldwide sabotage efforts against Cuba, later revealed that "There was lots of sugar being sent out from Cuba, and we were putting a lot of contaminants in it."[22]

2) The same year, a Canadian agricultural technician working as an adviser to the Cuban government was paid $5,000 by "an American military intelligence agent" to infect Cuban turkeys with a virus which would produce the fatal Newcastle disease.

Subsequently, 8,000 turkeys died. The technician later claimed that although he had been to the farm where the turkeys had died, he had not actually administered the virus, but had instead pocketed the money, and that the turkeys had died from neglect and other causes unrelated to the virus. This may have been a self-serving statement. The *Washington Post* reported that "According to U.S. intelligence reports, the Cubans—and some Americans—believe the turkeys died as the result of espionage."[23]

3) According to a participant in the project:

> During 1969 and 1970, the CIA deployed futuristic weather modification technology to ravage Cuba's sugar crop and undermine the economy. Planes from the China Lake Naval Weapons Center in the California desert, where high tech was developed, overflew the island, seeding rain clouds with crystals that precipitated torrential rains over non-agricultural areas and left the cane fields arid (the downpours caused killer flash floods in some areas).[24]

This said, it must be pointed out while it's not terribly surprising that the CIA would have attempted such a thing, according to one meteorologist consulted by the author it's unlikely to have been the cause of whatever changes in the weather took place.

4) In 1971, also according to participants, the CIA turned over to Cuban exiles a virus which causes African swine fever. Six weeks later, an outbreak of the disease in Cuba forced the slaughter of 500,000 pigs to prevent a nationwide animal epidemic. The outbreak, the first ever in the Western hemisphere, was called the "most alarming event" of the year by the United Nations Food and Agricultural Organization.[25]

5) Ten years later, the target may well have been human beings, as an epidemic of dengue hemorrhagic fever (DHF) swept

across the Cuban island. Transmitted by blood-eating insects, usually mosquitos, the disease produces severe flu symptoms and incapacitating bone pain. Between May and October 1981, over 300,000 cases were reported in Cuba with 158 fatalities, 101 of which were children under 15.[26]

The Centers for Disease Control and Prevention later reported that the appearance in Cuba of this particular strain of dengue, DEN-2 from Southeast Asia, had caused the first major epidemic of DHF ever in the Americas.[27] Fidel Castro announced that Cuba had asked the United States for a pesticide to help eradicate the fever-bearing mosquito, but had not been given any.[28]

In 1956 and 1958, declassified documents have revealed, the US Army loosed swarms of specially bred mosquitos in Georgia and Florida to see whether disease-carrying insects could be weapons in a biological war. The mosquitos bred for the tests were of the *Aedes Aegypti* type, the precise carrier of dengue fever as well as other diseases.[29]

In 1967 it was reported by *Science* magazine that at the US government center in Fort Detrick, Maryland, dengue fever was amongst those "diseases that are at least the objects of considerable research and that appear to be among those regarded as potential BW [biological warfare] agents."[30] Then, in 1984, a Cuban exile on trial in New York on an unrelated matter testified that in the latter part of 1980 a ship traveled from Florida to Cuba with:

> a mission to carry some germs to introduce them in Cuba to be used against the Soviets and against the Cuban economy, to begin what was called chemical war, which later on produced results that were not what we had expected, because we thought that it was going to be used against the Soviet forces, and it was used against our own people, and with that we did not agree.[31]

6) On a clear day, October 21, 1996, a Cuban pilot flying over Matanzas province observed a plane releasing a mist of some

substance about seven times. It turned out to be an American crop-duster plane operated by the US State Department, which had permission to fly over Cuba on a trip to Colombia via Grand Cayman Island. Responding to the Cuban pilot's report, the Cuban air controller asked the US pilot if he was having any problem. The answer was "no". On December 18, Cuba observed the first signs of a plague of *Thrips palmi*, a plant-eating insect never before detected in Cuba. It severely damages practically all crops and is resistant to a number of pesticides. Cuba asked the US for clarification of the October 21 incident. Seven weeks passed before the US replied that the State Department pilot had emitted only smoke, in order to indicate his location to the Cuban pilot.[32] By this time, the Thrips palmi had spread rapidly, affecting corn, beans, squash, cucumbers and other crops.

In response to a query, the Federal Aviation Administration stated that emitting smoke to indicate location is "not an FAA practice" and that it knew of "no regulation calling for this practice".[33]

In April 1997, Cuba presented a report to the United Nations which charged the US with "biological aggression" and provided a detailed description of the 1996 incident and the subsequent controversy.[34] In August, signatories of the Biological Weapons Convention convened in Geneva to consider Cuba's charges and Washington's response. On December 15, the group issued a report which stated that they had failed to reach a definitive conclusion and, because of the technical complexity of the issue and the passage of time, no further investigation would be undertaken.[35]

The full extent of American chemical and biological warfare against Cuba will never be known. Over the years, the Castro government has in fact blamed the United States for a number of other plagues which afflicted various animals and crops.[36] In 1977, newly-released CIA documents disclosed that the Agency "maintained a clandestine anti-crop warfare research program targeted during the 1960s at a number of countries throughout the world."[37]

Iraq

On March 3, 2005, at a news conference in Baghdad, an official in the health ministry of the occupied Iraqi government said that the United States had used internationally-banned weapons during its major offensive upon the city of Fallujah the previous November. Dr. Khalid ash-Shaykhli said that research studies, prepared by his medical team, proved that US occupation forces had used substances such as mustard gas, nerve gas, and other burning chemicals in their attacks in the war-torn city.[38]

The US military abroad—a deadly toxic legacy

It's not quite chemical or biological weaponry, but it's toxic, it sickens, and it kills. It's what thousands of American military installations in every corner of the world (hundreds in Germany alone) have left behind: serious environmental damage. The pollution is remarkably widespread, the record too extensive to offer more than a taste here, such as this snippet from a lengthy piece in the *Los Angeles Times:*

> U.S. military installations have polluted the drinking water of the Pacific island of Guam, poured tons of toxic chemicals into Subic Bay in the Philippines, leaked carcinogens into the water source of a German spa, spewed tons of sulfurous coal smoke into the skies of Central Europe and pumped millions of gallons of raw sewage into the oceans.[39]

The military has done the same in the United States at countless installations.[40]

Chapter 15

United States Use of Chemical and Biological Weapons at Home

In a January 1999 interview, President Clinton said that what kept him awake some nights was the fear of germ warfare.[1] It is safe to say that he did not have the Department of Defense or the CIA in mind as the purveyor of the source of his fear. Yet for two decades these two agencies conducted tests in the open air in the United States, exposing millions of Americans to large clouds of possibly dangerous bacteria and chemical particles. They did so without informing the potentially affected populations, without taking any precautions to protect the health and safety of these people, and with no followup monitoring of the effects.

Government officials have consistently denied that the biological agents used could be harmful despite an abundance of expert and objective scientific evidence that exposure to heavy concentrations of even apparently innocuous organisms can cause illness, at a minimum to the most vulnerable segments of the population—the elderly, children, and those suffering from a variety of ailments. "There is no such thing as a microorganism that cannot cause trouble," George Connell, assistant to the director of the Centers for Disease Control and Prevention, testified before the Senate in 1977. "If you get the right concentration at the right place, at the right time, and in the right person, something is going to happen."[2]

The Army has acknowledged that between 1949 and 1969, 239 populated areas from coast to coast as well as US territories were blanketed with various organisms during tests designed to measure patterns of dissemination in the air, weather effects, dosages, optimum placement of the source, and other factors.

Testing over such areas was supposedly suspended after 1969, but there is no way to be certain of this. In any event, open air spraying continued at Dugway Proving Ground in Utah.[3]

Following is a small sample of the tests carried out in the 1949-69 period:

Watertown, N.Y. area and Virgin Islands

1950: The Army used aircraft and homing pigeons to drop turkey feathers dusted with cereal rust spores to contaminate oat crops, to prove that a "cereal rust epidemic" could be spread as a biological warfare weapon.[4]

San Francisco Bay Area

September 20-27, 1950: Six experimental biological warfare attacks by the US Army from a ship, using *Bacillus globigii* and *Serratia marcescens,* at one point forming a cloud about two miles long as the ship traveled slowly along the shoreline of the bay. One of the stated objectives of the exercise was to study "the *offensive* possibilities of attacking a seaport city with a BW [biological warfare] aerosol" from offshore. (emphasis added) Beginning on September 29, patients at Stanford University's hospital in San Francisco were found to be infected by *Serratia marcescens*. This type of infection had never before been reported at the hospital. Eleven patients became infected, and one died.[5] According to a report submitted to a Senate committee in 1977 by a professor of microbiology at the State University of New York at Stony Brook: "an increase in the number of *Serratia marcescens* can cause disease in a healthy person and...serious disease in sick people."[6] In 2005, the Food and Drug Administration (FDA) stated that *Serratia marcescens* "can cause serious, life-threatening illness in patients with compromised immune systems."[7]

Between 1954 and 1967, other tests were carried out in the Bay Area, including some with a base of operations at Fort Cronkhite in Marin County.[8]

Minneapolis

1953: 61 releases of zinc cadmium sulfide in four sections of the city, involving massive exposure of people at home and children in school. The substance was later described by the US Environmental Protection Agency as "potentially hazardous because of its cadmium content", and a former Army scientist, writing in the professional journal *Atmosphere Environment*, in 1972, said that cadmium compounds, including zinc cadmium sulfide, are "highly toxic and the use of them in open atmospheric experiments presents a human health hazard". He stated that the symptoms produced by exposure to zinc cadmium sulfide include lung damage, acute kidney inflammation, and fatty degeneration of the liver.[9]

St. Louis

1953: 35 releases of zinc cadmium sulfide over residential, commercial and downtown areas, including the Medical Arts Building, which presumably contained a number of sick people whose illnesses could be aggravated by inhaling toxic particles.[10]

Washington, DC area

1953: Aerial spraying from a height of 75 feet of zinc cadmium sulfide combined with *lycopodium* spores. The areas sprayed included the Monocacy River Valley in Maryland and Leesburg, Virginia, 30 miles from the capital.[11]

In 1969, the Army conducted 115 open-air tests of zinc cadmium sulfide near Cambridge, Maryland.[12]

Earlier in the 1960s, the Army covertly disseminated a large number of bacteria in Washington's National Airport to evaluate how easy it would be for an enemy agent to scatter smallpox through the entire country by infecting air travelers. The bacterium used, *Bacillus subtilis*, is potentially harmful to the infirm and the elderly, whose immune system is impaired, and to those with cancer, heart disease or a host of other ailments, according to a professor of microbiology at the Georgetown University Medical Center. A similar experiment was carried out at the Washington Greyhound bus terminal.

Sometime during Richard Nixon's time in office (apparently 1969), the Army "assassinated" him with germs via the White House air conditioning system.[13]

And at a building used by the Food and Drug Administration, the Army surreptitiously placed an allegedly benign colored dye into the water system. Whether anyone suffered harm from drinking a certain quantity of that water is not known.[14]

Tampa Bay area, Florida

1955: The CIA conducted one or more open-air tests with whooping- cough bacteria around the area of Tampa Bay and perhaps elsewhere in the state. The number of whooping cough cases recorded in Florida jumped from 339 and one death in 1954 to 1080 and 12 deaths in 1955.[15]

Savannah, Georgia and Avon Park, Florida

1956-58: The Army, wishing to test "the practicality of employing *Aedes aegypti* mosquitos to carry a BW agent", released over wide areas hundreds of thousands, if not millions, of this mosquito, notorious as a carrier of yellow fever and dengue fever, both highly dangerous diseases. The Army stated that the mosquitos were uninfected, but prominent scientists said that, for several reasons, the experiment was not without risk, and was a "terrible idea".[16] The actual effects upon the targeted population are not known.

New York City

Feb. 11-15, 1956: A CIA-Army team sprayed New York streets and the Holland and Lincoln tunnels, using trick suitcases and a car with a dual muffler.[17]

June 6-10, 1966: The army report of this test was called "A Study of the Vulnerability of Subway Passengers in New York City to Covert Attack with Biological Agents". Trillions of *Bacillus subtilis variant niger* were released into the subway system during rush hours. One method was to use light bulbs filled with the bacteria; these were unobtrusively shattered at sidewalk level on subway ventilating grills or tossed onto the roadbeds inside the stations. Aerosol clouds were momentarily visible after a release of bacteria from the light bulbs. The report noted that "When the cloud engulfed people, they brushed their clothing, looked up at the grating apron and walked on."[18] The wind of passing trains spread the bacteria along the tracks; in the time it took for two trains to pass, the bacteria were spread from 15th Street to 58th Street.[19] It is not known how many people later became ill from being unsuspecting guinea pigs. The United States Army apparently exhibited no interest in this question.

Chicago

1960s: The Chicago subway system was the scene of an Army experiment similar to the one carried out in the New York City subway system, and a Chicago bus station may also have been a target.[20]

Utah

March 1968: Open-air nerve agent testing at the military's main chemical weapons center in the Utah desert (Dugway Proving Ground) caused the death of about 6,400 sheep when the nerve agent drifted away from the test range. The military eventually reimbursed ranchers and agreed to stop this particular testing.

Stockyards

November 1964 to January 1965: The Army conducted aerosol tests over stockyards in Texas, Missouri, Minnesota, South Dakota, Iowa, and Nebraska, using "anti-animal non-biological simulants".[21] It's not clear why stockyards were chosen, or what effect this might have had upon the meat consumed by the public.

Project Shipboard Hazard and Defense (SHAD)

1963-69: The Army carried out numerous exercises involving aircraft spraying American warships with thousands of servicemen aboard. A wide variety of chemical and biological warfare (CBW) agents were used to learn the vulnerabilities of these ships and personnel to such attacks and to develop procedures to respond to them. Amongst the CBW agents used were:

Coxiella burnetii: besides flu-like symptoms, can cause hepatitis or pneumonia, in rare cases damage to the heart, can be life-threatening.

Pasteurella tularenis: causes the infectious disease tularemia; can produce very serious symptoms; mortality rate of about six percent.

Zinc cadmium sulfide: see above.

Sarin nerve agent: classified by the Centers for Disease Control and Prevention as "volatile and lethal"; symptoms include difficulty breathing, dimness of vision, loss of bladder/bowel control, twitching, jerking, staggering, coma, and death.

Sulfer dioxide: strong irritant of the lungs and throat.

VX nerve gas: extremely lethal, one of the most toxic substances ever synthesized; penetrates the skin or lungs to disrupt the body's nervous system; can block breathing, leading to death.

Staphylococcal enterotoxin, Type B: "not generally thought of as a lethal agent; however, it may incapacitate soldiers for one to two weeks".

Bacillus globigit: a bacterium believed at the time to be harmless, but later discovered to be capable of causing infections in people with weakened immune systems.[22]

Most of the SHAD exercises took place in the Pacific Ocean near Hawaii, San Diego and the Marshall Islands, and in the Atlantic near Newfoundland.

The Department of Defense (DoD) reports on the exercises began to be released in 2001 in response to pressure from veterans and Congress.

The *New York Times* reported that a DoD medical official said it was unclear whether sailors had been intentionally exposed to the germ and chemical agents without the benefit of protective masks and gear. Also uncertain, he said, was whether any had given their permission to become human guinea pigs in medical experiments with the deadly substances. "When you read the overarching plans for the testing, people were to be protected," he said. "But when we get to individual reports, we do not see things like informed consent or individual protection. We don't have the records for what, if any, protection was given to people." The implication, he said, is that in some cases sailors may have been exposed to the chemical and germ dangers.[23]

It was reported in 2002 that some of those involved in the tests say they now suffer health problems linked to their exposure to the chemicals and germs. They were pressing the Veterans Affairs

Department to compensate them and the Defense Department to release more information about the tests.[24]

Dr. Robert Williscroft, 23-year veteran of the Navy and the National Oceanic and Atmospheric Administration, and a senior editor of the website DefenseWatch, has closely monitored the SHAD operation. He concluded in 2002: "Information released to date strongly indicates that the Navy exposed a relatively large number of American fighting men to biological and chemical toxins, with potentially serious long-term effects, without their knowledge or consent. It also appears that DoD officials are stonewalling any serious effort to establish the facts and offer appropriate relief and compensation to the unwitting victims."[25]

The Nuremberg Code

The International Military Tribunal at Nuremberg, Germany, 1946-1949, revealed many details of the Nazi medical experiments on involuntary subjects, leading the judges to formulate a set of principles that came to be called The Nuremberg Code; in effect a bill of rights for people selected for medical experimentation. The Code's first tenet states: "The voluntary consent of the human subject is absolutely essential." Very shortly thereafter, the US Army-CIA testing programs, described above, began, and although the tests were of course nowhere near as gruesome as those of the Nazis, and the subjects of the tests were not humans as such, but rather the behavior of certain substances released in the air, the fact remains that the testers knew that untold numbers of humans were being directly contaminated by the tests, and none of the reports of the tests mentions a word about obtaining the consent of any of these humans. If the testers did not "know" that the contaminating substances were potentially dangerous, it can only be because they didn't investigate this question in any depth, which is the same as saying that they didn't know because they didn't *want* to know.

Not to mention radiating the environment

During the period of 1948-1952, the US government conducted many *deliberate* releases of radioactive material, mainly from airplanes, which carried as much as 10 miles over populated areas, in order to study fallout patterns and the rate at which radioactivity decayed, and to study the feasibility of creating "an offensive radiation warfare device".[26]

And the face to face human experimentation

In terms of sheer numbers, there cannot be any parallel in all of recorded history...a government conducting innumerable medically dangerous and medically unethical experiments on its own people. For decades after the end of World War II, the US government conducted experiments with literally millions of human subjects, both civilian humans and military humans, for the purpose of measuring the effects upon them of: a) sundry chemical and biological materials, including nerve agents; b) nuclear radiation, including injecting many with plutonium; c) a host of mind-control drugs such as LSD, other hallucinogens, and assorted other exotic chemical concoctions.[27]

For the human experimentation, the various government agencies appear to have chosen as their subjects primarily those who had least political clout, such as servicemen and women, conscientious objectors, prison inmates, blacks, the poor, the retarded, the elderly, the young, mental patients...

> "It's a little cocktail. It'll make you feel better," Helen Hutchison recalled the doctor telling her in July 1946, during a visit to the Vanderbilt University Hospital Prenatal Clinic. It didn't make her feel better at all. It contained radioactive iron. She was one of 829 women to receive various doses of the potion over a two-year period. Both Hutchison and the daughter she carried went on to suffer a lifetime of

strange ailments. Hutchison's hair fell out at one point, she suffers from pernicious anemia, and she is highly sensitive to sunlight. Her daughter, now grown, suffers from an immune system disorder and skin cancer.[28]

By 1999 the American public had perhaps learned something. When it was disclosed that the federal government's Los Alamos National Laboratory in New Mexico planned to release a strain of bacteria into the atmosphere to test new biowarfare detectors, the public outcry was such that the Laboratory canceled the test. At a public hearing called to ease the public's fear, a Santa Fe resident asked a Laboratory representative: "If it's so safe, why don't you release it into the office of someone in Washington, D.C.?"[29]

A final thought...What if?

On June 9, 1969, Dr. Donald M. MacArthur, Deputy Director, Research and Engineering, Department of Defense, testified before Congress.

> Within the next 5 to 10 years, it would probably be possible to make a new infective microorganism which could differ in certain important aspects from any known disease-causing organisms. Most important of these is that it might be refractory [resistant] to the immunological and therapeutic processes upon which we depend to maintain our relative freedom from infectious disease.[30]

Chapter 16

US Encouraging the Use of CBW by Other Nations

Egypt

It was reported in 1969 that for some years the US Army had been instructing foreign specialists in chemical and biological warfare (CBW). A total of 550 foreigners from 36 nations, including Egypt, Israel, Iraq, Jordan, Lebanon, Saudi Arabia, Yugoslavia, and South Vietnam, had taken courses at the Army's Chemical School at Ft. McClellan, Alabama. The Egyptian specialists reportedly used their new American know-how to help plan the poison-gas attacks upon Yemen in 1967. The International Red Cross verified that Egyptian pilots dropped canisters of poison gases from planes over Yemen. Subsequently, the US Defense Intelligence Agency also confirmed this. Some 150 villagers gagged, coughed and bled to death.[1]

South Africa

According to testimony before the Truth and Reconciliation Commission in 1998, the United States encouraged South Africa's apartheid regime to develop a CBW program that was aimed at the country's black population. Dr. Wouter Basson, the South African general who headed the project from its inception in 1981, testified from notes he made of a meeting with US Maj. Gen. William Augerson: "He [Augerson] feels that chemical warfare is an ideal strategic weapon because infrastructure is preserved together with facilities, and only living people are killed. The warm climate of Africa is ideal for this type of weapon because the diffusion of the poison is better and the absorption is increased by perspiration and increased blood flow in the persons who are targets."[2]

South Africa's CBW program did in fact work on a number of projects that echoed US programs: using black soldiers as guinea pigs for experimental drugs; developing a toxin to cause a heart attack, which would appear to be the "natural" cause of death; contaminating drinking water with disease pathogens; using a variety of poisonous gases to paralyze and kill opponents in South Africa and neighboring states.[3]

Iraq

In his January 1998 State of the Union address, President Clinton spoke of how we must "confront the new hazards of chemical and biological weapons, and the outlaw states, terrorists and organized criminals seeking to acquire them." He castigated Iraq for "developing nuclear, chemical and biological weapons" and called for strengthening the Biological Weapons Convention. Who among his listeners knew, who among the media reported, that the United States had been the supplier to Iraq of much of the source biological materials Saddam Hussein's scientists required to create a biological warfare program?

According to reports of a US Senate Committee in 1994: From 1985, if not earlier, through 1989, a veritable witch's brew of biological materials were exported to Iraq by private American suppliers pursuant to application and licensing by the US Department of Commerce. Amongst these materials, which often produce slow, agonizing deaths, were:

Bacillus anthracis, cause of anthrax.

Clostridium botulinum, a source of botulinum toxin.

Histoplasma capsulatam, cause of a disease attacking lungs, brain, spinal cord and heart.

Brucella melitensis, a bacteria that can damage major

organs.

    Clostridium perfringens, a highly toxic bacteria causing systemic illness.

    Clostridium tetani, highly toxigenic.

    Also, *Escherichia coli* (E.coli); genetic materials; human and bacterial DNA. Dozens of other pathogenic biological agents were shipped to Iraq during the 1980s. The Senate Report pointed out that "These biological materials were not attenuated or weakened and were capable of reproduction."

    "It was later learned," the committee stated, "that these microorganisms exported by the United States were identical to those the United Nations inspectors found and removed from the Iraqi biological warfare program."

    The report noted further that US exports to Iraq included the precursors to chemical-warfare agents, plans for chemical and biological warfare production facilities, and chemical-warhead filling equipment.

    These exports continued to at least November 28, 1989 despite the fact that Iraq had been reported to be engaging in chemical warfare and possibly biological warfare against Iranians, Kurds, and Shiites since the early 80s as part of its war with Iran.[4] Presumably, the use of these weapons by Iraq—whom the US supported in the war—against Iran is what Washington expected would happen.

Hypocrisy of this magnitude has to be respected

For some six years, 1992-98, following the Gulf War, the United States, acting through the United Nations, forced Iraq to open up its country to inspection for "weapons of mass destruction". No building or structure was exempted. The wishes of the Iraqi government to place certain sites off limits were dismissed out of hand by US officials and the American media, who had a lot of fun with the issue. "What does Saddam have to hide?" was the prevailing attitude.

It so happened that near the end of this period, May 1997, the US Senate passed an act to implement the "Convention on the Prohibition of the Development, Production, Stockpiling and Use of Chemical Weapons and on Their Destruction" ["Chemical Convention"], an international treaty which had been ratified by more than 100 nations in its four-year life. But the Senate insisted on adding an amendment before it would ratify the Convention.

The Senate amendment, Section 307, stipulates that "the President may deny a request to inspect any facility in the United States in cases where the President determines that the inspection may pose a threat to the national security interests of the United States."

> Saddam Hussein had asked for no more than this for Iraq.
> It can be surmised that under the Senate amendment the White House, Pentagon, etc. would be off limits, as Saddam had insisted his presidential palaces should be, as well as the military unit responsible for his personal security, which an American colonel had demanded to inspect.

Moreover, we now know that in closing off certain places to the inspectors, Saddam was not being entirely paranoid or arbitrary, inasmuch as it was later revealed that for some time the United States had been supplying certain inspectors with the means of planting recording devices wherever they could gain access.

It may be further relevant that a detailed study of the first one-and-a-half years of the Chemical Convention's life has shown that Washington's record in complying with the Convention has been remarkably dismal, setting a rather bad example for other nations.[5]

Part III

A Rogue State versus the World

Chapter 17

A Concise History of United States Global Interventions, 1945 to the Present

Presented here is the most extensive published compilation of serious post-World War II American interventions into the life of other nations, covering many more cases than found in the author's book, *Killing Hope: U.S. Military and CIA Interventions Since World War II.* **(Please see this book for further details of some of the interventions and for sources not indicated below.)**

The Roman Empire

There was no corner of the known world where some interest was not alleged to be in danger or under actual attack. If the interests were not Roman, they were those of Rome's allies; and if Rome had no allies, the allies would be invented. When it was utterly impossible to contrive such an interest—why, then it was the national honor that had been insulted. The fight was always invested with an aura of legality. Rome was always being attacked by evil-minded neighbors...The whole world was pervaded by a host of enemies, it was manifestly Rome's duty to guard against their indubitably aggressive designs.... Even less than in the cases that have already been discussed, can an attempt be made here to comprehend these wars of conquest from the point of view of concrete objectives. Here there was neither a warrior nation in our sense, nor, in the beginning, a military despotism or an aristocracy of specifically military orientation. Thus there is but one way to an understanding: scrutiny of domestic class interests, the question of who stood to gain.

Joseph Schumpeter, 1919[1]

America is today the leader of a world-wide anti-revolutionary movement in the defence of vested interests. She now stands for what Rome stood for. Rome consistently supported the rich against the poor in all foreign communities that fell under her sway; and, since the poor, so far, have always and everywhere been far more numerous than the rich, Rome's policy made for inequality, for injustice, and for the least happiness of the greatest number.

Arnold Toynbee, 1961[2]

The American Empire

China, 1945-51

At the close of World War II, the US intervened in a civil war, taking the side of Chiang Kai-shek's Nationalists against Mao Tse-tung's Communists, even though the latter had been a much closer ally of the United States in the war. To compound the irony, the US used defeated Japanese soldiers to fight for its side. After their defeat in 1949, many Nationalist soldiers took refuge in northern Burma, where the CIA regrouped them, brought in other recruits from elsewhere in Asia, and provided a large supply of heavy arms and planes. During the early 1950s, this army proceeded to carry out a number of incursions into China, involving at times thousands of troops, accompanied by CIA advisers (some of whom were killed), and supplied by air drops from American planes.

France, 1947

Communist Party members had fought in the wartime resistance, unlike many other French who had collaborated with the Germans. After the war the Communists followed the legal path to form strong labor unions and vie for political office. But the United States was determined to deny them their place at the table, particularly since some unions were taking steps to impede the flow of arms to French forces seeking to reconquer their former colony of Vietnam with US aid. The US funneled very large amounts of money to the Socialist Party, the Communists' chief rival; sent in American Federation of Labor (AFL) experts to subvert the CP's union dominance and import scabs from Italy; supplied arms and money to Corsican gangs to break up Communist strikes, burn down party offices, and beat up and murder party members and strikers; sent in a psychological warfare team to complement all of these actions; and used the threat of a cutoff of food aid and other aid...all to seriously undermine Communist Party support and prestige. It worked.

A portion of the financing for these covert operations came from the funds of the Marshall Plan, which also helped finance the corruption of the Italian elections of 1948 (see below), and set up a special covert operations agency which later melded into the CIA.[3] These are a few of the hidden sides of the Marshall Plan, which has long been held up to the world as a shining example of America's unselfish benevolence.

At the same time, Washington was forcing the French government to dismiss its Communist ministers in order to receive American economic aid. Said Premier Paul Ramadier: "A little of our independence is departing from us with each loan we obtain."[4]

Marshall Islands, 1946-58

Driven by perceived Cold War exigencies, the United States conducted dozens of Intercontinental ballistic missile, nuclear bomb, and other nuclear tests on this trust territory in the Pacific, after forcing the residents of certain islands, notably Bikini Atoll, to relocate to other, uninhabited islands. In 1968, the former residents of Bikini were told by the Johnson administration that their island had been cleaned and was safe for habitation. Many went back, only to be told later that they had been subjected to massive doses of radiation and would have to leave again. In 1983, the US Interior Department declared that the islanders could return to their homes immediately—provided they ate no homegrown food until the late 21st century.[5] They have never returned.

Italy, 1947-1970s

In 1947, the US forced the Italian government to dismiss its Communist and Socialist cabinet members in order to receive American economic aid. The following year and for decades thereafter, each time a combined front of the Communists and Socialists, or the Communists alone, threatened to defeat the US-supported Christian Democrats in national elections, the CIA used every (dirty) trick in the book and trained its big economic, political, and psychological-warfare guns on the Italian people, while covertly funding the CD candidates. And it worked. Again and again. This perversion of democracy was done in the name of "saving democracy" in Italy. American corporations also contributed many millions of dollars to help keep the left from a share of power.

Greece, 1947-49

The United States intervened in a civil war, taking the side of the neo-fascists against the Greek left, who had fought the Nazis courageously. The neo-fascists won and instituted a highly brutal regime, for which the CIA created a suitably repressive internal security agency. For the next 15 years, Greece was looked upon much as a piece of real estate to be developed according to Washington's needs.

Philippines, 1945-53

The US military fought against the leftist Huk forces even while the Huks were still fighting against the Japanese invaders in the world war. After the war, the US organized Philippine armed forces to continue the fight against the Huks, finally defeating them and their reform movement. The CIA interfered grossly in elections, installing a series of puppets as president, culminating in the long dictatorship of Ferdinand Marcos, for whom torture was *la spécialité de la maison*. (see Elections chapter)

Korea, 1945-53

After World War II, the United States suppressed popular progressive organizations, who had been America's allies in the war—at times with brutal force—in favor of the conservatives who had collaborated with the Japanese. As a result, the best opportunities to unify North and South were derailed. This led to a long era of corrupt, reactionary, and ruthless governments in the South and the huge, war-crime filled American military intervention of 1950-53 in the "Korean War", which was far from the simple affair of North Korea invading South Korea on a particular day, which the world has been led to believe.

In 1999 we learned that, amongst many other such incidents, American soldiers had machine-gunned hundreds of helpless civilians and hundreds more were killed when the US purposely blew up bridges they were crossing.[6]

Albania, 1949-53

By infiltrating émigré guerrillas into the country, the US and Britain tried to overthrow the Communist government and install a new one that would have been pro-Western, albeit composed largely of monarchists and collaborators with Italian fascists and Nazis. Hundreds of the émigrés lost their lives or were imprisoned.

Eastern Europe, 1948-56

Allen Dulles, Director of the CIA, in a remarkable chess game, instigated a high Polish security official, Jozef Swiatlo, to use a controversial American, Noel Field, to spread paranoia amongst the security establishments of Eastern Europe, leading to countless purge trials, hundreds of thousands of imprisonments, and at least hundreds of deaths.[7]

Germany, 1950s

The CIA orchestrated a wide-ranging campaign of sabotage, terrorism, dirty tricks, and psychological warfare against East Germany. This was one of the factors which led to the building of the Berlin Wall in 1961.

The United States also created a secret civilian army in Germany, which drew up a list of 200 leading Social Democrats, 15 Communists, and various others who were to be "put out of the way" if the Soviet Union invaded.

This secret army had its counterparts all over Western Europe as part of "Operation Gladio", developed by the CIA and other intelligence services, and not answerable for its actions under the laws of any state. After NATO was formed in 1949, Gladio came under its discreet aegis. "Gladiators" were responsible for numerous acts of terrorism in Europe, foremost of which was the bombing of the Bologna railway station in 1980, claiming 86 lives. The purpose of the terrorism was to place the blame for these atrocities on the left and thus heighten public concern about a Soviet invasion; at the same time, discrediting leftist electoral candidates, for NATO feared that if the left came to power in the government of any of its members, they might pass legislation that would be a threat to the NATO installations or operations in that country.[8]

Iran, 1953

Prime Minister Mossadegh was overthrown by a CIA operation with some help from the British. Mossadegh had been elected to his position by a large majority of parliament, but he had made the fateful mistake of spearheading the movement to nationalize a British-owned oil company, the sole oil company operating in Iran. The coup restored the Shah to absolute power, initiating a period of 25 years of repression and torture; while the oil industry was restored to foreign ownership, with the US and Britain each getting 40 percent.

Guatemala, 1953-1990s

Humorist Dave Barry boils the Monroe Doctrine down to 3 simple precepts: 1) Other nations are not allowed to mess around with the internal affairs of nations in this hemisphere. 2) But we are. 3) Ha ha ha.

A CIA-organized coup overthrew the democratically-elected and progressive government of Jacobo Arbenz, initiating 40 years of military-government death squads, torture, disappearances, mass executions, and unimaginable cruelty, totaling more than 200,000 victims—indisputably one of the most inhumane chapters of the 20th century. The justification for the coup that was put forth for years, until it fell of its own weight, is that Guatemala had been on the verge of the proverbial Soviet takeover. In actuality, the Russians had so little interest in the country that it didn't even maintain diplomatic relations. The real problem was that Arbenz had taken over some of the uncultivated land of the US firm, United Fruit Company, which had extremely close ties to the American power elite. Moreover, in the eyes of Washington, there was the danger of Guatemala's social-democracy model spreading to other countries in Latin America.

Despite a 1996 "peace" accord between the government and rebels, respect for human rights remains as only a concept in Guatemala; death squads continue to operate with a significant measure of impunity against union activists and other dissidents; priests who call for greater concern for the poor are still branded as Marxists and receive death threats; torture rears its ugly head yet; the lower classes are as impoverished and illiterate as ever; the military endures as a formidable institution; the US continues to arm and train the Guatemalan military and carry out exercises with it; and key provisions of the peace accord concerning military reform have not been carried out.[9]

Costa Rica, mid-1950s, 1970-71

To liberal American political leaders, President José Figueres was the quintessential "liberal democrat", the kind of statesman they liked to think, and liked the world to think, was the natural partner of US foreign policy rather than the military dictators who somehow kept popping up as allies. Yet the United States tried to overthrow Figueres (in the 1950s, and apparently also in the 1970s when he was again president), and tried to assassinate him twice. The reasons? Figueres was not tough enough on the left, led Costa Rica to become the first country in Central America to establish diplomatic relations with the Soviet Union and Eastern Europe, and on occasion questioned American foreign policy, like the invasion of Cuba in 1961.

Middle East, 1956-58

The Eisenhower Doctrine stated that the United States "is prepared to use armed forces to assist" any Middle East country "requesting assistance against armed aggression from any country controlled by international communism". The English translation of this was that no one would be allowed to dominate, or have excessive influence over, the Middle East and its oil fields except the United States, and that anyone who tried would be, by definition, "communist". In keeping with this policy, the United States twice attempted to overthrow the Syrian government, staged several shows-of-force in the Mediterranean to intimidate movements opposed to US-supported governments in Jordan and Lebanon, landed 14,000 troops in Lebanon, and conspired to overthrow or assassinate Nasser of Egypt and his troublesome Middle-East nationalism.

Indonesia, 1957-58

Sukarno, like Nasser, was the kind of Third World leader the United States could not abide by: a nationalist who was serving the wrong national interest. He took neutralism in the Cold War seriously, making trips to the Soviet Union and China as well as to the White House. He nationalized many private holdings of the Dutch, the former colonial power. And he refused to crack down on the Indonesian Communist Party, which was walking the legal, peaceful road and making impressive gains electorally. Such policies could easily give other Third World leaders "wrong ideas". Thus it was that the CIA began throwing money into the elections, plotted Sukarno's assassination, tried to blackmail him with a phony sex film, and joined forces with dissident military officers to wage a full-scale war against the government, including bombing runs by American pilots. Sukarno survived it all.

Haiti, 1959

The US military mission, in Haiti to train the troops of noted dictator Francois Duvalier, used its air, sea and ground power to smash an attempt to overthrow Duvalier by a small group of Haitians, aided by some Cubans and other Latin Americans.

Western Europe, 1950s-1960s

For two decades, the CIA used dozens of American foundations, charitable trusts and the like, including a few of its own creation, as conduits for payments to all manner of organizations in Western Europe. The beneficiaries of this largesse were political parties, magazines, news agencies, journalist unions, other unions and labor organizations, student and youth groups, lawyers' associations, and other enterprises, all ostensibly independent, but nonetheless serving Washington's Cold-War, anti-communist, anti-socialist agenda; an agenda which also included a militarized and united Western Europe, allied to (and dominated by) the United States, and support for the Common Market and NATO, all part of the bulwark against the supposed Soviet threat.

British Guiana/Guyana, 1953-64

The United States and Great Britain made life extremely difficult for the democratically elected leader, Cheddi Jagan, finally forcing him from office (See Elections chapter). Jagan was another Third World leader who incurred Washington's wrath by trying to remain neutral and independent. Although a leftist—more so than Sukarno or Arbenz—his policies in office were not revolutionary. But he was still targeted, for he represented Washington's greatest fear: building a society that might be a successful example of an alternative to the capitalist model. John F. Kennedy had given a direct order for his ouster, as, presumably, had Eisenhower.

One of the better-off countries in the region under Jagan, Guyana, by the 1980s, was one of the poorest. Its principal export had become people.

Iraq, 1958-63

In July 1958, Gen. Abdul Karim Kassem overthrew the monarchy and established a republic. Though somewhat of a reformist, he was by no means any kind of radical. His action, however, awakened revolutionary fervor in the masses and increased the influence of the Iraqi Communist Party. By April of the following year, CIA Director Allen Dulles, with his customary hyperbole, was telling Congress that the Iraqi Communists were close to a "complete takeover" and the situation in that country was "the most dangerous in the world today".[10] In actuality, Kassem aimed at being a neutralist in the Cold War and pursued rather inconsistent policies toward the Iraqi Communists, never allowing them formal representation in his cabinet, nor even full legality, though they strongly desired both. He tried to maintain power by playing the Communists off against other ideological groups.[11]

A secret plan for a joint US-Turkish invasion of the country was drafted by the United States Joint Chiefs of Staff shortly after the 1958 coup. Reportedly, only Soviet threats to intercede on Iraq's side forced Washington to hold back. But in 1960, the United States began to fund the Kurdish guerrillas in Iraq who were fighting for a measure of autonomy[12] and the CIA undertook an assassination attempt against Kassem, which was unsuccessful.[13] The Iraqi leader made himself even more of a marked man when, in that same year, he began to help create the Organization of Petroleum Exporting Countries (OPEC), which challenged the stranglehold Western oil companies had on the marketing of Arab oil; and in 1962 he created a national oil company to exploit the nation's oil.

In February 1963, Kassem told the French daily, *Le Monde*,

that he had received a note from Washington—"in terms scarcely veiled, calling upon me to change my attitude, under threat of sanctions against Iraq...All our trouble with the imperialists [the US and the UK] began the day we claimed our legitimate rights to Kuwait."[14] (Kuwait was a key element in US and UK hegemonic designs over mid-east oil.) A few days after Kassem's remarks were published, he was overthrown in a coup led by the Baath Party and summarily executed; thousands of communists were also killed, many because their names had been turned over to the Baathists by the CIA.[15] The State Department soon informed the press that it was pleased that the new regime would respect international agreements and was not interested in nationalizing the giant Iraq Petroleum Co., of which the US was a major owner.[16] The new government, at least for the time being, also cooled its claim to Kuwait.

Papers of the British cabinet of 1963, later declassified, disclose that the coup had been backed by the British and the CIA.[17]

Soviet Union, 1940s-1960s

The US infiltrated many hundreds of Russian émigrés into the Soviet Union to gather intelligence about military and technological installations; commit assassinations; obtain current samples of identification documents; assist Western agents to escape; engage in sabotage, such as derailing trains, wrecking bridges, actions against arms factories and power plants; or instigate armed political struggle against Communist rule by linking up with resistance movements. There was also a mammoth CIA anti-Soviet propaganda campaign, highlighted by the covert publishing of well over a thousand books in English, a number by well-known authors, which were distributed all over the world, as well as hundreds in foreign languages.

Vietnam, 1945-73

"What we're doing in Vietnam is using the black man to kill the yellow man so the white man can keep the land he took from the red man."—Dick Gregory

The slippery slope began with the US siding with the French, the former colonizers, and with collaborators with the Japanese, against Ho Chi Minh and his followers, who had worked closely with the Allied war effort and admired all things American. Ho Chi Minh was, after all, some kind of "communist" (one of those bad-for-you label warnings). He had written numerous letters to President Truman and the State Department asking for America's help in winning Vietnamese independence from the French and finding a peaceful solution for his country. All his entreaties were ignored. For he was some kind of communist. Ho Chi Minh modeled the new Vietnamese declaration of independence on the American, beginning it with "All men are created equal. They are endowed by their Creator with..." But this would count for nothing in Washington. Ho Chi Minh was some kind of communist.

More than twenty years and more than a million dead later, the United States withdrew its military forces from Vietnam. Most people believe that the US lost the war. But by destroying Vietnam to its core, by poisoning the earth, the water, the air, and the gene pool for generations, Washington had in fact achieved its primary purpose: preventing the rise of what might have been a good development option for Asia, an alternative to the capitalist model. Ho Chi Minh was, after all, some kind of communist.

Cambodia, 1955-73

Prince Sihanouk, yet another leader who did not fancy being an American client. After many years of hostility towards his regime, including assassination plots and the infamous Nixon/Kissinger secret "carpet bombings" of 1969-70, Washington finally overthrew Sihanouk in a coup in 1970. This was all that was needed to impel Pol Pot and his Khmer Rouge forces to enter the fray. Five years later, they took power. But the years of American bombing had caused Cambodia's traditional economy to vanish. The old Cambodia had been destroyed forever.

Incredibly, the Khmer Rouge were to inflict even greater misery upon this unhappy land. And to multiply the irony, the United States supported Pol Pot and the Khmer Rouge after their subsequent defeat by the Vietnamese. (See Pol Pot chapter)

Laos, 1957-73

The Laotian left, led by the Pathet Lao, tried to effect social change peacefully, making significant electoral gains and taking part in coalition governments. But the United States would have none of that. The CIA and the State Department, through force, bribery, and other pressures, engineered coups in 1958, 1959 and 1960. Eventually, the only option left for the Pathet Lao was armed force. The CIA created its famous *Armeé Clandestine*—totaling 30,000, from every corner of Asia—to do battle, while the US Air Force, between 1965 and 1973, rained down more than two million tons of bombs upon the people of Laos, many of whom were forced to live in caves for years in a desperate attempt to escape the monsters falling from the sky. After hundreds of thousands had been killed, many more maimed, and countless bombed villages with hardly stone standing upon stone, the Pathet Lao took control of the country, following on the heels of events in Vietnam.

Thailand, 1965-73

While using the country to facilitate its daily bombings of Vietnam and Laos, the US military took the time to try to suppress insurgents who were fighting for economic reform, an end to police repression, and in opposition to the mammoth US military presence, with its huge airbases, piers, barracks, road building, and other major projects, which appeared to be taking the country apart and taking it over. Eventually, the American military personnel count in Thailand reached 40,000, with those engaged in the civil conflict—including 365 Green Beret forces—officially designated as "advisers", as they were in Vietnam.

To fight the guerillas, the US financed, armed, equipped, and trained police and military units in counter-insurgency, significantly increasing their numbers; transported government forces by helicopter to combat areas; were present in the field as well, as battalion advisers; and sometimes accompanied Thai soldiers on anti-guerrilla sweeps. In addition, the Americans instituted considerable propaganda and psychological warfare activities, and actually encouraged the Thai government to adopt a more forceful response.[18] However, the conflict in Thailand, and the US role, never approached the dimensions of Vietnam.

In 1966, the *Washington Post* reported that "In the view of some observers, continued dictatorship in Thailand suits the United States, since it assures a continuation of American bases in the country and that, as a US official put it bluntly, 'is our real interest in this place'."[19]

Ecuador, 1960-63

Infiltrating virtually every department of the government, up to and including the second and third positions of power, along with an abundant use of dirty tricks, enabled the CIA to oust President José María Velasco because of his refusal to go along with US Cuba policy and not clamping down hard on the left domestically; and when his replacement also refused to break relations with Cuba, a military leader in the pay of the CIA gave him an ultimatum, which he acceded to.

The Congo/Zaire, 1960-65, 1977-78

In June 1960, Patrice Lumumba—legally and peacefully—became the Congo's first prime minister after independence from Belgium. At Independence Day ceremonies before a host of foreign dignitaries, Lumumba called for the nation's economic as well as its political liberation, recounting a list of injustices against the natives by the white owners of the country. The man was obviously a "communist". And obviously doomed, particularly since Belgium retained its vast mineral wealth in Katanga province, and prominent Eisenhower administration officials had financial ties to the same wealth.

Eleven days later, Katanga seceded; in September Lumumba was dismissed by the president at the instigation of the United States; and in January 1961 he was assassinated, with CIA involvement, after Eisenhower had requested that Lumumba should depart from this life. There followed several years of civil conflict and chaos and the rise to power in 1965 of Mobutu Sese Seko, a man not a stranger to the CIA. Mobutu went on to rule the country for more than 30 years, with a level of corruption and cruelty that shocked even his CIA handlers. The Zairian people lived in abject poverty despite the country's extraordinary natural wealth, while Mobutu became a multibillionaire.

In both 1977 and 1978, the Carter administration rushed extensive military aid to Zaire, including airlifting Moroccan troops, to help Mobutu quell rebel uprisings and remain in power. President George H.W. Bush was later to remark that Mobutu was "our best friend in Africa".[20]

France/Algeria, 1960s

The CIA apparently supported a French military coup in Algeria to block that country's independence in the face of French president Charles de Gaulle's determination to grant independence. The US was concerned that an independent Algeria would have a "communist" government. Washington also hoped that the repercussions would topple de Gaulle, who was a major obstacle to American hegemonic plans for NATO. A few years later, evidence indicates, the CIA was involved in an aborted plot to assassinate the French president.

Brazil, 1961-64

President João Goulart was guilty of the usual crimes: He took an independent stand in foreign policy, resuming relations with socialist countries and opposing sanctions against Cuba; his administration passed a law limiting the amount of profits multinationals could transmit outside the country; a subsidiary of ITT, the US multinational, was nationalized; he promoted economic and social reforms. And US Attorney-General Robert Kennedy was uneasy about Goulart allowing "communists" to hold positions in government agencies. Yet the man was no radical. He was a millionaire landowner and a Catholic who wore a medal of the Virgin around his neck. That, however, was not enough to save him. In 1964, he was overthrown in a military coup which had covert American involvement and indispensable support. The official Washington line was...yes, it's unfortunate that democracy has been overthrown in Brazil...but still, the country has been saved from communism.

For the next 15 years, all the features of military dictatorship which have become Latin America's sad heritage were instituted: Congress was shut down, political opposition was reduced to virtual extinction, habeas corpus for "political crimes" was suspended, criticism of the president was forbidden by law, labor unions were taken over by government interveners, mounting protests were met by police and military firing into crowds, peasants' homes were burned down, priests were brutalized...disappearances, death squads, a remarkable degree and depravity of torture...the government had a name for its program: the "moral rehabilitation" of Brazil.

Washington was very pleased. Brazil broke relations with Cuba and became one of the United States' most reliable allies in Latin America.

Peru, 1965

The US military set up "a miniature Fort Bragg" in the Peruvian jungle and proceeded to wipe out several guerrilla groups, which had arisen in response to the deep-seated poverty of the Peruvian masses.

Dominican Republic, 1963-65

In February 1963, Juan Bosch took office as the first democratically elected president of the Dominican Republic since 1924. Here at last was John F. Kennedy's "liberal anti- communist", to counter the charge that the US supported only military dictatorships. Bosch's government was to be the long sought "showcase of democracy" that would put the lie to Fidel Castro. He was given the grand treatment in Washington shortly before he took office.

To Washington's dismay, however, Bosch was true to his beliefs. He called for land reform; low-rent housing; modest nationalization of business; foreign investment provided it was not excessively exploitative of the country; and other policies making up the program of any liberal Third World leader serious about social change. He was likewise serious about the thing called civil liberties: communists, or those labeled as such, were not to be persecuted unless they actually violated the law.

A number of American officials and congressmen expressed their discomfort with Bosch's plans, as well as his stance of independence from the United States. Land reform and nationalization are always touchy issues in Washington, the stuff that "creeping socialism" is made of. In several quarters of the US press Bosch was red-baited.

In September, the military boots marched. Bosch was out. The United States, which could discourage a military coup in Latin America with a frown, did nothing.

Nineteen months later, April 1965, a widespread popular revolt broke out, which promised to put the exiled Bosch back into power. The United States sent in 23,000 troops to help crush it.

Cuba, 1959 to present

The motto of the CIA: "Proudly overthrowing Fidel Castro since 1959."[21]

Castro came to power at the beginning of 1959. As early as March 10, a US National Security Council meeting included on its agenda the feasibility of bringing "another government to power in Cuba". There followed more than 40 years of terrorist attacks, bombings, a full-scale military invasion, sanctions, embargos, isolation, assassinations...Cuba had carried out The Unforgivable Revolution, a very serious threat of setting a "good example" (or "bad example" as Washington would see it) in Latin America.

The saddest part of this is that the world will never know just how good the example would have been, what kind of society Cuba could have produced if left alone, if not constantly under the gun and the threat of invasion, if allowed to relax its control at home. The idealism, the vision, the talent, the internationalism were all there. But we'll never know. And that of course has been the idea.

The Cuban government, its critics claim, sees the CIA behind every problem. In actuality, the CIA is behind only half of the problems. The problem is, the Cuban government can't tell which half.

Indonesia, 1965

A complex series of events, involving a supposed coup attempt, a counter-coup, and perhaps a counter-counter-coup, with American fingerprints apparent at various points, resulted in the ouster from power of Sukarno and his replacement by General Suharto and the Indonesian military, which was very closely tied to the US military. The massacre that then began immediately—of communists, communist sympathizers, suspected communists, suspected communist sympathizers, and none of the above—was called by the *New York Times* "one of the most savage mass slayings of modern political history". The estimates of the number killed in the course of a few years begin at half a million and go above a million.

It was later learned that the US embassy had compiled lists of "communists", from top echelons down to village cadres, as many as 5,000 names, and turned them over to the army, which then hunted those persons down and killed them. The Americans would then check off the names of those who had been killed or captured. "It really was a big help to the army," said one US diplomat. "They probably killed a lot of people, and I probably have a lot of blood on my hands. But that's not all bad. There's a time when you have to strike hard at a decisive moment."

Ghana, 1966

When Kwame Nkrumah tried to lessen his country's dependence on the West by strengthening economic and military ties to the Soviet Union, China and East Germany, he effectively sealed his fate. A CIA-backed military coup sent the African leader into exile, from which he never returned. A 1966 CIA document, later declassified, revealed that the Agency was in close contact with the military plotters and had been reporting to Washington for a year on the military's plans to oust Nkrumah; the last such report was the day before the coup. There is no indication that the CIA ever informed Nkrumah of any of these plots.[22]

Uruguay, 1969-72

The 1960s was the era of the Tupamaros, perhaps the cleverest, most resourceful, most sophisticated, least violent, Robin Hood-like urban guerrillas the world has ever seen. They were too good to be allowed to endure. A team of American experts arrived, to supply the police with all the arms, vehicles, communications gear, etc. they needed; to train them in assassination and explosives techniques, to teach methods of interrogation *cum* torture, to set up an intelligence service *cum* death squad. It was all-out war against the Tupamaros and any suspected sympathizers. The Tupamaros lost.

In 1998, Eladio Moll, a retired Uruguayan Navy rear admiral and former intelligence chief, testifying before a commission of the Uruguayan Chamber of Deputies, stated that during Uruguay's "dirty war" (1972-1983), orders came from the United States concerning captive Tupamaros. "The guidance that was sent from the U.S.," said Moll, "was that what had to be done with the captured guerrillas was to get information, and that afterwards they didn't deserve to live."[23]

Chile, 1964-73

Salvador Allende was the worst possible scenario for the Washington power elite, who could imagine only one thing worse than a Marxist in power—an *elected* Marxist in power, one who honored the constitution, and became increasingly popular. This shook the very foundation stones upon which the anti-communist tower was built: the doctrine, painstakingly cultivated for decades, that "communists" can take power only through force and deception, that they can retain that power only through terrorizing and brainwashing the population.

After sabotaging Allende's electoral endeavor in 1964, and failing to do so in 1970, despite their best efforts, the CIA and the rest of the American foreign policy machine left no stone unturned in their attempt to destabilize the Allende government over the next three years, paying particular attention to undermining the economy and building up military hostility. Finally, in September 1973, the military, under General Pinochet, overthrew the government, Allende dying in the process.

Thus it was that they closed the country to the outside world for a week, while the tanks rolled and the soldiers broke down doors; the stadiums rang with the sounds of execution and the bodies piled up along the streets and floated in the river; the torture centers opened for business, dogs trained to sexually molest female prisoners were set loose; the subversive books were thrown to the bonfires; soldiers slit the trouser legs of women, shouting that "In Chile women wear dresses!"; the poor returned to their natural state; and the men of the world in Washington and in the halls of international finance opened up their checkbooks. In the end, more than 3,000 dissidents were killed or disappeared, many thousands tortured.[24]

The FBI accommodated the new government by trying to track down Chilean leftists in the United States, while Secretary of State Henry Kissinger assured Pinochet in Chile that "In the United States, as you know, we are sympathetic with what you are trying to do here.... We wish your government well."[25]

Greece, 1967-74

A military coup took place in April 1967, just two days before the campaign for national elections was to begin, elections which appeared certain to bring the veteran liberal leader George Papandreou back as prime minister. The coup had been a joint effort of the Royal Court, the Greek military, the CIA, and the American military stationed in Greece, and was followed immediately by the traditional martial law, censorship, arrests, beatings, and killings, the victims totaling some 8,000 in the first month. This was accompanied by the equally traditional declaration that this was all being done to save the nation from a "communist takeover". Torture, inflicted in the most gruesome of ways, often with equipment supplied by the United States, became routine.

George Papandreou was not any kind of radical. He was a liberal anti-communist type. But his son Andreas, the heir-apparent, while only a little to the left of his father, had not disguised his wish to take Greece out of the Cold War, and had questioned remaining in NATO, or at least as a satellite of the United States.

Andreas Papandreou was arrested at the time of the coup and held in prison for eight months. Shortly after his release, he and his wife Margaret visited the American ambassador, Phillips Talbot, in Athens. Papandreou related the following:

> I asked Talbot whether America could have intervened the night of the coup, to prevent the death of democracy in Greece. He denied that they could have done anything about it. Then Margaret asked a critical question: What if the coup had been a Communist or a Leftist coup? Talbot

answered without hesitation. Then, of course, they would
have intervened, and they would have crushed the coup.

South Africa, 1960s-1980s

The CIA collaborated closely with South African intelligence, one
of the principal focuses being the African National Congress, the
leading anti-apartheid organization which had been banned and
exiled. The Agency cooperated in suppressing internal dissent,
provided specific warnings of planned attacks by the ANC,
and information about ANC members residing in neighboring
countries; on at least one occasion, in Mozambique 1981, this led
to South Africa sending an assassination squad to wipe out the
fingered individuals. The CIA was also responsible for the capture
of ANC leader Nelson Mandela. Additionally, for a number of
years in the 1970s and 80s, the US supported South Africa in the
UN, and the CIA violated the UN's arms embargo against South
Africa (of which the US was a declared supporter) by covertly
providing the country with weapons and supporting its efforts to
militarily determine the political makeup of Southern Africa.[26]

Bolivia, 1964-75

An armed popular revolt in 1952 had defeated the military and
reduced it to a small, impotent and discredited force. But under
US guidance and aid, there was a slow but certain rejuvenation
of the armed forces. By 1964, the military, with the indispensable
support of the CIA and the Pentagon, was able to overthrow
President Victor Paz, whom the United States had designated a
marked man because of his refusal to support Washington's Cuba
policies. The US continued to dictate who should lead Bolivia
long after.

In 1967, a CIA operation, employing some of the Agency's

Cuban exile agents, tracked down Che Guevara, resulting in his summary execution.

Australia, 1972-75

The CIA channeled millions of dollars to the Labor Party's opposition, but failed to block Labor's election. When the party took power in December 1972, it immediately rankled Washington by calling home Australian military personnel from Vietnam and denouncing US bombing of Hanoi, among other actions against the war. The government also displayed less than customary reverence for the intelligence and national security games so dear to the heart of the CIA. Edward Gough Whitlam, the new prime minister, was slowly but surely sealing his fate. Through complex supra- legal maneuvering, the US, the British, and the Australian opposition were eventually able to induce Governor-General John Kerr—who had a long history of involvement with CIA fronts—to "legally" dismiss Whitlam in 1975.

Iraq, 1972-75

As a favor to a very important ally, the Shah of Iran, President Nixon and National Security Advisor Henry Kissinger provided military aid to the Kurds fighting for their autonomy in Iraq, Iran's perennial foe. Though the military aid was to total some $16 million, the object—unknown to the Kurds—was not to win them their autonomy, but to sap the Iraqi resources and distract them from Iran. Said a CIA memo of 1974: "Iran, like ourselves, has seen benefit in a stalemate situation...in which Iraq is intrinsically weakened by the Kurds' refusal to relinquish semi- autonomy. Neither Iran nor ourselves wish to see the matter resolved one way or the other." The congressional Pike committee, later investigating the CIA, commented: "This policy was not imparted to [the Kurds], who were encouraged to continue fighting. Even in the context of covert action, ours was a cynical enterprise."

In 1975, oil politics brought Iraq and Iran together, and the latter, along with the United States, abandoned the Kurds to a terrible fate. At a crucial point, the Kurds were begging Kissinger for help, but he completely ignored their pleas. Kurd forces were decimated; several hundred of their leaders were executed. Later, when questioned about this by the Pike Committee, Kissinger responded: "Covert action should not be confused with missionary work."[27]

Portugal, 1974-76

A bloodless military coup in 1974 brought down the US-supported 48-year fascist regime that was the world's only remaining colonial power. This was followed by a program centered on nationalization of major industries, workers control, a minimum wage, land reform, and other progressive measures. Washington and multinational officials who were on the board of directors of the planet were concerned. Destabilization became the order of the day: covert actions; attacks in the US press; subverting trade unions; subsidizing opposition media; economic sabotage through international credit and commerce; heavy financing of selected candidates in elections; a US cut-off of Portugal from certain military and nuclear information commonly available to NATO members; NATO naval and air exercises off the Portuguese coast, with 19 NATO warships moored in Lisbon's harbor, regarded by most Portuguese as an attempt to intimidate the provisional government.[28] The Portuguese revolution was doomed. The CIA-financed candidates took and retained power for years.

East Timor, 1975-99

While East Timor, which lies at the eastern end of the Indonesian archipelago, was undergoing a process of decolonization from Portugal in 1975, various political groupings were formed on the island. In August one of the parties, the UDT, attempted a coup against Portuguese rule, which was almost certainly instigated by Indonesia. A brief civil war broke out and by September a movement of the left, Fretilin, had prevailed, and in November declared East Timor's independence from Portugal. Nine days later, Indonesia invaded East Timor. The invasion was launched the day after US President Gerald Ford and Secretary of State Henry Kissinger had left Indonesia after giving President Suharto permission to use American arms, which, under US law, could not be used for aggression. Indonesia was Washington's most valuable ally in Southeast Asia and, in any event, the United States was not inclined to look kindly on any leftist government.[29]

Indonesia soon achieved complete control over East Timor, with the help of American arms and diplomatic support. Daniel Moynihan, who was US ambassador to the UN at the time, later wrote that the "United States wished things to turn out as they did, and worked to bring this about. The Department of State desired that the United Nations prove utterly ineffective in whatever measures it undertook. This task was given to me, and I carried it forward with no inconsiderable success.[30]

Amnesty International estimated that by 1989, Indonesian troops had killed 200,000 people out of a population of between 600,000 and 700,000. The United States stood virtually alone in the world with its consistent support of Indonesia's claim to East Timor, and downplayed the slaughter to a remarkable degree; at the same time supplying Indonesia with all the military hardware and training it needed to carry out the job. Despite denials to the contrary, Washington continued this military aid up to and including the period of extensive massacres of pro- independence Timorese in 1999 by Indonesian soldiers and their militia allies, yet another ultra-bloody entry on Suharto's record.[31]

In 1995, a senior official of the Clinton administration, speaking of Suharto, said: "He's our kind of guy."[32]

Angola, 1975-1980s

The United States, China and South Africa supported one side of the civil war, while the Soviet Union and Cuba supported the other side. It dragged on bloodily, horribly, and pointlessly for decades, perhaps half a million lives lost, widespread hunger, and what is said to be the highest amputee rate in the world, caused by the innumerable land mines. In the early years, Henry Kissinger personally prevented what might well have been a peaceful solution, but the man was wholly obsessed with countering Soviet moves anywhere on the planet—significant or trivial, real or imagined, *fait accompli* or anticipated. In the 1990s, Washington finally tried to rein in its client, Jonas Savimbi, head of UNITA, to keep him from prolonging the war, but it would have been immensely better for the people of Angola if the US had not intervened at all in Angolan politics beginning in the early 1960s. The Russians would then have had no interest. Nor Henry Kissinger. Savimbi died in 2002, initiating the beginning of the end of the Angolan civil war.

Jamaica, 1976

Prime Minister Michael Manley got on Washington's bad side, by supporting the wrong faction in Angola, by establishing diplomatic relations with Cuba, and by going up against the transnational aluminum companies. The United States employed many tactics in an attempt to defeat Manley's bid for reelection in 1976, but failed. (See Elections chapter)

Honduras, 1980s

The US turned Honduras into an instant colony in the early 1980s, a military base with thousands of American troops, to support counter-insurgency operations in El Salvador and Guatemala, and, above all, to serve as a staging area, supply center, and refuge for the Contras and their war against the Nicaraguan government. Inasmuch as the uninterrupted continuance of such operations in Honduras required a quiescent population, the US gave the Honduran military and police the training, arms, equipment, and funds needed to efficiently suppress dissidents—the anti-American types (who mockingly referred to their country as the U.S.S. Honduras), those involved in solidarity campaigns for the Salvadoran rebels and the Sandinistas of Nicaragua, and those striving for social change within Honduras, though still far from becoming a guerrilla threat.[33] "American diplomats," observed the *New York Times* in 1988, "exercise more control over domestic politics in Honduras than in any other country in the hemisphere, and in private that fact is universally acknowledged here."[34]

Nicaragua, 1979-90

When the Sandinistas overthrew the Somoza dictatorship in 1979, it was clear to Washington that they might well be that long-dreaded beast—"another Cuba". Under President Carter, attempts to sabotage the revolution took diplomatic and economic forms. Under Reagan, violence was the method of choice. For eight terribly long years, the people of Nicaragua were under attack by Washington's proxy army, the Contras, formed from Somoza's vicious National Guardsmen and other supporters of the dictator. It was all-out war, aiming to destroy the progressive social and economic programs of the government, burning down schools and medical clinics, raping, torturing, mining harbors, bombing and strafing. These were the charming gentlemen Ronald Reagan liked to call "freedom fighters".

In 1990, the US seriously interfered in national elections, resulting in the defeat of the Sandinistas by Washington-approved political forces.[35]

As with Cuba, we'll never know what kind of progressive society the Sandinistas might have created if allowed to live in peace and not have to spend half their budget on fighting a war. Oxfam, the international development organization, said that from its experience of working in 76 developing countries, Nicaragua under the Sandinistas was "exceptional in the strength of that government's commitment...to improving the condition of the people and encouraging their active participation in the development process."[36]

Since returning to the rule of the free market, Nicaragua had become one of the poorest nations in the hemisphere, with more than half its people suffering from malnutrition and with illiteracy widespread.

Philippines, 1970s-1990s

Another scenario of poverty, social injustice, death squads, torture, etc. leading to wide-ranging protest and armed resistance...time once again for the US military and CIA to come to the aid of the government in suppressing such movements. In 1987 it was revealed that the Reagan administration had approved a $10 million, two-year plan for increased CIA involvement in the counter-insurgency campaign.[37] The CIA undertook large-scale psychological warfare operations and US military advisers routinely accompanied Philippine troops during their maneuvers.[38] The Philippines has long been the most strategic location for US war-making in Asia, the site of several large American military bases, which have been the object of numerous protests by the citizens. In 1991, the US embassy informed the media that embassy polls indicated that 68 percent, 72 percent, even 81 percent of the Philippine people favored the bases. The polls, however, never existed. "I made the numbers up," an embassy official conceded.[39]

Seychelles, 1979-81

The country's leader, France Albert René, amongst other shortcomings in the eyes of Washington, was a socialist, pursued non-alignment in the Cold War, wanted to turn the Indian Ocean into a nuclear-free zone, and was not happy that his island nation was the home of a US Air Force satellite tracking station. For this he was the object of various US destabilization conspiracies beginning in 1979. In November 1981, the CIA reportedly was behind a mercenary invasion of the country, which originated in South Africa and got no further than an armed battle at the Seychelles airport.[40]

Diego Garcia, late 1960s to present

In the late 1960s and early 1970s, a few thousand inhabitants of the Chagos Islands in the Indian Ocean were summarily uprooted by Great Britain and shipped against their will to Mauritius and the Seychelles, each more than a thousand miles away. No one helped them resettle or paid for the homes they lost. They simply were forced to become squatters in foreign lands. The reason for this was to make room for a US military base on the biggest of the Chagos islands, Diego Garcia. A secret agreement between British Prime Minister Harold Macmillan and US President John F. Kennedy in 1961 designated the island as an Anglo-American "point of strategic support" against the Soviet Union. Washington wanted to establish a communications and refueling center for its fleet there but required that the Chagos archipelago be excluded from the decolonization process London was then engaged in and that its inhabitants be evacuated "for security reasons".

The families who lived on the island and sustained themselves with vegetable farming, fishing, and coconut products, found themselves stripped of their possessions and shipped without any assistance to the urban slums of Port-Louis in Mauritius and Victoria in the Seychelles. Not surprisingly, their communities proceeded to be ravaged by alcoholism, drug use, and misery, while the United States, armed with a fifty year lease renewable for an additional twenty year period, transformed Diego Garcia into a fortress. The island's harbors and airports have since welcomed many American Navy ships and served as a long distance departure base for B-52 and B-1 bombers. The US military base, built by Halliburton and completed in 1973, holds a decisive position in the support of other US bases in Africa, the Middle East, and Southeast Asia. Following the terrorist attacks of September 11, 2001 against the United States, the island played an essential role in American bombing missions over Afghanistan and Iraq. It also served as a sort of Guantánamo annex, holding prisoners suspected of belonging to al-Qaeda in the utmost secrecy.

For some years, the island's former inhabitants have been fighting against their fate in the courts. In November 2000, the London High Court ruled that the "transfer" was "illegal" and recognized the grounds for the islanders "right of return" to their ancestral land. The British and American governments have completely ignored this ruling. The value of Diego Garcia to the US empire is such that returning the territory to the natives is simply out of the question. The base employs several thousand civilian workers from other countries like the Philippines, but the island's natives are not permitted to set foot on their former homeland. The British and the Americans don't want any kind of claim made or demonstration. There are now more than 2,000 US troops, anchorage for 30 warships, a nuclear dump, a satellite spy station, shopping malls, bars and a golf course. "Camp Justice" the Americans call it.[41]

Article 7 of the Statute of the International Criminal Court (1998) describes the "deportation or forcible transfer of population ... by expulsion or other coercive acts" as a crime against humanity.

South Yemen, 1979-84

Partly to cater to the wishes of next-door Saudi Arabia, and partly as a Cold-War reflex, the US supported paramilitary forces in South Yemen to undermine the government, which was perceived as the proverbial "Soviet satellite", as opposed to North Yemen, which was seen to be the proverbial "pro-Western" good guys. North and South had been fighting on and off for years. The US sent North Yemen military aid and trained paramilitary forces to blow up bridges and carry out other acts of sabotage in the South. In March 1982, a 13-man paramilitary team was captured in the South; under torture, they confessed (honestly) to a CIA training connection and 12 were executed; Washington's operation soon came to an end. Reagan's CIA Director, William Casey, a genuine anti-Soviet primitive, had been convinced that the South Yemenis were part of a Soviet-run international terrorist network, along with Cubans, the Italian Red Brigades, and the IRA.[42] In reality, since 1979, the Soviet Union had been providing military support and advisers to both North and South, sometimes at the very same time, and even helped North Yemen to put down a leftwing guerrilla movement.[43] In 1990, North and South combined into one country, the Republic of Yemen. The Cold War as vaudeville.

South Korea, 1980

In May, the United States—which had the first and last word on matters military in South Korea—acting on a government request, released some South Korean forces from the combined US- Korean command to be used by military strongman Chun Doo Hwan to suppress an uprising of students and workers in the city of Kwangju.[44] They were protesting martial law, the arrest of dissidents and their families and friends, fraudulent elections, torture, and unmet social needs. A brutal crackdown followed, estimates of the death toll ranging between several hundred and 2,000, with a number of gross atrocities committed by the armed forces.[45] The US support came from the Carter administration, heralded as human-rights advocates. Said a State Department spokesman: "Our situation, for better or worse, is that Korea is a treaty ally, and the US has a very strong security interest in that part of the world."[46]

In February 1981, Chun was honored by being invited to the White House as President Reagan's first state visitor; the US and South Korea engaged in the first joint military exercises of the new administration; the administration asked Congress to delay publication of the annual worldwide report on human rights while the South Korean president was still in Washington, to avoid embarrassing him; and Reagan, in his toast to Chun, was moved to declare: "You've done much to strengthen the tradition of 5,000 years' commitment to freedom."[47] In 1996, a Korean court convicted Chun of treason and murder, and sentenced him to death, for his role in the Kwangju massacre.

Chad, 1981-82

The Reagan administration's obsession with Moammar Qaddafi of Libya knew no limits: geographical, legal or ethical. Libya maintained a military force in neighboring Chad at the request of that government—which was faced with armed insurgents—and to serve Libya's desire for a friendly government on its border. The United States wanted to replace the Chadian government with one not very friendly to Libya, at the same time giving free rein to anti-Qaddafi Libyan exiles in Chad to mount attacks on Libya from across the border.

Thus it was that the US, along with France, the former colonial power in Chad, employed bribes and political pressures to induce the Chad government to ask the Libyans to leave—which Libya reluctantly did—and to replace them with forces of the Organization of African Unity. The OAU was given a vague mandate to maintain security in Chad. This proved to be a sort of Trojan horse. The CIA rebuilt an opposition Chadian force in the Sudan and provided it with money, arms, political support, and technical assistance. Then, as the OAU stood by doing nothing, this army, led by Hissen Habré, succeeded in overthrowing the Chadian government in June 1982.[48] With US support, Habré went on to rule for eight years, during which his secret police reportedly killed tens of thousands, tortured as many as 200,000, and disappeared an undetermined number. In 2000, some of his torture victims succeeded in having him indicted in Senegal, where he resided, calling him "Africa's Pinochet".[49]

Grenada, 1979-83

How impoverished, small, weak or far away must a country be before it is not a threat to the US Government? In a 1979 coup, Maurice Bishop and his followers had taken power in this island country of 110 thousand, and though their actual policies were not as revolutionary as Castro's, Washington was again driven by its fear of "another Cuba", particularly when public appearances by the Grenadian leaders in other countries of the region met with great enthusiasm.

American destabilization tactics against the Bishop government began soon after the Reagan administration came into office, featuring outrageous disinformation and deception. Then, in October 1983, Bishop was overthrown by an ultra-leftist faction of his own party and the United States seized on this to launch an invasion, overthrow the new government, and put into power individuals more beholden to US foreign policy objectives. The invasion was attended by yet more transparent lies, created by Washington to justify its gross violations of international law. One of the stories advanced, which Reagan termed "of overriding importance", was the need to evacuate many hundreds of Americans from the island, mainly students at a medical college, who were supposedly in a dangerous position because of the new regime and the chaos surrounding its accession to power.

After the United States had suffered 135 killed or wounded; after some 400 Grenadian casualties, and 84 Cubans, mainly construction workers, after all this plus bombing and destruction, a White House spokesman was asked by journalists if there was any concrete information about threats to Americans in Grenada. Replied the White House spokesman: "Nothing that I know of."

Suriname, 1982-84

A plot by the United States to overthrow the government because it allegedly was falling into "the Cuban orbit". It was to be an invasion by some 300 men, half US and South American and half Surinamese. The CIA had actually informed Congress of its plan to use a paramilitary force, which President Reagan had authorized. Congress was not enthused, but William Casey and his CIA cowboys went ahead with their planning anyway, and were induced to call it off only after the scheme was discovered by the internal security agency of the Netherlands, the former colonial power in Suriname, when it was known as Dutch Guiana.

Libya, 1981-89

The official reason for the Reagan administration's intense antipathy toward Moammar Qaddafi was that he supported terrorism. In actuality, the Libyan leader's crime was not his support for terrorist groups per se, but that he was supporting the *wrong* terrorist groups; i.e., Qaddafi was not supporting the same terrorists that Reagan was, such as the Nicaraguan Contras, UNITA in Angola, Cuban exiles in Miami, the governments of El Salvador and Guatemala, and the US military in Grenada. The one band of terrorists the two men supported in common was the Moujahedeen in Afghanistan.

On top of this, Washington has long had a deep-seated antipathy toward Middle East oil-producing countries that it can't exert proper control over. And Qaddafi was uppity; he had even overthrown a rich ruling clique and instituted a welfare state. He and his country would have to be put in their place. In 1981, US planes shot down two Libyan planes in Libyan air space. This was followed by attempts to assassinate the man, operations to overthrow him, economic sanctions, and, in 1986, the bombing of one of Qaddafi's residences, killing scores of people, including his young daughter. There was as well a major disinformation campaign, reporting one piece of nonsense after another, including conspicuous exaggerations of Qaddafi's support for terrorism, and shifting the blame for the 1988 bombing of PanAm 103 to Libya and away from Iran and Syria when the Gulf War campaign required the support of the latter two countries.[50] To Washington, Libya was like magnetic north: the finger always pointed there.

Fiji, 1987

In April, only a month after taking office in a democratic election, Prime Minister Timoci Bavrada was ousted in a military coup. Bavrada, of the Labour Party, made Washington unhappy by identifying himself with the non-aligned movement, and even more so by taking office with a pledge to reinstate Fiji as a nuclear free zone, meaning that nuclear-powered or nuclear-weapons- carrying ships could not make port calls. When Bavrada's predecessor, R.S.K. Mara, instituted the same policy in 1982, he was put under great US pressure to drop it. Declared the former US ambassador to Fiji that year, William Bodde, Jr., "a nuclear free zone would be unacceptable to the US, given our strategic needs...the US must do everything possible to counter this movement."[51] The following year, Mara dropped the policy. Bavrada would clearly not be so easily swayed. He had taken office as part of a Nuclear-Free-Pacific coalition.

Two weeks after Bavrada took office, American UN Ambassador Vernon Walters visited the island. The former Deputy Director of the CIA has had a history of showing up shortly before, during, or shortly after CIA destabilization operations. Walters met with Bavrada, ostensibly to discuss UN matters. He also met with Lt. Col. Sitiveni Rabuka, third-in-command of the Army. Two weeks later, Rabuka led a military coup which ousted Bavrada.

During Bavrada's month in office, a multi-layered "Libyan scare" campaign suddenly and inexplicably broke out in the Pacific area. The Reagan administration had already been exposed for its phony Libya-scare campaign in the United States. When the Fiji coup took place, Rabuka and his supporters pointed to the Libyan "threat" as justifying the coup.[52]

There are more of such "coincidences" in this drama, including appearances in Fiji before the coup of the National Endowment for Democracy (see chapter 19) and its funding, some of the CIA's labor mafia, and units of the US military in the Pacific.[53]

The day after the coup, a Pentagon source, while denying US involvement, declared: "We're kinda delighted...All of a sudden our ships couldn't go to Fiji, and now all of a sudden they can."[54]

Panama, 1989

Just weeks after the fall of the Berlin Wall, the United States showed its joy that a new era of world peace was now possible by invading Panama, as Washington's mad bombers struck again. On December 20, 1989, a large tenement barrio in Panama City was wiped out; 15,000 people were left homeless. Counting several days of ground fighting between US and Panamanian forces, 500-something natives dead was the official body count—i.e., what the United States and the new US-installed Panamanian government admitted to. Other sources, examining more evidence, concluded that thousands had died. Additionally, some 3,000 Panamanians were wounded, 23 Americans died, 324 were wounded.

Question from reporter: "Was it really worth it to send people to their death for this? To get Noriega?"

George H.W. Bush: "Every human life is precious, and yet I have to answer, yes, it has been worth it."

Manuel Noriega had been an American ally and informant for years until he outlived his usefulness. But getting him was hardly a major motive for the attack. Bush wanted to send a clear message to the people of Nicaragua, who had an election scheduled in two months, that this might be their fate if they reelected the Sandinistas. Bush also wanted to flex some military muscle to illustrate to Congress the need for a large combat-ready force despite the very recent dissolution of the "Soviet threat". The official explanation for the American ouster was Noriega's drug trafficking. But Washington had known about this for years without being particularly alarmed by it, if at all. And they could easily have gotten their hands on the man without wreaking such terrible devastation upon the Panamanian people.[55]

Afghanistan, 1979-92

The striking repression of women in Afghanistan carried out by the Taliban Islamic fundamentalists is well known. Much less publicized is that in the late 1970s and most of the 1980s Afghanistan had a government committed to bringing the incredibly underdeveloped country into the 20th century, including giving women equal rights. The United States, however, poured billions of dollars into waging a terrible war against this government, simply because it was supported by the Soviet Union. By aiding the fundamentalist opposition, Washington knowingly and deliberately increased the probability of a Soviet intervention.[56] And when that occurred, the CIA became the grand orchestrator: hitting up Middle-Eastern countries for huge financial support, on top of that from Washington; pressuring and bribing neighboring Pakistan to rent out its country as a military staging area and sanctuary; supplying a great arsenal of weaponry and military training.

In the end, the United States and the Taliban "won", and the women, and the rest of Afghanistan, lost. More than a million dead, three million disabled, five million refugees; in total about half the population.

El Salvador, 1980-92

Salvador's dissidents tried to work within the system. But with US support, the government made that impossible, using repeated electoral fraud and murdering hundreds of protestors and strikers. In 1980, the dissidents took to the gun, and civil war. Washington responded immediately.

Officially, the US military presence in El Salvador was limited to an advisory capacity. In actuality, military and CIA personnel played a more active role on a continuous basis. About 20 Americans were killed or wounded in helicopter and plane crashes while flying reconnaissance or other missions over combat areas, and considerable evidence surfaced of a US role in the ground fighting as well. The war came to an official end in 1992 with these results: 75,000 civilian deaths; the US Treasury depleted by six billion dollars; a handful of the wealthy still owned the country; the poor remained as ever; dissidents still had to fear right-wing death squads; there would be no profound social change in El Salvador.

Haiti, 1987-94

After supporting the Duvalier family dictatorship for 30 years, which came to an inglorious end in 1986, the United States then opposed the reformist priest, Jean-Bertrand Aristide, who was rising in popularity and was elected to the presidency in 1991. Meanwhile, the CIA was working intimately with death squads, torturers and drug traffickers.

With this as background, in 1994 the Clinton White House found itself in the awkward position of having to pretend—because of all their rhetoric about "democracy"—that they supported the democratically-elected Aristide's return to power after he had been ousted in a 1991 military coup, eight months after taking office. After delaying his return for more than two years, Washington finally had its military restore Aristide to office, but only after obliging the priest to guarantee that he would not help the poor at the expense of the rich, literally; and that he would stick closely to free-market economics. This meant that Haiti would continue to be the assembly plant of the Western Hemisphere, with its workers receiving starvation wages, literally. If Aristide had thoughts about breaking the agreement forced upon him, he had only to look out his window—US troops were stationed in Haiti for the remainder of his term.

Bulgaria, 1990-91

In November 1999, President Clinton visited Bulgaria and told a crowd in Sofia that he hailed them for throwing off communism and holding fair elections.[57] What he failed to mention was that after one of their fair elections had been won by the communists, the US government had proceeded to overthrow them.

In 1990, the National Endowment for Democracy (NED) and the Agency for International Development (AID) poured more than $1.7 million into Bulgaria in an attempt to defeat the Bulgarian Socialist Party (the former Communist Party) in the June 1990 national election. On the basis of population, this was equivalent to a foreign power injecting some $47 million into an American electoral campaign. The main recipient of NED and AID largesse was the leading opposition party, the Union of Democratic Forces.[58] Much to the shock and dismay of Washington, the BSP won.

This would not do. Washington's ideological bottom line was that the Bulgarian Socialist Party could not, and would not, be given the chance to prove that a democratic, socialist-oriented mixed economy could succeed in Eastern Europe while the capitalist model was already beginning to disillusion people all around it. Thus it was that NED and AID stepped in with additional generous funding and technical help specifically to those opposition groups which carried out a campaign of chaos lasting almost five months: very militant and disruptive street demonstrations, paralyzing labor strikes, sit-ins, hunger strikes, arson...parliament was surrounded, the government was under siege...until finally the president was forced to resign, followed by some of his ministers; lastly, the prime-minister gave up his office.

In 1991, NED again threw hundreds of thousands of dollars into the election; this time, what NED calls the "democratic forces" won.[59]

Albania, 1991-92

A tale very similar to that of Bulgaria. A Communist government won overwhelming endorsement in the March 1991 elections, followed immediately by two months of widespread unrest, including street demonstrations and a general strike lasting three weeks, which finally led to the collapse of the new government by June.[60] The National Endowment for Democracy had been there also, providing $80,000 to the labor movement and $23,000 "to support party training and civic education programs".[61]

A new election was held in March 1992. During the election campaign, US political strategists and diplomats, including the American ambassador, openly accompanied candidates of the Democratic Party (the Communists' chief opposition) on their stumping tours and got out the message that said—frankly and explicitly—If the Communists win again, there will be no US aid, and "a lot of Western investors and governments are going to direct their aid elsewhere". NED, once again, was there with all kinds of gifts to make things easier for "the good guys", including brand new Jeep Cherokees.[62] The Democratic Party won.

Somalia, 1993

It was supposed to be a mission to help feed the starving masses. Before long, the US was trying to rearrange the country's political map by eliminating the dominant warlord, Mohamed Aidid, and his power base. On many occasions beginning in June US helicopters strafed groups of Aidid's supporters or fired missiles at them; the firing was at times indiscriminate, with a number of innocent civilians perishing. The helicopters also fired missiles, without warning, into a hospital crowded with patients and staff, with the expected blood and destruction, because of the belief that Aidid's forces had taken refuge there. In July, the target was a private home, where members of Aidid's political movement were holding a meeting; at least 54 people were killed, including clan elders and religious leaders. Reporting on this, the *Washington Post* said that "the debate in the United States centered on questions about the propriety of U.S. troops killing people inside the meeting without giving them the chance to surrender." Then, in October, a daring attempt by some 120 elite American forces to kidnap two leaders of Aidid's clan resulted in a horrendous bloody battle. The final tally was five US helicopters shot down, 18 Americans dead, 73 wounded; 500 to 1000 Somalis killed, many more injured.

It's questionable that getting food to hungry people was as important as the fact that four American oil giants held exploratory rights to large areas of Somali land and were hoping that US troops would put an end to the prevailing chaos which threatened their highly expensive investments. There was also the Pentagon's ongoing need to sell itself to those in Congress who were trying to cut the military budget in the post-cold war world. "Humanitarian" actions and (unnecessary) amphibious landings by US Marines on the beach in the glare of TV cameras were thought to be good selling points. Washington designed the operation in such a way that the show would be run by the US military and not the United Nations, under whose aegis it supposedly fell.

In any event, by the time the Marines landed, the worst of the famine was over. It had peaked months before.[63]

Iraq, 1991-2003

Mental hospitals and prisons are filled with people who claim to have heard voices telling them to kill certain people, often people they'd never met before, people who'd never done them any harm, or threatened any harm.

American soldiers went to the Middle East in 1991 to kill just such people after hearing a voice command them: the voice of George H.W. Bush.

Relentless bombing for more than 40 days and nights, against one of the most advanced nations in the Middle East, devastating its ancient and modern capital city; 177 million pounds of bombs falling on the people of Iraq, the most concentrated aerial onslaught in the history of the world to that time; depleted uranium weapons incinerating people, leading to cancers and sundry congenital problems; blowing up chemical and biological weapon and oil facilities, a terrible poisoning of the atmosphere; burying Iraqi soldiers alive, deliberately; the infrastructure destroyed, with dreadful effects on health; draconian sanctions continued into the 21st century, multiplying the health problems; more than a million children dead from all of these factors, even more adults. UNICEF, in an August 1999 report, stated that in southern and central Iraq, the death rate for children under five had more than doubled in the years of the sanctions.

For twelve years, until the 2003 American invasion, the US and Great Britain continued to launch missiles against the burned-out ash called Iraq, as their planes flew over the country on virtually a daily basis, guarding the so-called no-fly zones, the authority for which Washington and London derived from each other, not the United Nations as they would have the world believe; tens of thousands of sorties, thousands of bombs, many hundreds killed, the Iraqis claimed. Said US Brigadier General William Looney, a director of this operation:

> If they turn on their radars we're going to blow up their goddamn SAMs. They know we own their country. We own their airspace.... We dictate the way they live and talk. And that's what's great about America right now. It's a good thing, especially when there's a lot of oil out there we need.[64]

It can be said that the United States has inflicted more vindictive punishment and ostracism upon Iraq than upon Germany or Japan after World War II.

Noam Chomsky has written: "It's been a leading, driving doctrine of US foreign policy since the 1940s that the vast and unparalleled energy resources of the Gulf region will be effectively dominated by the United States and its clients, and, crucially, that no independent, indigenous force will be permitted to have a substantial influence on the administration of oil production and price."

This may have been Iraq's crime, not that they invaded Kuwait in 1990, an invasion actually encouraged by the United States and provoked by Kuwait itself, which was stealing oil from Iraq; an invasion that gave the US all the pretext it needed to take action. Iraq's invasion of Kuwait was, after all, no more than Indonesia had done to East Timor, with Washington's blessing.

Colombia, 1990s to present

Colombia, one of the most violent countries in the world, is amongst the very top recipients of US military aid, with well over a thousand American military personnel and private US contract workers posted there, in a growing number of military installations, to aid in a counter-insurgency against leftist guerrillas. The United States has aided government bombing raids and other military functions by providing helicopters, intelligence information about guerrilla movements, satellite images, and communications intercepts. At times, US planes fly overhead during combat operations.[65]

The public rationale given by Washington for taking sides in a civil war has been "to fight drug trafficking". To drive home this point, US officials routinely refer to the two leading guerrilla groups, FARC and ELN, as "narco-terrorists." Though the guerrillas do finance themselves in part through protecting and "taxing" drug producers, they have never been drug trafficking entities per se; in any event, almost everyone in Colombia has been corrupted by the drug culture. The main recipient of American aid, the Colombian military, has been involved in drug trafficking, at the same time being intimately linked to right-wing paramilitary forces, which have been even more active in drug trafficking and in protecting drug producers.[66] In November 1998, a Colombian Air Force cargo plane that landed at Fort Lauderdale, Florida was found to contain 1,639 pounds of cocaine. In 1996, Colombian Air Force officers tried to smuggle heroin to the United States aboard the plane used by then-President Ernesto Samper.[67] Samper himself was labeled a "drug trafficker" by a senior Clinton administration official.[68]

In 2004, when Alvaro Uribe was the Colombian president and a key US partner in the drug war, a 1991 report from US Defense Intelligence Agency officials in Colombia came to light, which stated that Uribe, then a Senator, was a "close personal friend of Pablo Escobar", the infamous drug kingpin. Uribe, the report added, "was linked to a business involved in narcotics activities in the United States" and "has worked for the Medellín cartel," the narcotics trafficking organization led by Escobar; moreover, Uribe had participated in Escobar's parliamentary campaign and as Senator he had "attacked all forms of the extradition treaty" with the US,[69] which has been used frequently to send Colombian drug traffickers to the United States. In 2000 the wife of US Army Col. James Hiett, was charged with sending four shipments of heroin from Colombia to the United States. Col. Hiett was the commander of the US Army's anti-drug operation in Colombia.[70]

And in 2005, five American soldiers were arrested after 15 kilograms of cocaine were found aboard a US military plane that took off from Colombia and flew to El Paso, Texas.[71]

And so it goes in Colombia.

As US Senator Patrick Leahy pointed out in 1999, in speaking of Colombia: "What we are really seeing is a ratcheting up of a counter-insurgency policy masquerading as a counter-drug policy."[72]

In a 1994 report, Amnesty International estimated that more than 20,000 people had been killed in Colombia since 1986, mainly by the military and its paramilitary allies—"not in the 'drug wars' but for political reasons". Many of the victims were "trade unionists, human-rights activists and leaders of legal left-wing movements." Amnesty charged that "U.S.-supplied military equipment, ostensibly delivered for use against narcotics traffickers, was being used by the Colombian military to commit these abuses in the name of 'counter-insurgency'."[73]

A March 1997 letter by members of the House Foreign Operations Subcommittee to Secretary of State Madeleine Albright stated that "efforts by the Colombian government to take action to curb the increased abuses committed by paramilitary groups, or to curb extrajudicial executions, disappearances, torture, political killings and other forms of human rights abuses committed by security forces [the regular military] are not sufficient to warrant the provision of over $100 million in military assistance and the resumption of lethal aid."[74]

The lethal aid, however, continued. Washington suspects that the Colombian guerrillas, if they ever took power, would just not fit in very well in the globalized economy of the New World Order, although the fact is that the guerrillas are not what they used to be. Demands for land reform and other revolutionary programs have been largely replaced by a military and money-making process, killing government forces in revenge for the killing of their comrades, kidnapping and extortion of the wealthy and prominent, and killing villagers who won't join them or who are suspected of helping the government.

Yugoslavia, 1995-99

In April 1996, President Clinton visited Russia during a pause in the brutal military struggle between Moscow and its breakaway province of Chechnya. At a press conference, the president declared:

> You say that there are some who say we should have been more openly critical. I think it depends upon your first premise; do you believe that Chechnya is a part of Russia or not? I would remind you that we once had a Civil War in our country in which we lost on a per-capita basis far more people than we lost in any of the wars of the 20th century over the proposition that Abraham Lincoln gave his life for, that no State had a right to withdraw from our Union.[75]

Three years later Clinton destroyed much of Yugoslavian industry, culture and infrastructure, in effect rejecting the idea that President Slobodan Milosevic had the right to try to prevent the province of Kosovo from withdrawing from the Federal Republic of Yugoslavia. The United States, under the cover of NATO, intervened in a civil war less violent than the American civil war; indeed, a lot less violent, and of shorter duration, than several other civil conflicts going on in the world at the same time, such as in Turkey, Sri Lanka, Indonesia/East Timor, Angola, and other places in Africa; yet it was the supposed extreme (and one-sided?) violence of Serbia against the Kosovars that tore at the heartstrings of the kindly American and NATO leaders.

To those who argue that the US couldn't be saving the entire world, it must be pointed out that far from simply not saving certain peoples, Washington had been actively *supporting* Turkey and Indonesia for years in their mailed-fist military suppressions, and helped Croatia carry out, and then cover up, its "ethnic cleansing" of the Krajina Serbs in 1995.[76] Turkey, in fact, had nearly threatened to veto the NATO decision that it could act on Kosovo unless Ankara was assured that this policy could never be applied to Turkey's treatment of Kurds.[77]

But it was imperative for the United States that certain principles be established: 1) that NATO—in the absence of the Cold War, the Soviet Union, and the Warsaw Pact—still had a purpose in life; 2) that NATO had the right to intervene anywhere, even outside of its own geographical boundaries, and without having to seek explicit authority from the UN Security Council; 3) that NATO was to be the military arm of the New World Order (corporate headquarters located in Washington, DC).

Yugoslavia was not inclined to worship these principles; nor, as we have seen in the Introduction, had the Serbs shown proper reverence for joining the club of globalized American allies *cum* obedient junior partners. Most of their industry and financial sector was still state owned. They had not even banned the word "socialism" from polite conversation yet. Mad raving dinosaurs they were! All in all, an ideal humanitarian bombing target. The fact that Milosevic was an authoritarian leader was of no significance except for its propaganda value.

So Yugoslavia, which for years had feared an attack from the East (the Soviet Union), instead was devastated by the Western "free world". While the bombing attacks were being carried out, Serbian TV was also targeted, because it was broadcasting things *which the United States did not like*. The bombs took the lives of many of the station's staff, and both legs of one of the survivors, which had to be amputated to free him from the wreckage.[78]

"Once you kill people because you don't like what they say," observed noted British foreign correspondent, Robert Fisk, "you change the rules of war."[79]

Perhaps the strangest aspect of the whole conflict is the collective amnesia that appears to have afflicted countless intelligent, well-meaning people, who are convinced that the US/ NATO bombing took place *after* the mass forced deportation of ethnic Albanians from Kosovo was well underway; which is to say that the bombing was launched to *stop* this "ethnic cleansing". In actuality, the systematic forced deportations of large numbers of people did not begin until a few days after the bombing began, and was clearly a reaction to it, born of extreme anger and powerlessness. This is easily verified by looking at a daily newspaper for the few days before the bombing began the night of March 23/24, and the few days after. Or simply look at the *New York Times* of March 26, page 1, which reads:

> ... with the NATO bombing already begun, a deepening sense of fear took hold in Pristina [the main city of Kosovo] that the Serbs would *now* vent their rage against ethnic Albanian civilians in retaliation. [emphasis added]

On March 27, we find the first reference to a "forced march" or anything of that sort.

But the propaganda version is already set in marble.

Ecuador 2000

On January 21, in this nation where the majority live in poverty, a very large number of Indian peasants rose up in desperation and marched to the capital city of Quito, where they were joined by labor unions and some junior military officers (most members of the army being Indian). This coalition presented a list of economic demands, seized the Congress and Supreme Court buildings, and forced the president to resign; he was replaced by a junta from the ranks of the coalition. Washington was alarmed. Besides its knee-reflex hostility to anything that looks like a leftist revolution or coup, it had big plans for military bases in Ecuador; and

Colombia—already plagued by leftist movements—was next door.

The US quickly stepped in to educate the Ecuadorean military leaders in the facts of imperial life. The American embassy in Quito; Peter Romero, Assistant Secretary of State for Latin America and Western Hemispheric Affairs; Sandy Berger, National Security Adviser to President Clinton; and Undersecretary of State Thomas Pickering all made phone calls to Ecuadorian officials to threaten a cutoff in aid and other support, warning that "Ecuador will find itself isolated", informing them that the United States would never recognize any new government the coalition might set up, and that there would be no peace in Ecuador unless the military backed the vice president as the new leader. And the vice president must continue to pursue neoliberal "reforms", the kind of IMF structural adjustment policies which had played a major role in inciting the Indian uprising in the first place.

Within hours the heads of the Ecuadorian army, navy and air force declared their support for the vice president. The leaders of the uprising fled into hiding. And that was the end of the Ecuadorian revolution of the year 2000.[80] This was neither the first nor the last serious uprising in Ecuador against US/IMF policies of privatization, removal of subsidies, etc., which have led to crushing inflation, loss of services, and hunger.

Afghanistan 2001 to present

The United States asked the world to believe that its bombing of Afghanistan, begun in October 2001, was in direct retaliation for the attacks on New York and Washington on September 11. But amongst the thousands of victims of the American bombing and subsequent warfare not one was ever identified as having a connection to the events of that tragic day. The September 11 terrorists had chosen symbolic buildings to attack and the United

States then chose a symbolic country to retaliate against.

The attacks on Afghanistan killed more innocent civilians than were killed in the United States on September 11 as well as taking the lives of countless "combatants" (i.e., anyone who defended against the invasion of the land they were living in).

Most of the so-called "terrorists" of foreign nationality residing in Afghanistan at the time, including those training at al Qaeda camps, had come there to help the Taliban in their civil war; for them it was a religious mission, none of Washington's concern.

The American occupation of Afghanistan served the purpose of setting up a new government that would be sufficiently amenable to Washington's international objectives, including the installation of military bases and electronic listening stations and the running of secure oil and gas pipelines through Afghanistan from the Caspian Sea region to the Indian Ocean. American oil barons had their hearts set on this scenario for years. The oilmen had been quite open about it, giving frank testimony before Congress on the matter.[81]

In addition to causing the death of thousands of Afghans, the following have been among the consequences of the US actions in Afghanistan: countless homes and other buildings have been destroyed; depleted uranium has begun to show its ugly face; the warlords have returned to extensive power; opium cultivation is booming anew; crime and violence are once again a daily fact of life in the cities' neighborhoods, which had been made safer by the Taliban; the president is nothing less than an American puppet (he and several of his ministers are actually Afghan- Americans); the country is occupied by foreign troops (i.e., American) who often treat the population badly, including the use of torture; US forces seize Afghans and take them away without explanation and keep them incommunicado indefinitely, some being sent to the 21st century's Devils Island in Guantánamo Base, Cuba; in Kabul, the number of children suffering from malnutrition is almost double what it was before the American invasion;[82] Afghanistan has become a protectorate of the US and NATO.

Although the awful Taliban regime has been removed, it must be kept in mind that the Taliban would never have come to power in the first place if the United States, in the 1980s and 90s, had not played an essential role in the overthrow of a secular and fairly progressive government, which allowed women much more freedom than they'll ever have under the current government.

Venezuela 2001—2004

In 2000, for the second time, Hugo Chávez was elected president by a wide margin. But in the eyes of Washington officials, Chávez was no more than a man guilty of the following offenses:

He branded the post-September 11 US attacks on Afghanistan as "fighting terrorism with terrorism", demanding an end to "the slaughter of innocents"; holding up photographs of children said to have been killed in the American bombing attacks, he said their deaths had "no justification, just as the attacks in New York did not, either."[83] The US Ambassador told Chávez "to keep his mouth shut on these important issues."[84]

To add to his crimes, Chávez was very friendly with Fidel Castro and sold oil to Cuba at discount rates or in exchange for medical and other services. His defense minister asked the permanent US military mission in Venezuela to vacate its offices in the military headquarters in Caracas, saying its presence was an anachronism from the Cold War.[85] Chávez did not cooperate to Washington's satisfaction with the US war against the Colombian guerrillas.[86] And he refused to provide US intelligence agencies with information on Venezuela's large Arab community.[87]

He also promoted a regional free-trade bloc and united Latin American petroleum operations as ways to break free from

US economic dominance, as well as opposing the Free Trade Area of the Americas, a globalization program high on Washington's agenda.

And much more in the same vein, which the Washington aristocracy is unaccustomed to encountering from the servant class. Uncle Sam has been inspired to topple numerous governments which displayed considerably less disrespect for him than Venezuela did.

At the same time, Chávez was trying to institute all manner of reforms to relieve the suffering of the poor (who comprise about 80 percent of the population), a program not likely to win favor with a class-conscious, privatization-minded US government and Venezuelan upper and middle classes.

On April 11, 2002 a military coup toppled Chávez, who was taken to a remote location. Through a startling series of circumstances, Chávez was returned to power two days later. But during those two days, Pedro Carmona, the chairman of Venezuela's largest chamber of commerce, was installed as president. He proceeded to dissolve the legislature, the Supreme Court, the attorney general's office, the national electoral commission, and the state governorships and suspended the constitution.

And what was the reaction of the US government to this sharp slap in the face of democracy, civil liberties, and law, that fits the textbook definition of dictatorship?

The Bush administration did not call it a coup. The White House term of choice was "a change of government". They blamed Chávez for what had taken place, maintaining that his ouster was prompted by peaceful protests and justified by the Venezuelan leader's own actions. It occurred, said White House spokesman Ari Fleischer, "as a result of the message of the Venezuelan people."[88]

The State Department also expressed its support for the coup, declaring that "undemocratic actions committed or encouraged by the Chávez administration provoked yesterday's crisis in Venezuela".[89]

As the coup was being hatched, the United States met with all the key players, either in Venezuela or in Washington: Pedro Carmona, who became president; Vice Admiral Carlos Molina, Air Force Col. Pedro Soto, and several other officers who in February had publicly demanded Chávez's removal; opposition legislators, and others. A US diplomat revealed that Molina and Soto had each received $100,000 from a Miami bank account for denouncing Chávez.[90]

"We felt we were acting with U.S. support," Molina said of the coup. "We agree that we can't permit a communist government here. The U.S. has not let us down yet. This fight is still going on because the government is illegal."[91]

The officers who took part in the overthrow of Chávez "understood the U.S. State Department's repeated statements of concern over the Chávez administration as a tacit endorsement of their plans to remove him from office if the opportunity arose."..."The State Department had always expressed its preoccupation with Chávez," retired military officer Fernando Ochoa said after the coup. "We interpreted that as" an endorsement of his removal.[92]

Washington also financed the plotters. The National Endowment for Democracy (NED) was on the scene, as it has been for so many other Washington destabilization operations, giving in excess of a million dollars in the two years preceding the coup to organizations opposed to Chávez. These organizations initiated work stoppages and protest demonstrations which galvanized opposition to the Venezuelan leader.

Following the aborted coup, the opposition tried to unseat Chávez through a recall referendum, a drive that was funded in part, if not in full, by NED. This too failed.[93]

Iraq 2003 to present

It was indeed remarkable—that the United States could openly announce to the world its determination to invade a sovereign nation and overthrow its government, a nation that had not attacked the US, that had not threatened to attack the US, that knew it would mean instant mass suicide for them if they attacked the US. American leaders told one story after another about why Iraq was a threat, a chemical threat, a biological threat, a nuclear threat, an imminent threat, a threat increasing in danger with each passing day, that Iraq was a terrorist state, that Iraq was tied to al Qaeda, only to have each story amount to nothing. The United States told the world again and again that Iraq must agree to having the UN weapons inspectors back in, and when Iraq agreed to this Washington made it clear that this was not good enough to save them.

Did any of this make sense? This sudden urgency of fighting a war in the absence of a fight? Creating fiction after fiction to justify it? It did make sense if one understands that the war, which began with bombing attacks on March 20, 2003, was not about Sadaam Hussein and his evilness, or his weapons, or terrorism, but rather had to do with such things as expansion of the American Empire, oil, the care and feeding of American corporations, and Israel.

After the conquest—the thousand-pound gorilla subduing the 90-year-old woman in a wheel chair to the cheers of Americans yelling "USA Number 1! USA Number 1!"—came the resistance. How could it be otherwise? What kind of people like being bombed, invaded, occupied, tortured, subjected to daily humiliations, their loved ones torn apart by missiles, their homes, hospitals, schools and jobs destroyed? The great majority of the Iraqi people had better lives under Saddam Hussein than under the American occupation; amongst the many things they've lost is their secular society—in the new Iraq, Islamic religious police are now on the prowl, imposing the kind of awful punishments that made the Taliban infamous. And more and more, the US occupiers are making use of Saddam's own security forces to fight the resistance.

In any event, the removal of Saddam Hussein, even if Washington was truly and morally moved by his evilness, could not justify the American onslaught. What kind of world would we have if any country could invade any other country because it didn't like the leader of that country? The harm done to international law and the United Nations has been considerable.

Haiti 2004

On February 28, 2004, American military and diplomatic personnel arrived at the home of President Jean-Bertrand Aristide in Port- au-Prince to inform him that his private American security agents must either leave immediately to return to the United States or fight and die; that the remaining 25 of the American security agents hired by the Haitian government, who were to arrive the next day, had been blocked by the United States from coming; that foreign and Haitian rebels were nearby, heavily armed, determined and ready to kill thousands of people in a bloodbath. Aristide was pressured to sign a "letter of resignation" before he was flown into exile by the United States.[94]

And then US Secretary of State Colin Powell, in the sincerest voice he could muster, told the world that Aristide "was not kidnapped. We did not force him onto the airplane. He went onto the airplane willingly. And that's the truth."[95]

Powell sounded as sincere as he had sounded a year earlier when he gave the UN a detailed inventory of the chemical, biological and nuclear weapons in Iraq. He did not explain why the United States disbanded Aristide's personal security forces. He did not explain why the United States was not protecting Aristide from the rebels, which the US could have done with the greatest of ease, without so much as firing a single shot. He did not explain why Aristide would "willingly" give up his presidency. The world is still waiting for answers to these questions.

The answers lie with this: Jean-Bertrand Aristide was on record, by word and deed, repeatedly, as not being a great lover of globalization or capitalism. This was not the kind of man the imperial mafia wanted in charge of the assembly plant of the Western Hemisphere. It was only a matter of time before they took action.

Chapter 18

Perverting Elections

It shall be unlawful for a foreign national directly or through any other person to make any contribution of money or other thing of value, or to promise expressly or impliedly to make any such contribution, in connection with an election to any political office or in connection with any primary election...

Title 2, United States Code Amended (USCA), Section 441e(a)

Thus the legal basis, if not the political, for the indignation expressed by both Republican and Democratic members of Congress at revelations in 1996 that the Chinese may have tried to use covert campaign donations to influence American policy.

Washington policymakers, however, have long reserved the unrestrained right to pour large amounts of money into elections of other countries (including those which also prohibit foreign contributions) and taint their electoral systems in numerous other ways, as we shall see below.

Elections and this thing called democracy

For more than a decade, the sentiment has been proclaimed on so many occasions by the president and other political leaders, and dutifully reiterated by the media, that the thesis: "Cuba is the only non-democracy in the Western Hemisphere" is now nothing short of received wisdom in the United States.

Let us examine this thesis carefully for it has a highly interesting implication.

Throughout the period of the Cuban revolution, 1959 to the present, Latin America has witnessed a terrible parade of human rights violations—systematic, routine torture; legions of "disappeared" people; government-supported death squads picking off selected individuals; massacres *en masse* of peasants, students and other groups, shot down in cold blood. The worst perpetrators of these acts during this period have been the military and associated paramilitary squads of El Salvador, Guatemala, Brazil, Argentina, Chile, Colombia, Peru, Mexico, Uruguay, Haiti and Honduras.

Not even Cuba's worst enemies have made serious charges against the Castro government for any of these violations, and if one further considers education and health care, "both of which," said President Clinton, "work better [in Cuba] than most other countries",[1] and both of which are guaranteed by the United Nations "Universal Declaration of Human Rights" and the "European Convention for the Protection of Human Rights and Fundamental Freedoms", then it would appear that during the more-than-45 years of its revolution, Cuba has enjoyed one of the very best human-rights records in all of Latin America.

If, despite this record, the United States can insist that Cuba is the only "non-democracy" in the Western Hemisphere, we are left with the inescapable conclusion that this thing called "democracy", as seen from the White House, may have little or nothing to do with many of our most cherished human rights. Indeed, numerous pronouncements emanating from Washington officialdom over the years make it plain that "democracy", at best, or at most, is equated solely with elections and civil liberties. Neither jobs, food or shelter, nor education or health care are part of the equation.

Thus, a nation with hordes of hungry, homeless, untended sick, barely literate, unemployed, and/or tortured people, whose loved ones are being disappeared and/or murdered with state connivance, can be said to be living in a "democracy"—its literal Greek meaning of "rule of the people" implying that this is the kind of life the people actually *want*—provided that every two years or four years they have the right to go to a designated place and put an X next to the name of one or another individual who promises to relieve their miserable condition, but who will, typically, do virtually nothing of the kind; and provided further that in this society there is at least a certain minimum of freedom—how much being in large measure a function of one's wealth—for one to express one's views about the powers-that-be and the workings of the society, without undue fear of punishment, regardless of whether expressing these views has any influence whatsoever over the way things are.

It is not by chance that the United States has defined democracy in this narrow manner. Throughout the Cold War, the absence of "free and fair" multiparty elections and adequate civil liberties were what marked the Soviet foe and its satellites. These nations, however, provided their citizens with a relatively decent standard of living so far as things like employment, food, health care, education, social safety nets, vacations, etc. At the same time, many of America's Third World allies in the Cold War—members of what Washington liked to refer to as "The Free World"—were human-rights disaster areas, who could boast of little other than the 60-second democracy of the polling booth and a tolerance for dissenting opinion so long as it didn't cut too close to the bone or threaten to turn into a movement.

Naturally, with team lineups like these, the only way to win Cold-War propaganda points was to extol your team's brand of virtue and condemn the enemy's lack of it, designating the former "democracy" and the latter "totalitarianism".

Thus it is, that Americans are raised to fervently believe that no progress can be made in any society in the absence of elections. They are taught to equate elections with democracy, and democracy with elections. And no matter how cynical they've grown about electoral politics and ballot counting at home, few of them harbor any doubt that the promotion of free and fair elections has long been a basic and sincere tenet of American foreign policy.

In light of this, let us examine the actual historical record. (Note: For many of the following cases, further details can be found in Chapter 17 herein and the author's book, *Killing Hope: U.S. Military and CIA Interventions Since World War II.*)

Philippines, 1950s

Flagrant manipulation by the CIA of the nation's political life, featuring stage-managed elections with extensive disinformation campaigns, heavy financing of candidates, writing their speeches, drugging the drinks of one of the opponents of the CIA-supported candidate so he would appear incoherent; plotting the assassination of another candidate. The Agency covertly set up an organization called National Movement for Free Elections, the better to promote its agenda, and trusting citizens joined up all over the country. The *New York Times* was also trusting. It praised the Philippine's political and electoral development, declaring that "It is not without reason that the Philippines has been called "democracy's showcase in Asia".[2]

Italy, 1948-1970s

Multifarious campaigns to repeatedly sabotage the electoral chances of the Communist Party and ensure the election of the Christian Democrats, long-favored by Washington.

Lebanon, 1950s

The CIA provided funds to support the campaigns of President Camille Chamoun and selected parliamentary candidates; other funds were targeted against candidates who had shown less than total enchantment with US interference in Lebanese politics.[3]

Indonesia, 1955

A million dollars were dispensed by the CIA to a centrist coalition's electoral campaign in a bid to cut into the support for President Sukarno's party and the Indonesian Communist Party.[4]

Vietnam, 1955

The US was instrumental in South Vietnam canceling the elections scheduled to unify North and South because of the certainty that the North Vietnamese communist leader, Ho Chi Minh, would easily win.[5]

British Guiana/Guyana, 1953-64

For 11 years, two of the oldest democracies in the world, Great Britain and the United States, went to great lengths to prevent Cheddi Jagan—three times the democratically elected leader— from occupying his office. Using a wide variety of tactics— from general strikes and disinformation to terrorism and British legalisms—the US and Britain forced Jagan out of office twice during the period.[6]

Japan, 1958-1970s

The CIA emptied the US treasury of millions to finance the conservative Liberal Democratic Party in parliamentary elections, "on a seat-by-seat basis", while doing what it could to weaken and undermine its opposition, the Japanese Socialist Party. The result was 38 years in power for the Liberal Democratic Party, comparable to the reign of the Christian Democrats in Italy, also sponsored by the CIA; these tactics kept both Japan and Italy from developing a strong multi-party system.[7]

The 1961-63 edition of the State Department's annual

Foreign Relations of the United States, published in 1996, includes an unprecedented disclaimer that, because of material left out, a committee of distinguished historians thinks, "this published compilation does not constitute a 'thorough, accurate, and reliable documentary record of major United States foreign policy decisions'," as required by law. The deleted material involved US actions from 1958-1960 in Japan, according to the State Department's historian.[8]

Nepal, 1959

By the CIA's own admission, it carried out an unspecified "covert action" on behalf of B.P. Koirala to help his Nepali Congress Party win the national parliamentary election. The NCP won a majority of seats in the new legislature and Koirala became prime minister. It was Nepal's first national election ever, and the CIA was there to initiate them into the wonderful workings of democracy.[9]

Laos, 1960

CIA agents stuffed ballot boxes to help a hand-picked strongman, Phoumi Nosavan, set up a pro-American government.[10]

Brazil, 1962

The CIA and the Agency for International Development expended millions of dollars during federal and state elections in support of candidates opposed to President João Goulart, who won anyway. The Agency also dipped into its bag of dirty tricks to torment the campaigns of various other candidates.[11]

Dominican Republic, 1962

In October 1962, two months before election day, US Ambassador John Bartlow Martin got together with the candidates of the two major parties and handed them a written notice, in Spanish and English, which he had prepared. It read in part: "The loser in the forthcoming election will, as soon as the election result is known, publicly congratulate the winner, publicly recognize him as the President of all the Dominican people, and publicly call upon his own supporters to so recognize him.... Before taking office, the winner will offer Cabinet seats to members of the loser's party. (They may decline)."[12]

The United States also worked with the Dominican government to deport some 125 people—supporters of the former dictator Trujillo as well as "Castro/Communists"—to the US and elsewhere, who were not allowed to return until after the election. This was "to help maintain stability so elections could be held", as Martin put it.[13]

As matters turned out, the winner, Juan Bosch, was ousted in a military coup seven months later, a slap in the face of democracy which neither Martin nor any other American official did anything about.

Guatemala, 1963

The US overthrew the regime of General Miguel Ydigoras because he was planning to step down in 1964, leaving the door open to an election; an election that Washington feared would be won by the former president, liberal reformer and critic of US foreign policy, Juan José Arévalo. Ydigoras's replacement made no mention of elections.[14]

Bolivia, 1966

The CIA bestowed $600,000 upon President René Barrientos and lesser sums to several right-wing parties in a successful effort to influence the outcome of national elections. Gulf Oil contributed two hundred thousand more to Barrientos.[15]

Chile, 1964-70

Major US interventions into national elections in 1964 and 1970, and congressional elections in the intervening years. Socialist Salvador Allende fell victim in 1964, but won in 1970 despite a multimillion-dollar CIA operation against him. The Agency then orchestrated his downfall in a 1973 military coup.[16]

Portugal, 1974-5

In the years following the coup in 1974 by military officers who talked like socialists, the CIA revved up its propaganda machine while funneling many millions of dollars to support "moderate" candidates, in particular Mario Soares and his (so-called) Socialist Party. At the same time, the Agency enlisted social- democratic parties of Western Europe to provide further funds and support to Soares. It worked. The Socialist Party became the dominant power.[17]

Australia, 1974-75

Despite providing considerable support for the opposition, the United States failed to defeat the Labor Party, which was strongly against the US war in Vietnam and CIA meddling in Australia. The CIA then used "legal" methods to unseat the man who won the election.

Jamaica, 1976

A CIA campaign to defeat social democrat Michael Manley's bid for reelection, featuring disinformation, arms shipments, labor unrest, economic destabilization, financial support for the opposition, and attempts upon Manley's life. Despite it all, he was victorious.[18]

Panama, 1984, 1989

In 1984, the CIA helped finance a highly questionable presidential electoral victory for one of Manuel Noriega's men. The opposition cried "fraud", but the new president was welcomed at the White House. By 1989, Noriega was no longer a Washington favorite, so the CIA provided more than $10 million dollars to those opposing Noriega's candidate as well as providing for clandestine radio and TV broadcasts to influence the vote. When the Noriega man "won", Washington, on this occasion, expressed its moral indignation about the fraudulent election.[19]

Nicaragua, 1984, 1990

In 1984, the United States, trying to discredit the legitimacy of the Sandinista government's scheduled election, covertly persuaded the leading opposition coalition to not take part. A few days before election day, some other rightist parties on the ballot revealed that US diplomats had been pressing them to drop out of the race as well.[20] The CIA also tried to split the Sandinista leadership by placing phony full-page ads in neighboring countries.[21] But the Sandinistas won handily in a very fair election monitored by hundreds of international observers.

Six years later, the National Endowment for Democracy (NED), Washington's specially created stand-in for the CIA, poured in millions of dollars to defeat Daniel Ortega and the Sandinistas in the February elections. NED helped organize the Nicaraguan opposition, UNO, building up the parties and organizations that formed and supported this coalition. The successful UNO was the only political party to receive US aid, even though eight other opposition parties fielded candidates.[22]

Perhaps most telling of all, the Nicaraguan people were made painfully aware that a victory by the Sandinistas would mean a continuation of the relentlessly devastating war being waged against them by Washington through their proxy army, the Contras.

Haiti, 1987-1988

After the Duvalier dictatorship came to an end in 1986, the country prepared for its first free elections ever. However, Haiti's main trade union leader declared that Washington was working to undermine the left. US aid organizations, he said, were encouraging people in the countryside to identify and reject the entire left as "communist". Meanwhile, the CIA was involved in a range of support for selected candidates until the US Senate Intelligence Committee ordered the Agency to cease its covert electoral action.[23]

Bulgaria, 1990-1991 and Albania, 1991-1992

With no regard for the fragility of these nascent democracies, the US interfered broadly in their elections and orchestrated the ousting of their elected socialist governments.

Russia, 1996

For four months (March-June), a group of veteran American political consultants worked secretly in Moscow in support of

Boris Yeltsin's presidential campaign. Although the Americans were working independently, President Clinton's political guru, Dick Morris, acted as their middleman to the administration, and Clinton himself told Yeltsin in March that he wanted to "make sure everything the United States did would have a positive impact" on the Russian's electoral campaign. Boris Yeltsin was being counted on to run with the globalized-free market ball and it was imperative that he cross the goal line. The Americans scripted a Clinton-Yeltsin summit meeting in April to allow the Russian to "stand up to the West", to match what the Russian Communist Party Yeltsin's main opponent—was insisting they would do if they won.

The Americans emphasized sophisticated methods of message development, polling, focus groups, crowd staging, direct- mailing, etc., urged more systematic domination of the state- owned media, and advised against public debates with the Communists. Most of all they encouraged the Yeltsin campaign to "go negative" against the Communists, painting frightening pictures of what the Communists would do if they took power, including much civic upheaval and violence, and, of course, a return to the worst of Stalinism. With a virtual media blackout against them, the Communists were extremely hard pressed to respond to the attacks or to shout the Russian equivalent of "It's the economy, stupid."

It is impossible to measure the value of the American consultants' contributions to the Yeltsin campaign, for there's no knowing which of their tactics the Russians would have employed anyhow if left to their own devices, how well they would have applied them, or how things would have turned out. But we do know that before the Americans came on board, Yeltsin was favored by only six percent of the electorate. In the first round of voting, he edged the Communists 35 percent to 32, and was victorious in the second round 54 to 40 percent. "Democracy," declared *Time* magazine, "triumphed."[24]

Mongolia, 1996

The National Endowment for Democracy worked for several years with the opposition to the governing Mongolian People's Revolutionary Party (the former Communists, who had won the 1992 election) to achieve a very surprising electoral victory. In the six-year period leading up to the 1996 elections, NED spent close to a million dollars in a country with a population of some 2.5 million, the most significant result of which was to unite the opposition into a new coalition, the National Democratic Union. Borrowing from Newt Gingrich's Contract With America, the NED drafted a "Contract With the Mongolian Voter", which called for private property rights, a free press and the encouragement of foreign investment.[25] The MPRR had already instituted Western-style economic reforms, which had led to widespread poverty and wiped out much of the communist social safety net. But the new government promised to accelerate the reforms, including the privatization of housing.[26] The *Wall Street Journal* was ecstatic that "shock-therapy" was now going to become even more shocking, as with the sale of state enterprises. The newspaper's editorial was entitled "Wisdom of the Steppes".[27] The new government was one that Washington could expect to be more hospitable to American corporations and intelligence agencies than the MPRR had been. Indeed, by 1998 it was reported that the US National Security Agency had set up electronic listening posts in Outer Mongolia to intercept Chinese army communications, and the Mongolian intelligence service was using nomads to gather intelligence in China itself.[28]

Bosnia, 1998

Effectively an American protectorate, with Carlos Westendorp— the Spanish diplomat appointed to enforce Washington's offspring:

the 1995 Dayton peace accords—as the colonial Governor-General, known officially as the "high representative". Before the September elections for a host of offices, Westendorp removed 14 Croatian candidates from the ballot because of alleged biased coverage aired in Bosnia by neighboring Croatia's state television and politicking by ethnic Croat army soldiers. After the election, Westendorp fired the elected president of the Bosnian Serb Republic, accusing him of creating instability. In this scenario those who appeared to support what the US and other Western powers wished were called "moderates", and allowed to run for and remain in office. Those who had other thoughts were labeled "hard-liners", and ran the risk of a different fate. When Westendorp was chosen to assume this position of "high representative" in Bosnia in May 1997, *The Guardian* of London wrote that "The US secretary of state, Madeleine Albright, praised the choice. But some critics already fear that Mr. Westendorp will prove too lightweight and end up as a cipher in American hands."[29] (In both 2001 and 2005, the "high representative" removed one of the three men elected to Bosnia's tripartite presidency. In the latter instance, it was Britisher Paddy Ashdown firing Dragan Covic. Covic had won his position, for a four-year term, in the October 2002 elections with 61.5 per cent of the Bosnian Croat vote.)[30]

Nicaragua 2001

Sandinista leader Daniel Ortega was once again a marked man. US State Department officials tried their best to publicly associate him with terrorism, including just after September 11 had taken place, and to shamelessly accuse Sandinista leaders of all manner of violations of human rights, civil rights, and democracy. The US ambassador literally campaigned for Ortega's opponent, Enrique Bolaños. A senior analyst in Nicaragua for Gallup, the international pollsters, was moved to declare: "Never in my whole life have

I seen a sitting ambassador get publicly involved in a sovereign country's electoral process, nor have I ever heard of it."

The US also exerted relentless pressure on the Conservative Party and succeeded in making them withdraw from the election so as to avoid splitting the conservative vote against the Sandinistas, the State Department's No. 2 man personally visiting the country to make this appeal. Then there were ads in the newspapers, signed by Jeb Bush, to make it appear that his brother the president was personally supporting Bolaños.

At the close of the campaign, Bolaños announced: "If Ortega comes to power, that would provoke a closing of aid and investment, difficulties with exports, visas and family remittances. I'm not just saying this. The United States says this, too. We cannot close our eyes and risk our well-being and work. Say yes to Nicaragua, say no to terrorism."

In the end, the Sandinistas lost the election by about ten percentage points after steadily leading in the polls during much of the campaign.[31]

Bolivia 2002

The American *bête noire* here was Evo Morales, Amerindian, former member of Congress, socialist, running on an anti-neoliberal, anti-big business, and anti-coca eradication campaign.

The US Ambassador declared: "The Bolivian electorate must consider the consequences of choosing leaders somehow connected with drug trafficking and terrorism." Following September 11, painting Officially Designated Enemies with the terrorist brush was *de rigueur* US foreign policy rhetoric.

The US Assistant Secretary of State for Western Hemisphere Affairs warned that American aid to the country would be in danger if Mr. Morales was chosen. Then the ambassador and other US officials met with key figures from Bolivia's main political parties in an effort to shore up support for Morales's opponent, Sanchez de Lozada. Morales lost the vote.[32]

Slovakia 2002

To defeat Vladimir Meciar, former prime minister, a man who did not share Washington's *weltanschauung* about globalization, the US ambassador explicitly warned the Slovakian people that electing him would hurt their chances of entry into the European Union and NATO. The US ambassador to NATO then arrived and issued his own warning. The National Endowment for Democracy was also on hand to influence the election. Meciar lost.[33]

El Salvador 2004

Washington's target in this election was Schafik Handal, candidate of the FMLN, the leftist former guerrilla group. He said he would withdraw El Salvador's 380 troops from Iraq as well as reviewing other pro-US policies; he would also take another look at the privatizations of Salvadoran industries, and would reinstate diplomatic relations with Cuba.

His opponent was Tony Saca of the incumbent Arena Party, a pro-US, pro-free market organization of the extreme right, which in the bloody civil war days had featured death squads and the infamous assassination of Archbishop Oscar Romero.

During a February visit to the country, the US Assistant Secretary of State for Western Hemisphere Affairs, met with all the presidential candidates except Handal. He warned of possible repercussions in US-Salvadoran relations if Handal were elected. Three Republican congressmen threatened to block the renewal of annual work visas for some 300,000 Salvadorans in the United States if El Salvador opted for the FMLN. And Congressman Thomas Tancredo of Colorado stated that if the FMLN won, "it could mean a radical change" in US policy on remittances to El Salvador.

Washington's attitude was exploited by Arena and the generally conservative Salvadoran press, who mounted a scare campaign, and it became widely believed that a Handal victory could result in mass deportations of Salvadorans from the United States and a drop in remittances.

Arena won the election with about 57 percent of the vote to some 36 percent for the FMLN.

After the election, the US ambassador declared that Washington's policies concerning immigration and remittances had nothing to do with any election in El Salvador. There appears to be no record of such a statement being made in public *before* the election when it might have had a profound positive effect for the FMLN.[34]

Afghanistan 2004

The US ambassador to Afghanistan, Zalmay Khalilzad, went around putting great pressure on one candidate after another to withdraw from the presidential race so as to insure the victory for Washington's man, the incumbent, Hamid Karzai in the October election. There was nothing particularly subtle about it. Khalilzad told each one what he wanted and then asked them what they needed. Karzai, a long-time resident in the United States, was Washington's hand-picked, packaged, and groomed candidate, described by the *Washington Post* as "a known and respected figure at the State Department and National Security Council and on Capitol Hill."

"Our hearts have been broken because we thought we could have beaten Mr. Karzai if this had been a true election," said Sayed Mustafa Sadat Ophyani, campaign manager for Younis Qanooni, Karzai's leading rival. "But it is not. Mr. Khalilzad is putting a lot of pressure on us and does not allow us to fight a good election campaign."

This was not the first time Khalilzad had been accused of meddling in Afghan politics. Delegates to gatherings that named Karzai interim president in 2002 and ratified Afghanistan's new Constitution in December 2003 also accused the ambassador of interfering, even of paying delegates for their support.[35]

None of the major candidates actually withdrew from the election, which Karzai won with about 56 percent of the votes.

> *Mr. Castro, once, just once, show that you're unafraid of a real election.*
>
> George W. Bush, 2002[36]

Further evidence of Washington's love affair with elections

There have also been the occasions where the United States, while (perhaps) not interfering in the election process, was, however, involved in overthrowing a democratically-elected government, such as in Iran 1953, Guatemala 1954, the Congo 1960, Ecuador 1961, Bolivia 1964, Greece 1967, and Fiji 1987.

On many occasions, US interventions resulted in free, or any, elections being done away with completely for large stretches of time, as in Iran, South Korea, Guatemala, Brazil, Congo, Indonesia, Chile, and Greece.

Chapter 19

Trojan Horse: The National Endowment for Democracy

How many Americans could identify the National Endowment for Democracy? An organization which often does exactly the opposite of what its name implies. The NED was set up in the early 1980s under President Reagan in the wake of all the negative revelations about the CIA in the second half of the 1970s. The latter was a remarkable period. Spurred by Watergate—the Church committee of the Senate, the Pike committee of the House, and the Rockefeller Commission, created by the president, were all busy investigating the CIA. Seemingly every other day there was a new headline about the discovery of some awful thing, even criminal conduct, the CIA had been mixed up in for years. The Agency was getting an exceedingly bad name, and it was causing the powers-that-be much embarrassment.

Something had to be done. What was done was not to stop doing these awful things. Of course not. What was done was to shift many of these awful things to a new organization, with a nice sounding name—The National Endowment for Democracy. The idea was that the NED would do somewhat overtly what the CIA had been doing covertly for decades, and thus, hopefully, eliminate the stigma associated with CIA covert activities.

It was a masterpiece. Of politics, of public relations, and of cynicism.

Thus it was that in 1983, the National Endowment for Democracy was set up to "support democratic institutions throughout the world through private, nongovernmental efforts". Notice the "nongovernmental"—part of the image, part of the myth. In actuality, virtually every penny of its funding comes from the federal government, as is clearly indicated in the financial statement in each issue of its annual report. NED likes to refer to itself as an NGO (Non-governmental organization) because this helps to maintain a certain credibility abroad that an official US government agency might not have. But NGO is the wrong category. NED is a GO.

"We should not have to do this kind of work covertly," said Carl Gershman in 1986, while he was president of the Endowment. "It would be terrible for democratic groups around the world to be seen as subsidized by the C.I.A. We saw that in the 60's, and that's why it has been discontinued. We have not had the capability of doing this, and that's why the endowment was created."[1]

And Allen Weinstein, who helped draft the legislation establishing NED, declared in 1991: "A lot of what we do today was done covertly 25 years ago by the CIA."[2]

In effect, the CIA has been laundering money through NED.

The Endowment has four principal initial recipients of funds: the International Republican Institute; the National Democratic Institute for International Affairs; an affiliate of the AFL-CIO (such as the American Center for International Labor Solidarity); and an affiliate of the Chamber of Commerce (such as the Center for International Private Enterprise). These institutions then disburse funds to other institutions in the US and all over the world, which then often disburse funds to yet other organizations.

In a multitude of ways, NED meddles in the internal affairs of numerous foreign countries by supplying funds, technical know- how, training, educational materials, computers, faxes, copiers, automobiles, and so on, to selected political groups, civic organizations, labor unions, dissident movements, student groups, book publishers, newspapers, other media, etc. NED typically refers to the media it supports as "independent" despite the fact that these media are on the US payroll.

NED programs generally impart the basic philosophy that working people and other citizens are best served under a system of free enterprise, class cooperation, collective bargaining, minimal government intervention in the economy, and opposition to socialism in any shape or form. A free-market economy is equated with democracy, reform, and growth; and the merits of foreign investment in their economy are emphasized.

From 1994 to 1996, NED awarded 15 grants, totaling more than $2,500,000, to the American Institute for Free Labor Development, an organization used by the CIA for decades to subvert progressive labor unions.[3] AIFLD's work within Third World unions typically involved a considerable educational effort very similar to the basic NED philosophy described above. The description of one of the 1996 NED grants to AIFLD includes as one its objectives: "build union-management cooperation".[4] Like many things that NED says, this sounds innocuous, if not positive, but these in fact are ideological code words meaning "keep the labor agitation down...don't rock the status-quo boat". The relationship between NED and AIFLD very well captures the CIA origins of the Endowment.[5]

NED has funded centrist and rightist labor organizations to help them oppose those unions which were too militantly pro- worker. This has taken place in France, Portugal and Spain amongst many other places. In France, during the 1983-4 period, NED supported a "trade union-like organization for professors and students" to counter "left-wing organizations of professors". To this end it funded a series of seminars and the publication of posters, books and pamphlets such as "Subversion and the Theology of Revolution" and "Neutralism or Liberty".[6] ("Neutralism" here refers to being unaligned in the cold war.)

NED describes one of its 1997-98 programs thusly: "To identify barriers to private sector development at the local and federal levels in the Federal Republic of Yugoslavia and to push for legislative change...[and] to develop strategies for private sector growth."[7] Critics of Yugoslav President Slobodan Milosevic, a socialist, were supported by NED grants for years.[8]

In short, NED's programs are in sync with the basic needs and objectives of the New World Order's economic globalization, just as the programs have for years been on the same wavelength as US foreign policy.

Interference in elections

NED's Statement of Principles and Objectives, adopted in 1984, asserts that "No Endowment funds may be used to finance the campaigns of candidates for public office." But the ways to circumvent the spirit of such a prohibition are not difficult to come up with; as with American elections, there's "hard money" and there's "soft money".

As described in the "Elections" and "Interventions" chapters, NED successfully manipulated elections in Nicaragua in 1990 and Mongolia in 1996; helped to overthrow democratically elected governments in Bulgaria in 1990 and Albania in 1991 and 1992; and worked to defeat the candidate for prime minister of Slovakia in 2002 who was out of favor in Washington. And from 1999 to 2004, NED heavily funded members of the opposition to President Hugo Chavez in Venezuela to subvert his rule and to support a referendum to unseat him.

Additionally, in the 1990s and afterward, NED supported a coalition of groups in Haiti known as the Democratic Convergence, who were united in their opposition to Jean-Bertrand Aristide and his progressive ideology, while he was in and out of the office of the president.[9]

The Endowment has made its weight felt in the electoral-political process in numerous other countries.

NED would have the world believe that it's only teaching

the ABCs of democracy and elections to people who don't know them, but in virtually all the countries named above, in whose electoral process NED intervened, there had already been free and fair elections held. The problem, from NED's point of view, is that the elections had been won by political parties not on NED's favorites list.

The Endowment maintains that it's engaged in "opposition building" and "encouraging pluralism". "We support people who otherwise do not have a voice in their political system," said Louisa Coan, a NED program officer.[10] But NED hasn't provided aid to foster progressive or leftist opposition in Mexico, El Salvador, Guatemala, Nicaragua, or Eastern Europe—or, for that matter, in the United States—even though these groups are hard pressed for funds and to make themselves heard. Cuban dissident groups and media are heavily supported however.

NED's reports carry on endlessly about "democracy", but at best it's a modest measure of mechanical political democracy they have in mind, not economic democracy; nothing that aims to threaten the powers-that-be or the way-things-are, unless of course it's in a place like Cuba.

The Endowment played an important role in the Iran-Contra affair of the 1980s, funding key components of Oliver North's shadowy "Project Democracy" network, which privatized US foreign policy, waged war, ran arms and drugs, and engaged in other equally charming activities. At one point in 1987, a White House spokesman stated that those at NED "run Project Democracy".[11] This was an exaggeration; it would have been more correct to say that NED was the public arm of Project Democracy, while North ran the covert end of things. In any event, the statement caused much less of a stir than if—as in an earlier period—it had been revealed that it was the CIA which was behind such an unscrupulous operation.

NED also mounted a multi-level campaign to fight the leftist insurgency in the Philippines in the mid-1980s, funding a host of private organizations, including unions and the media.[12] This was a replica of a typical CIA operation of pre-NED days.

And between 1990 and 1992, the Endowment donated a quarter-million dollars of taxpayers' money to the Cuban-American National Foundation, the ultra-fanatic anti-Castro Miami group. The CANF, in turn, financed Luis Posada Carriles, one of the most prolific and pitiless terrorists of modern times, who had been involved in the blowing up of a Cuban airplane in 1976, which killed 73 people. In 1997, he was involved in a series of bomb explosions in Havana hotels,[13] and in 2000 imprisoned in Panama when he was part of a group planning to assassinate Fidel Castro with explosives while the Cuban leader was speaking before a large crowd, although eventually, the group was tried on lesser charges.

The NED, like the CIA before it, calls what it does supporting democracy. The governments and movements whom the NED targets call it destabilization.[14]

Chapter 20

The United States versus the World at the United Nations

America, we have all been taught for more than half a century, is the leader of "The Free World". If this is so, it's proper to ask: Where are the followers? Where is the evidence that Washington's world view and foreign policy sways other governments and leaders by virtue of anything other than the United States being a 10,000-pound gorilla zillionaire? Where is the loyalty and admiration engendered by intellectual or moral leadership? To enlist support for its wars in Korea, Vietnam, Yugoslavia, Afghanistan (twice), and Iraq (twice), the US has had to resort to bribery, threats, and chicanery. At the United Nations, with noteworthy regularity, Washington has found itself—often alone, sometimes joined by one or two other countries—standing in opposition to General Assembly resolutions aimed at furthering human rights, peace, nuclear disarmament, economic justice, the struggle against South African apartheid and Israeli lawlessness, and other progressive causes.

The table below shows a portion of this pattern. It covers an arbitrarily chosen 10-year period, 1978 through 1987, and is composed of the following sections:

1978-1981: All voting in the General Assembly examined; only those resolutions for which the US cast a solitary "no" vote or was joined by one or two other nations are listed.

1982-1983: All voting in the General Assembly examined; only those resolutions for which the US cast a solitary "no" vote are listed.

1984-1987: Only a sample of General Assembly resolutions are shown, primarily for diversity.

In total, almost 150 examples are given. The number of abstentions is not shown. There were many other resolutions in this period where Israel cast a solitary "no" vote and the US was the sole abstainer.

Voting on resolutions of the Security Council and the Economic and Social Council are not included here, but these votes show a very similar pattern. In the Council, a solitary US "no" vote is of course enough to defeat a measure.

The 1983 US invasion of Grenada was almost universally condemned in Latin America, with only the military dictatorships of Chile, Guatemala and Uruguay expressing support. The United Nations voted its disapproval overwhelmingly. To this President Reagan responded: "One hundred nations in the UN have not agreed with us on just about everything that's come before them where we're involved, and it didn't upset my breakfast at all."[1]

One of the evils of communist states, we were always told, was that they were oblivious to world opinion.

...a decent respect to the opinions of mankind...

The Declaration of Independence

Date/Issue	Resolution Number	Yes-No vote
1978		

Dec. 15   33/75   119-2 (US, Israel)

Urges the Security Council, especially its permanent members, to take all necessary measures for insuring UN decisions on the maintenance of international peace and security

Dec. 18   33/110   110-2 (US, Israel)

Request for report on the living conditions of Palestinians in occupied Arab countries

Dec. 18   33/113C   97-3 (US, Israel, Guatemala)

Condemnation of Israeli human rights record in occupied territories

Dec. 19   33/136   119-1 (US)

Calls upon developed countries to increase quantity and quality of development assistance to underdeveloped countries

1979

Jan. 24   33/183M   114-3 (US, France, UK)

To end all military and nuclear collaboration with apartheid South Africa

Jan. 29   33/196   111-1 (US)

Protectionism of developing countries' exports

Nov. 23   34/46   136-1 (US)

Alternate approaches within the UN system for improving the enjoyment of human rights and fundamental freedoms

Nov. 23   34/52E   121-3 (US, Israel, Australia)

Return of inhabitants expelled by Israel.

Dec. 11   34/83J   120-3 (US, UK, France)

Negotiations on disarmament and cessation of nuclear arms race.

Dec. 12   34/90A   111-2 (US, Israel)

Demand that Israel desist from certain human rights violations

Dec. 12   34/93D   132-3 (US, UK, France)

Strengthening arms embargo against South Africa

Dec. 12   34/93I   134-3 (US, UK, France)

Assistance to the oppressed people of South Africa and their liberation movement

Dec. 14   34/100   104-2 (US, Israel)

Against support for intervention in the internal or external affairs of States

Dec. 14   34/113   120-2 (US, Israel)

Request for report on the living conditions of Palestinians in occupied Arab countries

Dec. 14   34/133   112-3 (US, Israel, Canada)

Assistance to Palestinian people

Dec. 14   34/136   118-2 (US, Israel)

Sovereignty over national resources in occupied Arab territories

Dec. 17   34/158   121-2 (US, Israel)

Prepare and carry out the UN Conference on Women

Dec. 17   34/160   122-2 (US, Israel)

Include Palestinian women in agenda of UN Conference on Women

Dec. 19   34/199   112-1 (US)

Safeguarding rights of developing countries in multinational trade negotiations

1980

Nov. 3   35/13E   96-3 (US, Israel, Canada)

Requests Israel to return displaced persons

Dec. 5   35/57   134-1 (US)

Establishment of a New International Economic Order to promote the growth of underdeveloped countries and international economic co-operation.

Dec. 5   35/75   118-2 (US, Israel)

Condemns Israeli policy re the living conditions of Palestinian people

Dec. 11   35/119   134-3 (US, UK, France)

Implementation of the Declaration on the Granting of Independence to Colonial Countries and Peoples

Dec. 11   35/122C   118-2 (US, Israel)

Israeli human rights practices in occupied territories. [Same day, similar resolutions, 35/122E—119-2 vote, and 35/122F—117-2]

Dec. 11   35/136   132-3 (US, Israel, Canada)

Endorse Program of Action for Second Half of UN Decade for Women

Dec. 12   35/145A   111-2 (US, UK)

Cessation of all nuclear test explosions

Dec. 12   35/154   110-2 (US, Albania)

Declaration of non-use of nuclear weapons against non-nuclear states

Dec. 15   35/169C   120-3 (US, Israel, Australia)

To further the "inalienable rights of the Palestinian people"

Dec. 15   35/174   120-1 (US)

Emphasizing that the development of nations and individuals is a human right

Dec. 16   35/206J   137-3 (US, UK, France)

Assistance to oppressed people of South Africa and their national liberation movement

1981

Oct. 28   36/12   145-1 (US)

Anti-racism; condemns apartheid in South Africa and Namibia

Oct. 28   36/13   124-1 (US)

Condemns collaboration of certain States and transnational corporations with the South African government

Oct. 28   36/15   114-2 (US, Israel)

Demand that Israel cease excavations of certain sites in E. Jerusalem

Nov. 9   36/18   123-1 (US)

To promote co-operative movements in developing countries (agricultural, savings and credits, housing, consumer protection, social services, etc.)

Nov. 9   36/19   126-1 (US)

The right of every state to choose its economic and social system in accord with the will of its people, without outside interference in whatever form it takes

Nov. 13   36/27   109-2 (US, Israel)

Condemns Israel for its bombing of an Iraqi nuclear installation

Dec. 1   36/68   133-3 (US, UK, Guatemala)

Condemns activities of foreign economic interests in colonial territories

Dec. 4   36/73   109-2 (US, Israel)

Condemns Israeli policy re living conditions of the Palestinian people

Dec. 9   36/84   118-2 (US, UK)

Cessation of all test explosions of nuclear weapons

Dec. 9   36/87B   107-2 (US, Israel)

Establishment of a nuclear-weapon free zone in the Middle East

Dec. 9   36/92J   78-3 (US, Canada, Brazil)

World-wide action for collecting signatures in support of

measures to prevent nuclear war, curb the arms race and promote disarmament

Dec. 9   36/96B   109-1(US)

Urges negotiations on prohibition of chemical and biological weapons

Dec. 9   36/98   101-2 (US, Israel)

Demands Israelis renounce possession of nuclear weapons

Dec. 10   36/120A   121-2 (US, Israel)

Strengthening the Special Unit on Palestinian Rights

Dec. 10   36/120B   119-3 (US, Israel, Canada)

Economic assistance to Palestinians

Dec. 10   36/120E   139-2 (US, Israel)

Israel should comply with UN resolutions relevant to the historic character of Jerusalem

Dec. 14   36/133   135-1 (US)

Declares that education, work, health care, proper nourishment, national development, etc. are human rights

Dec. 16   36/146A   141-2 (US, Israel)

Israel should desist from removal and resettlement of Palestinian refugees in the Gaza Strip and destruction of their shelters

Dec. 16   36/146B   121-3 (US, Israel, Canada)

Rights of displaced Palestinians to return to their homes

Dec. 16   36/146C   117-2 (US, Israel)

Palestinian refugees are entitled to the revenue derived from their property

Dec. 16   36/146G   119-2(US, Israel)

Establishment of University of Jerusalem for Palestinian refugees

Dec. 16   36/147C   111-2 (US, Israel)

Israeli violations of human rights in occupied territories

Dec. 16   36/147F   114-2 (US, Israel)

Condemns Israeli closing of universities in occupied territories

Dec. 16   36/149B   147-2 (US, Israel)

Calls for the establishment of a new and more just world information and communications order

Dec. 16   36/150   139-2 (US, Israel)

Opposes Israel's decision to build a canal linking the Mediterranean Sea to the Dead Sea

Dec. 17   36/172C   136-1 (US)

Condemns aggression by South Africa against Angola and other African states.

Dec. 17   36/172H   129-2 (US, UK)

To organize an international conference of trade unions on sanctions against South Africa

Dec. 17   36/172L   126-2 (US, UK)

To encourage various international actions against South Africa

Dec. 17   36/172N   139-1(US)

Support of sanctions and other measures against South Africa

Dec. 17   36/172O   138-1 (US)

Cessation of further foreign investments and loans for South Africa

Dec. 17   36/173   115-2 (US, Israel)

Permanent sovereignty over national resources in occupied Palestine and other Arab territories

Dec. 17   36/226B   121-2 (US, Israel)

Non-applicability of Israeli law over the Golan Heights

Dec. 18   36/234B   127-1 (US)

UN accounting changes for 1980-1

1982 [only solitary US votes]

Oct. 28   37/7   111-1

World Charter for protection of the ecology

Nov. 15   37/11   136-1

Setting up UN conference on succession of states in respect to state property, archives, and debts

Dec. 3   37/47   124-1

Appeal for universal ratification of the convention on the suppression and punishment of apartheid

Dec. 9   37/69E   141-1

Promoting international mobilization against apartheid

Dec. 9   37/69G   138-1

Drafting of international convention against apartheid in sports

Dec. 9   37/69H   134-1

Cessation of further foreign investments and loans for South Africa

Dec. 9   37/73   111-1

Need for a comprehensive nuclear-test-ban treaty

Dec. 9   37/78A   114-1

Request to US and USSR to transmit a status report on their nuclear arms negotiations [USSR abstained]

Dec. 9   37/83   138-1

Prevention of arms race in outer space

Dec. 10   37/94B   131-1

Support of UNESCO's efforts to promote a new world information and communications order

Dec. 13   37/98A   95-1

Necessity of a convention on the prohibition of chemical and bacteriological weapons

Dec. 16   37/103   113-1

Development of the principles and norms of international law relating to the new economic order

Dec. 17   37/131   129-1

Measures concerning the UN Joint Staff Pension Board, including prevention of exclusion of certain UN employees

Dec. 17   37/137   146-1

Protection against products harmful to health and the environment

Dec. 18   37/199   131-1

Declares that education, work, health care, proper nourishment, national development, etc. are human rights

Dec. 20   37/204   141-1

Motion for a review of the implementation of the Charter of Economic Rights and Duties of States

Dec. 21   37/237/XI   132-1

Adequacy of the conference facilities of the Economic Commission for Africa at Addis Ababa

Dec. 21   37/251   146-1

Development of the energy resources of developing countries

Dec. 21   37/252   124-1

Restructuring international economic relations toward establishing a new international economic order

1983

Nov. 22   38/19   110-1

International Convention on the Suppression and Punishment of the Crime of Apartheid

Nov. 22   38/25   131-1

The right of every state to choose its economic and social system in accord with the will of its people, without outside interference in whatever form it takes

Dec. 5   38/39E   149-1

Disseminating material and organizing conferences in the campaign against apartheid

Dec. 5   38/39I   140-1

Urges the Security Council to consider sanctions against South Africa as a protest against apartheid

Dec. 5   38/39K   145-1

Authorizes the International Convention against Apartheid in Sports to continue its consultations

Dec. 15   38/70   147-1

Outer space should be used for peaceful purposes; prevention of an arms race in outer space

Dec. 16   38/124   132-1

Declares that education, work, health care, proper nourishment, national development, etc. are human rights

Dec. 19   38/128   110-1

Development of the principles and norms of international law relating to the new world economic order

Dec. 19   38/150   137-1

Transport and communications Decade in Africa

Dec. 20   38/182   116-1

Prohibition of the development and manufacture of new types and systems of weapons of mass destruction

Dec. 20   38/183M   133-1

Requests nuclear-arms States to submit to General Assembly annual reports on measures taken for prevention of nuclear war and reversing the arms race

Dec. 20   38/187A   98-1

Urges intensification of negotiations to achieve an accord on a prohibition of chemical and bacteriological weapons

Dec. 20   38/188G   113-1

Requests a study on the naval arms race

Dec. 20   38/188H   132-1

A study concerning how military expenditures threaten world security and survival and impede development

Dec. 20   38/202   126-1

Strengthening the capacity of the UN to respond to natural and other disasters

1984 [selected resolutions]

Nov. 8   39/9   134-2 (US, Israel)

Cooperation between the UN and the League of Arab States

Nov. 16   39/14   106-2 (US, Israel)

Condemns Israeli attack against Iraqi nuclear installation

Nov. 23   39/21   145-1

Report of the Committee on the Elimination of Racial Discrimination

Dec. 5   39/411   119-2 (US, UK)

Reaffirming the right of St. Helena to independence

Dec. 5   39/42   121-2 (US, UK)

Condemns support of South Africa in its Namibian and other policies

Dec. 11   39/49A   127-2 (US, Israel)

Rights of the Palestinian people

Dec. 11   39/49D   121-3 (US, Israel, Canada)

Convening a Middle-East peace conference

Dec. 12   39/62   125-1

Prohibition of development and manufacture of new types of weapons of mass destruction

Dec. 12   39/65B   84-1

Prohibition of chemical and bacteriological weapons

Dec. 13   39/72G   146-2 (US, UK)

International action to eliminate apartheid

Dec. 13   39/73   138-2 (US, Turkey)

Law of the sea.

Dec. 14   39/95A   120-2 (US, Israel)

Israeli human rights violations in occupied territories

Dec. 14   39/95H   143-2 (US, Israel)

Condemns assassination attempts against Palestinian mayors and calls for apprehension and prosecution of the perpetrators

Dec. 17   39/147   94-2 (US, Israel)

Condemns Israel's refusal to place its nuclear facilities under International Atomic Energy Agency safeguards

Dec. 17   39/148N   123-1

Nuclear-test ban, cessation of nuclear-arms race, nuclear

disarmament

Dec. 17   39/151F   141-1

Request to continue UN study on military research and development

Dec. 17   39/161B   143-1

Commemorating the 25th anniversary of the Declaration on the Granting of Independence to Colonial Countries and Peoples

Dec. 18   39/224   146-2 (US, Israel)

Economic and social assistance to the Palestinian people

Dec. 18   39/232   118-2 (US, Israel)

Support of the UN Industrial Development Organization

Dec. 18   39/233   120-1

Industrial Development Decade for Africa

Dec. 18   39/243   123-2 (US, Israel)

Staff and administrative questions re the Economic Commission for Western Asia

1985

Dec. 13   40/114   134-1

Indivisibility and interdependence of economic, social, cultural, civil, and political rights

Dec. 13   40/124   130-1

Alternative approaches within the UN system for improving the enjoyment of human rights and fundamental freedoms

Dec. 13   40/148   121-2 (US, Israel)

Measures to be taken against Nazi, Fascist and neo-Fascist activities

Dec. 17   40/445   133-1

International cooperation in the interrelated areas of money, finance, debt, resource flow, trade and development

1986

Oct. 27   41/11   124-1

Zone of peace and co-operation in the South Atlantic

Dec. 3   41/68A   148-1

New world information order, led by UNESCO, to eliminate existing imbalances in the information and communications fields

Dec. 4   41/90   126-1

Review of the Implementation of the Declaration of the Strengthening of International Security

Dec. 4   41/91   117-1

Need for result-oriented political dialogue to improve the international situation

Dec. 4   41/92   102-2 (US, France)

Establishment of a comprehensive system of international peace and security

Dec. 4   41/128   146-1

Declaration on the right to development

Dec. 4   41/151   148-1

Measures to improve the situation and ensure the human rights and dignity of all migrant workers

Dec. 8   41/450   146-1

Protection against products harmful to health and the environment

1987

Oct. 15   42/5   153-2 (US, Israel)

Cooperation between the UN and the League of Arab States

Nov. 12   42/18   94-2 (US, Israel)

Need for compliance in the International Court of Justice concerning military and paramilitary activities against Nicaragua

Dec. 2   42/69J   145-2 (US, Israel)

Calls upon Israel to abandon plans to remove and resettle Palestinian refugees of the West Bank away from their homes and property

Dec. 7   42/101   150-0-1 (US sole abstainer)

A call for a "convention on the rights of the child"

Dec. 7   42/159   153-2 (US, Israel)

Measures to prevent international terrorism, study the underlying political and economic causes of terrorism, convene a conference to define terrorism and to differentiate it from the struggle of people for national liberation

Dec. 8   42/162B   140-1

Financing the training of journalists and strengthening communication services in the underdeveloped world

Dec. 11   42/176   94-2 (US, Israel)

Ending trade embargo against Nicaragua

Dec. 11   42/198   154-1

Furthering international co-operation regarding the external debt problems

Dec. 11   42/441   131-1

Preparation of summary records for a UN conference on Trade and Development

Necessity of ending the US embargo against Cuba

1992 59-2 (US, Israel)*
1993 88-4 (US, Israel, Albania, Paraguay)
1994 101-2 (US, Israel)
1995 117-3 (US, Israel, Uzbekistan)
1996 138-3 (US, Israel, Uzbekistan)**
1997 143-3 (US, Israel, Uzbekistan)
1998 157-2 (US, Israel)
1999 155-2 (US, Israel)

2000 167-3 (US, Israel, Marshall Is.)
2001 167-3 (US, Israel, Marshall Is.)
2002 173-3 (US, Israel, Marshall Is.)
2003 179-3 (US, Israel, Marshall Is.)
2004 179-4 (US, Israel, Marshall Is., Palau)

* Romania also voted "no", by mistake.
** For the first time, all 15 European Union countries voted yes.

It should be remembered that for years American political leaders and media were fond of labeling Cuba an "international pariah".

No "right to food"

As noted above, in 1981, 1982 and 1983, the United States was alone in voting against a declaration that education, work, health care, proper nourishment, and national development are human rights. In 1996, at a United Nations-sponsored World Food Summit, the matter of nutrition was brought to a head when the US took issue with an affirmation by the summit of the "right of everyone to have access to safe and nutritious food". The United States insisted that it does not recognize a "right to food". Washington instead championed free trade as the key to ending the poverty at the root of hunger, and expressed fears that recognition of a "right to food" could lead to lawsuits from poor nations seeking aid and special trade provisions.[2]

The United States may lose the votes, but it gets its way

Climate change

Pressure from Washington and the oil industry resulted in the replacement, in April 2002, of atmospheric scientist Dr. Robert Watson as chairman of the Intergovernmental Panel on Climate

Change (IPCC), which was set up in 1988 by the United Nations Environment Program and the World Meteorological Organization to assess man-made climate change. Watson was defeated for re-election to his position by a candidate from India backed by the United States after a behind-the-scenes diplomatic campaign by the US to persuade developing countries to vote against Watson, according to diplomats.

Watson had led the panel since 1996 and was also the chief scientist of the World Bank. He had been vocal in warning governments about the danger of fossil fuel emissions contributing to global warming. A leaked memo from ExxonMobil had asked the White House, "Can Watson be replaced now at the request of the U.S.?"

Steve Sawyer, a Greenpeace climate change specialist who attended the IPCC meeting in Geneva, declared: "Even the most cynical would be shocked by the heavy-handed tactics of the US delegation's bald display of their fossil fuel-backed politics in Geneva today." He said the US had sent notes to African states calling on them to support Watson's opponent. Diplomats in Washington confirmed that the US had pursued an active campaign against Watson.[3]

Human rights

Mary Robinson, former president of Ireland, whose work as United Nations High Commissioner for Human Rights was acclaimed by human rights groups across the world, was forced to retire in September 2002 because the United States strongly lobbied against her reappointment. She had been outspoken in her criticism of US efforts to undermine the International Criminal Court, its lack of regard for civilian casualties in the war waged in Afghanistan, its treatment of prisoners at Guantánamo Bay, and even an "internal" US matter like the death penalty. Washington also could not forgive her for her stands on Middle East issues or for her endorsement the previous year of the results of the UN's Durban Conference on Racism, which both the US and Israel walked out of.

"I am not somebody just to walk away...I would have stayed [but] there seems to have been strong resistance from just one country," said Robinson shortly before her retirement.[4]

Preparation for the Iraqi invasion

In 2000, the US Congress passed the African Growth and Opportunity Act (AGOA), the usual euphemistically-named agreement that promises the usual trade benefits to underdeveloped countries in return for the usual selling of their soul, like privatization of virtually everything, deregulation, ending price controls and subsidies on food and other goods, giving foreign multinationals the same rights as local companies, etc., etc. AGOA had an added requirement: agreeing not to "engage in activities that undermine United States national security or foreign policy interests". In November 2002 the United States invoked this provision in complaining to Mauritius that its UN ambassador, Jagdish Koonjul, was not lining up with sufficient zeal behind Washington's latest draft resolution on weapons inspections in Iraq at the Security Council. The ambassador was hurriedly recalled by his government.[5]

Chemical weapons

José Bustani of Brazil was the head of the Organization for the Prohibition of Chemical Weapons (OPCW), created to guarantee implementation of the 1994 Chemical Weapons Convention, which provides for destruction of the world's chemical weapons within 10 years, starting from April 1997. In May 2000, as a tribute to his extraordinary record of overseeing the destruction of chemical weapons and most of the world's chemical weapon facilities, Bustani was re-elected unanimously by the member states for a second five-year term, even though he had yet to complete his first one. In 2001, US Secretary of State Colin Powell wrote to him to thank him for his "very impressive" work. But the following year he earned Washington's intense ire by siding with severe criticism of US arms export policy, and then sealed his fate by suggesting that Iraq should become a member of the OPCW. Bustani, seeking to overcome the impasse concerning Iraq's alleged weapons of mass destruction, offered to send in his own inspectors. This infuriated the United States, which wanted to get rid of President Saddam Hussein's government in Iraq but knew they would find it difficult to win backing for military action if Iraq agreed to join the OPCW and admitted arms inspectors. Washington was uncompromising in demanding that Bustani resign and not seek a second term.

"Director general Bustani has said that he will not resign at the request of one or a few countries," said an OPCW spokesman. "He sees his resistance of this pressure as necessary to protect the independence of an international organisation [and] is particularly concerned about the precedent this might set for other international organizations."

The organization tried its best to resist but the US was relentless in its arm twisting and threats to defund; i.e., destroy, the organization, and in April 2002, it succeeded in getting Bustani ousted.[6]

Israel-Palestine

The reappointment of Peter Hansen as head of the UN Relief and Works Agency (UNRWA) was blocked by the Bush administration in January 2005 after a campaign by conservative and Jewish groups in the US and the Israeli government accused him of being an "Israel hater". Some European and Arab governments were keen for Hansen to stay on at the end of his nine-year tenure but the US supported Israel's assertion that Hansen was biased and soft on "terrorists".

"I was willing to stay," said Hansen. "There are certain facts about the views of certain groups in the US and Israel about how I have carried out my functions and those groups influenced the decision not to reappoint me." He had infuriated the Israeli government with public criticisms of their military's widespread destruction of Palestinian homes, which he described as a grave breach of international humanitarian law. Hansen also spoke out against the killing of children by indiscriminate Israeli gunfire hitting UN-run schools, and Israeli policies that contributed to economic collapse and growing hunger among about a million refugees in Gaza.

"I don't have a record of being an Israel hater," Hansen said, "but I can't in all honesty not criticise Israel's actions that harm Palestinian refugees. My job is not to put myself at the midpoint between the Israeli view and the refugees' view. My job was to represent the refugees."

UN Secretary-General Kofi Annan gave Hansen the bad news, telling him: "I don't have the political capital with the Americans to keep you."[7]

US military abuses in Afghanistan

In April 2005, the United Nation's top human-rights investigator in Afghanistan was forced out under American pressure just days after he presented a report criticizing the US military for its treatment of prisoners. Cherif Bassiouni had annoyed the US military since his appointment a year earlier by repeatedly trying, without success, to interview alleged Taliban and al-Qaeda prisoners at the two biggest US bases in Afghanistan, Kandahar and Bagram. Bassiouni's report highlighted the detaining of suspects without trial, holding them in secret prisons, and the terrible conditions under which they were imprisoned.

The UN eliminated Bassiouni's job after Washington pressed for his mandate to be changed so that it would no longer cover the US military. The Egyptian-born law professor, based in Chicago, had presented his criticisms in a 24-page report to the UN Commission on Human Rights in Geneva. The report, based on a year spent traveling around Afghanistan interviewing Afghans, international agency staff, and the Afghan Human Rights Commission, estimated that around 1,000 Afghans had been detained, and accused US troops of breaking into homes, arresting residents and abusing them.[8]

Some other items you may have missed about the US at the UN

In 1949, the United States induced UN Secretary-General Trygve Lie to agree to a written secret agreement with the US State Department whereby, in violation of basic liberties and of the United Nations Charter, applicants for and incumbents in UN Secretariat positions would be "screened", without their knowledge, by US agents. Although directed in the first instance against American citizens—who, numbering about 2,000, then constituted approximately half of the UN headquarters personnel— the influence of this clandestine agreement extended to UN employees of other nationalities, and permeated UN specialized agencies abroad. The agreement was an attempt to formalize a policy that had already been well established: a State Department policy aimed at excluding committed internationalists from the international civil service and aligning that service with partisan US attitudes.[9]

In 1952, "on the basis of confidential information supplied by the United States Government", Lie dismissed three American

Secretariat employees who had invoked the Fifth Amendment against self-incrimination before a US Senate subcommittee on internal security. Seven other American employees, who had done the same, were placed on compulsory leave with pay.[10]

In 1983, the American Deputy UN Ambassador told other UN members that if they wanted to move UN headquarters out of the United States, the Reagan administration would do nothing to stop them. Said Charles Lichenstein: "We will put no impediments in your way. The members of the US mission will be down at the docks waving you farewell as you sail into the sunset."[11]

And in 2005, the man chosen to be the new US ambassador to the United Nations was John R. Bolton, a man on record for saying things like: "There is no such thing as the United Nations. There is an international community that occasionally can be led by the only real power left in the world and that is the United States when it suits our interest and we can get others to go along."..."Many Republicans in Congress—and perhaps a majority—not only do not care about losing the General Assembly vote but actually see it as a 'make my day' outcome."...If the UN building "lost ten stories it wouldn't make a bit of difference."[12]

Chapter 21

Eavesdropping on the planet

Any sound that Winston made, above the level of a very low whisper, would be picked up by it...There was of course no way of knowing whether you were being watched at any given moment.... You had to live—did live, from habit that became instinct—in the assumption that every sound you made was overheard, and, except in darkness, every movement scrutinized.

George Orwell, *1984*

O rwell didn't have it quite right about the darkness. Night-vision technology is becoming more science-fictionish even as you read this. And he wrote of one country, Oceania. A large country to be sure, but certainly not the entire world. George might have been truly shocked to learn how things in the world of government surveillance of citizens would actually turn out, even before 1984, yet more so in the two decades after his envisioned future year.

Can people in the 21st century imagine a greater invasion of privacy on all of earth, in all of history? If so, they merely have to wait for technology to catch up with their imagination.

Like a mammoth vacuum cleaner in the sky, the National Security Agency (NSA) sucks it all up: home phone, office phone, cellular phone, email, fax, telex...satellite transmissions, fiber-optic communications traffic, microwave links...voice, text, images...captured by satellites continuously orbiting the earth, then processed by high-powered computers...if it runs on electromagnetic energy, NSA is there, with high, high tech. Seven days a week. Twenty-four hours a day. Perhaps billions of messages sucked up each day. No one escapes. Not presidents, prime ministers, the UN Secretary-General, the pope, the Queen of England, embassies, transnational corporation CEOs, friend, foe, your Aunt Lena...if God has a phone, it's being monitored... maybe your dog isn't being tapped. The oceans will not protect you. American submarines have been attaching tapping pods to deep underwater cables for decades.

Under a system codenamed ECHELON—launched in the 1970s to spy on Soviet satellite communications—the NSA and its junior partners in Britain, Australia, New Zealand, and Canada operate a network of massive, highly automated interception stations, covering the globe amongst them. In multiple ways, each of the countries involved is breaking its own laws, those of other countries, and international law—the absence of court-issued warrants permitting surveillance of specific individuals is but one example. Any of the partners can ask any of the others to intercept its own domestic communications. It can then truthfully say it does not spy on its own citizens.

In 1999, the House Intelligence Committee of the US Congress sought internal NSA documents about its compliance with the law that prohibits it from deliberately eavesdropping on Americans, either in the United States or overseas, unless the Agency can establish probable cause to believe that they are agents of a foreign government committing espionage or other crimes. NSA just stonewalled the committee.[1]

Apart from specifically-targeted individuals and institutions, the ECHELON system works by indiscriminately intercepting huge quantities of communications and using computers to identify and extract messages of interest from the mass of unwanted ones. Every intercepted message—all the embassy cables, the business deals, the sex talk, the birthday greetings—is searched for keywords, which could be anything the searchers think might be of interest. All it takes to flag a communication is for one of the parties to use a couple or so of the key words in the ECHELON "dictionary"—"He lives in a lovely old **white house** on **Bush** Street, right near me. I can **shoot** over there in two minutes." Within limitations, computers can "listen" to telephone calls and recognize when keywords are spoken. Those calls are extracted and recorded separately, to be listened to in full by humans.[2] The list of specific targets at any given time is undoubtedly wide ranging, at one point including the likes of Amnesty International and Christian Aid.[3]

ECHELON is carried out without official acknowledgment of its existence, let alone any democratic oversight or public or legislative debate as to whether it serves a decent purpose. In Great Britain, when Members of Parliament have raised questions about the activities of NSA and its ever-expanding base in Menwith Hill, North Yorkshire, the government has consistently refused to supply any information. Members of the US Congress have not even raised questions.

The base in England is now NSA's largest listening post in the world. Sprawling across 560 acres, it has an operations center and on-site town, including houses, shops, a chapel, a sports center, and its own uninterruptible electricity supply.[4]

The extensiveness of the ECHELON global network is a product of decades of intense Cold War activity. Yet with the end of the Cold War, its budget—far from being greatly reduced—was increased, and the network has grown in both power and reach; yet another piece of evidence that the Cold War was not a battle against something called "the international communist conspiracy".

The European Parliament in the late 1990s began to wake up to this intrusion into the continent's affairs. The parliament's Civil Liberties Committee commissioned a report, which appeared in 1998 and recommended a variety of measures for dealing with the increasing power of the technologies of surveillance. It bluntly advised: "The European Parliament should reject proposals from the United States for making private messages via the global communications network [Internet] accessible to US intelligence agencies." The report urged a fundamental review of the involvement of the NSA in Europe, suggesting that the agency's activities be either scaled down, or become more open and accountable. It also denounced Britain's role as a double-agent, spying on its own European partners.[5]

"It is profoundly shocking and should provoke a general outcry," Jean-Pierre Millet, a French lawyer specializing in computer crime, told the French newspaper *Le Figaro*. "Britain's European partners have a right to be furious but [the British] won't abandon their pact with the US."[6]

Commercial espionage

Despite concerns about NSA activities in Europe expressed by governments and members of the European Parliament since the end of the Cold War the US has continued to expand ECHELON surveillance in Europe, partly because of heightened interest in commercial espionage—to uncover industrial information that would provide American corporations with an advantage over foreign rivals.

German security experts discovered several years ago that ECHELON was engaged in heavy commercial spying in Europe. Victims included such German firms as the wind generator manufacturer Enercon. In 1998, Enercon developed what it thought was a secret invention, enabling it to generate electricity from wind power at a far cheaper rate than before. However, when the company tried to market its invention in the United States, it was confronted by its American rival, Kenetech, which announced that it had already patented a near-identical development. Kenetech then brought a court order against Enercon to ban the sale of its equipment in the US. In a rare public disclosure, an NSA employee, who refused to be named, agreed to appear in silhouette on German television to reveal how he had stolen Enercon's secrets by tapping the telephone and computer link lines that ran between Enercon's research laboratory and its production unit some 12 miles away. Detailed plans of the company's invention were then passed on to Kenetech.[7]

In 1994, Thomson S.A., located in Paris, and Airbus Industrie, based in Blagnac Cedex, France, also lost lucrative contracts, snatched away by American rivals aided by information covertly collected by NSA and CIA.[8] The same agencies also eavesdropped on Japanese representatives during negotiations with the United States in 1995 over auto parts trade.[9]

German industry has complained that it is in a particularly vulnerable position because the government forbids its security services from conducting similar industrial espionage. "German politicians still support the rather naive idea that political allies should not spy on each other's businesses. The Americans and the British do not have such illusions," said journalist Udo Ulfkotte, a specialist in European industrial espionage, in 1999.[10]

That same year, Germany demanded that the United States recall three CIA operatives for their activities in Germany involving economic espionage. The news report stated that the Germans "have long been suspicious of the eavesdropping capabilities of the enormous U.S. radar and communications complex at Bad Aibling, near Munich", which is in fact an NSA intercept station. "The Americans tell us it is used solely to monitor communications by potential enemies, but how can we be entirely sure that they are not picking up pieces of information that we think should remain completely secret?" asked a senior German official.[11] Japanese officials most likely have been told a similar story by Washington about the more than a dozen signals intelligence bases which Japan has allowed to be located on its territory.[12]

Encryption and the greatest intelligence scam of the 20th century

In their quest to gain access to more and more private information, the NSA, the FBI, and other components of the US national security establishment have been engaged for years in a campaign to require American telecommunications manufacturers and carriers to design their equipment and networks to optimize the authorities' wiretapping ability, and to impose a national civilian cryptography standard designed to allow the government to decode encrypted communications at will. The power to favor or block approval of a company's exports has been one of the carrot-and-stick tools employed by the security establishment. Some industry insiders say they believe that some US machines approved for export contain NSA "back doors" (also called "trap doors").

The United States has been trying to persuade European Union countries as well to allow it "back-door" access to encryption programs, claiming that this was to serve the needs of law-enforcement agencies. However, a report released by the European Parliament in May 1999 asserted that Washington's plans for controlling encryption software in Europe had nothing to do with law enforcement and everything to do with US industrial espionage. The NSA has also dispatched FBI agents on break-in missions to snatch code books from foreign facilities in the United States, and CIA officers to recruit foreign communications clerks abroad and buy their code secrets, according to veteran intelligence officials.[13]

For decades, beginning in the 1950s, the Swiss company Crypto AG sold the world's most sophisticated and secure encryption technology. The firm staked its reputation and the security concerns of its clients on its neutrality in the Cold War or any other war. The purchasing nations, some 120 of them— including prime US intelligence targets such as Iran, Iraq, Libya and

Yugoslavia—confident that their communications were protected, sent messages from their capitals to their embassies, military missions, trade offices, and espionage dens around the world, via telex, radio, and fax. And all the while, because of a secret agreement between the company and NSA, these governments might as well have been hand delivering the messages to Washington, uncoded. For their Crypto AG machines had been rigged before being sold to them, so that when they used them the random encryption key could be automatically and clandestinely transmitted along with the enciphered message. NSA analysts could read the messages as easily as they could the morning newspaper. German intelligence was in on it as well and may even have been the actual owner of Crypto AG.

In 1986, because of US public statements concerning the La Belle disco bombing in West Berlin, the Libyans began to suspect that something was rotten with Crypto AG's machines and switched to another Swiss firm, Gretag Data Systems AG. But it appears that NSA had that base covered as well. In 1992, after a series of suspicious circumstances over the previous few years, Iran came to a conclusion similar to Libya's, and arrested a Crypto AG employee who was in Iran on a business trip. He was eventually ransomed, but the incident became well known and the scam began to unravel in earnest.[14]

Microsoft Windows

NSA has done something similar with computers. In September 1999, leading European investigative reporter Duncan Campbell revealed that NSA had arranged with Microsoft to insert special "keys" into Windows software, in all versions from 95-OSR2 onwards. An American computer scientist, Andrew Fernandez of Cryptonym in North Carolina, had disassembled parts of the Windows instruction code and found the smoking gun—Microsoft's developers had failed to remove the debugging symbols used to test this software before they released it. Inside the code were the labels for two keys. One was called "KEY". The other was called "NSAKEY". Fernandez presented his finding at a conference at which some Windows developers were also in attendance. The developers did not deny that the NSA key was built into their software, but they refused to talk about what the key did, or why it had been put there without users' knowledge. Fernandez says that NSA's "back door" in the world's most commonly used operating system makes it "orders of magnitude easier for the US government to access your computer."[15]

In February 2000, it was disclosed that the Strategic Affairs Delegation (DAS), the intelligence arm of the French Defense Ministry, had prepared a report in 1999 which also asserted that NSA had helped to install secret programs in Microsoft software. According to the DAS report, "it would seem that the creation of Microsoft was largely supported, not least financially, by the NSA, and that IBM was made to accept the [Microsoft] MS-DOS operating system by the same administration." The report stated that there had been a "strong suspicion of a lack of security fed by insistent rumours about the existence of spy programmes on Microsoft, and by the presence of NSA personnel in Bill Gates' development teams." The Pentagon, said the report, was Microsoft's biggest client in the world.[16]

Cowardly new world

Recent years have seen disclosures that in the countdown to their invasion of Iraq in 2003, the United States had listened in on UN Secretary-General Kofi Annan, UN weapons inspectors in Iraq, and all the members of the UN Security Council during a period when they were deliberating about what action to take in Iraq.

It's as if the American national security establishment feels that it has an inalienable *right* to listen in; as if there had been a constitutional amendment, applicable to the entire world, stating that "Congress shall make no law abridging the freedom of the government to intercept the personal communications of anyone." And the Fourth Amendment had been changed to read: "Persons shall be secure in their persons, houses, papers, and effects, against unreasonable searches and seizures, except in cases of national security, real or alleged."

Chapter 22

Kidnapping and looting

I n 1962, the United States kidnapped about 125 people from the Dominican Republic, and took them to the US and elsewhere.

A suspected drug smuggler was spirited out of Honduras and taken to the US in 1988, although the Honduran constitution prohibits the extradition of Honduran citizens for trial in other countries. Presumably, in this case, it was carried out with the approval of the Honduran government under US pressure.

In December 1989, the American military grabbed Manuel Noriega in Panama and hustled him off to Florida.

In April of the following year, the Drug Enforcement Administration paid bounty hunters to abduct Dr. Humberto Alvarez Machain from his medical office in Guadalajara, Mexico, fly him to El Paso, Texas, and turn him over to the DEA. Machain was suspected of being involved in a 1985 murder of a DEA agent in Guadalajara and the Mexican government refused to extradite him.

A Cypriot businessman, Hossein Alikhani, accused of violating US sanctions against Libya, was lured on board a plane in the Bahamas in 1992 in a US Customs sting and abducted to Miami.[1]

In December 1997 Washington succeeded in forcing the Colombian government to remove a prohibition against extradition. The result, as of 2005, was that 239 Colombians charged with drug offenses had been shipped to the United States. Yet in 2005, when five American soldiers stationed in Colombia as part of the war on drugs were charged with trying to smuggle cocaine into the US, the United States hustled them out of the country and back home, despite the demand by Colombian legislators that they should be tried in Colombia. "In practical terms, these military personnel committed the alleged crime in Colombia, and according to the extradition treaty, which is bilateral, they should be tried here," said one legislator. The American ambassador, however, declared that the five soldiers enjoyed diplomatic immunity.[2]

Rendition

Both before and since the terrorist attack of September 11, 2001, the CIA has been in the practice of kidnapping individuals suspected of some kind of tie to terrorism, at times based on no more than a tip from a single informant of unknown credibility. Bypassing local and international extradition procedures and other legal formalities, these Agency abductions, hundreds in number, have been carried out in many countries of Asia, the Middle East, Europe, and Africa with the victims taken by CIA or Defense Department planes to Saudi Arabia, Egypt, Syria, Jordan, Uzbekistan, Pakistan, Morocco, Malawi, the US military base in Guantánamo Bay, Cuba, and other countries, as well as the United States, in addition to the secret archipelago of CIA detention; taken to these places to be interrogated (read "tortured"). In some cases, US intelligence agents remain closely involved in the interrogation. At times the abductee has died in custody. On occasion, the kidnapping has been carried out with the knowledge and assistance of the local government. The process is known as "rendition".

The United States insists that it asks for and receives an assurance from the foreign governments involved that the rendered persons will be treated humanely. But later testimonies from a number of these prisoners have recounted tales of torture. Why, it must be asked, are these men rendered in the first place if not to be tortured? Does the United States not have any speakers in foreign languages to conduct interrogations?[3]

One of the most striking examples of this practice occurred in

Bosnia. In 2001, US authorities tipped off the Bosnian government to an alleged plot by a group of five Algerians and a Yemeni living in Bosnia to blow up the American and British embassies in Sarajevo. The Bosnians held the men for three months, during which time an investigation failed to substantiate any criminal charges against them. On January 17, 2002, the Bosnian Supreme Court ruled that they should be released. As the men left prison, they were grabbed and herded into waiting unmarked cars by masked figures. They wound up in Guantánamo.[4]

Robert Baer, veteran CIA field operative, has described the renditions as such: "They are picking up people really with nothing against them, hoping to catch someone because they have no information about these [terrorist] networks."[5]

In June 1992, the US Supreme Court, ruling in the Alvarez Machain case (see above), declared that although it may be "shocking" in its violation of basic principles of international law, kidnapping foreign citizens in their own country is a legally acceptable way to get them to face charges in a US court for violating American law. Chief Justice William H. Rehnquist was willing to record for history his observation that the extradition treaty between the United States and Mexico could be ignored because the treaty didn't explicitly say "no kidnapping allowed".[6]

Law Professor Herman Schwartz wrote in 1992: "Kidnapping another country's citizens has long been considered a gross violation of international law and of proper behavior among civilized nations. [The United States] fought a war in 1812 with Great Britain over this. As the legal adviser to the Reagan State Department asked a few years ago, 'How would we feel if some foreign nation...seized some terrorist suspect in New York City, or Boston, or Philadelphia...because we refused, through the normal channels of international, legal communications, to extradite the individual?'"[7]

If people can be taken with impunity, how much easier with papers and other material goods.

Europe

In the dying days of World War II, the fascist leaders of Hungary escaped to the West with a trainload of loot belonging to the Hungarian Jewish bourgeoisie—from furs and stamp collections to artwork and oriental rugs, and at least one crate of wedding rings confiscated from Holocaust victims. The train got as far as Austria, where American Army forces stopped them. US officers, and likely the lower ranks as well, helped themselves to all manner of goodies. After the war, despite repeated pleas from the Hungarian Jewish community, very few of the valuables were returned to their original owners. In 1949, Washington transferred 1,181 paintings to Austria in violation of international treaties stipulating that "cultural property" looted during the Second World War should be returned to "the country of origin". The Truman administration wished to prevent such treasures from falling into the hands of Communist regimes in Eastern Europe; better in the hands of the Austrians, the willing accomplices of Adolf Hitler.[8]

Guatemala

In the wake of the CIA-engineered coup of 1954, the United States took possession of more than 50,000 documents from Guatemalan government agencies, private organizations, and leading figures of the overthrown regime, in the hope of uncovering the hand of The International Communist Conspiracy behind the government of Jacobo Arbenz. This, after all, has been Washington's official rationale to this day for overthrowing Arbenz. If this is what was indeed discovered in the documents, it has not been made public.[9]

Grenada

In the midst of its invasion of the island in October 1983, the United States found time to rifle through government files and take a large quantity of documents back home. Washington officials then proceeded to give selected documents to the press to publish—such as those dealing with meetings of Grenadian government leaders and military cooperation agreements with foreign countries—hoping that this would lend credence to the official US government position that Cuba and Russia were planning to take over the island and use it as a springboard for destabilizing the entire Caribbean. The documents, however, evidenced no such thing. Indeed, CIA Director William Casey was later to admit that the documents "were not a real find".[10]

Panama

During their invasion of December 1989, the United States confiscated thousands of boxes of government documents, which they refused to return.[11] The occupying American forces roamed the land free from the restraints of any higher power. Along the way they helped themselves to all manner of other documents, files, and archives from the offices of the media, political parties (particularly those of the left), labor unions, etc.[12]

The US also seized more than 52,000 weapons, as well as armored personnel carriers and rocket launchers. Panama later asked for compensation for the materiel.[13]

There has been no return of anything nor any compensation paid.[14]

Germany

Sometime shortly after the collapse of the East German government in 1990, the CIA managed to spirit away the top-secret archives of the country's intelligence agency, the Stasi. For the next nine years, the United States refused to return the material—with the exception of some bits and pieces now and then—despite the repeated requests of the German government. President Clinton for some time refused to even discuss the matter with German chancellor Gerhard Schroeder. Finally, in October 1999, the CIA announced that they would turn over what appears to be a substantial portion of the files, but the Agency would still retain a large number of selected files. The Stasi files contain information on numerous individuals whose identity the CIA would prefer not be exposed, presumably including their own agents who were spying on West Germany, whom the Stasi knew about; many other files might be valuable to the Agency because the individuals would be highly vulnerable to blackmail, for whatever purpose they could be used for by the CIA.[15]

Iraq

In the wake of the Persian Gulf War in 1991, Kurdish groups captured some 18 tons of Iraqi government documents, which the United States later took possession of. The papers now reside at the University of Colorado at Boulder and are open to the public.[16] Iraq, while still sovereign before the American occupation of 2003, never asked for the return of the documents, perhaps realizing the utter futility and demeaning nature of such a request.

Haiti

While returning Jean-Bertrand Aristide to power in 1994, the US military helped themselves to an estimated 160,000 documents, audio and videotapes (some of torture sessions), and "trophy photos" of mutilated victims, belonging to the Haitian military and paramilitary organizations. During the ensuing years, the United

States refused to hand back its booty unless it could select which ones to return, censoring any it wished, and unless Haiti agreed to certain detailed restrictions on the use of the material. The decades-long CIA involvement with sundry Haitian dictatorships, armed forces, death squads, torturers, drug traffickers, and miscellaneous corruption gave Washington more than enough reason to keep the material from wide dissemination. However, Haitian President Rene Preval, who succeeded Aristide, stated: "Our position is we want all the documents back, unaltered, period."

The Haitian government asked for the documents several times beginning in 1995, in private correspondence, press conferences, and international arenas. Among the supporters of its requests were the joint human rights mission to Haiti of the United Nations and Organization of American States, scores of present and former members of the US Congress, religious and solidarity groups in the United States and abroad, three Nobel Peace Prize winners, Amnesty International, and Human Rights Watch. The UN Human Rights Commission demanded the return of the documents so that the truth of "where the responsibility lies in each case" of human rights violations could be determined. The British Foreign Office also raised the issue with the US State Department. Advocates for the return of the documents said that the absence of evidence concerning some of those who took part in the 1991 coup that overthrew the democratically-elected Aristide contributed to the insecurity and injustice in the years following his reinstatement.

For several years, Haiti and its supporters in the United Nations Commission on Human Rights and in the General Assembly tried to bring to a vote a resolution calling for the United States to return the documents. But the US delegation was able to maneuver the proceedings to block such a vote.[17]

Finally, in September 2001, the United States returned thousands of pages of documents gathered from the offices of the Haitian military and the paramilitary group FRAPH. It was believed, however, that the names of US citizens had been erased from the returned documents.[18]

Chapter 23

How the CIA Sent Nelson Mandela to Prison for 28 Years

When Nelson Mandela was released from prison in February 1990, President George Bush personally telephoned the black South African leader to tell him that all Americans were "rejoicing at his release".[1]

This was the same Nelson Mandela who was imprisoned for almost 28 years because the CIA tipped off South African authorities as to where they could find him.

And this was the same George Bush who was once the head of the CIA and who for eight years was second in power of an administration whose CIA and National Security Agency collaborated closely with the South African intelligence service, providing information about Mandela's African National Congress.[2] The ANC was a progressive nationalist movement whose influence had been felt in other African countries; accordingly it had been perceived by Washington as being part of the legendary International Communist Conspiracy. In addition to ideology, other ingredients in the cooking pot the United States and South Africa both ate from was that the latter served as an important source of uranium for the United States, and the US was South Africa's biggest supporter at the United Nations.

On August 5, 1962, Nelson Mandela had been on the run for 17 months when armed police at a roadblock outside Howick, Natal flagged down a car in which he was pretending to be the chauffeur of a white passenger in the back seat. How the police came to be there was not publicly explained. In late July 1986, however, stories appeared in three South African newspapers (picked up shortly thereafter by the London press and, in part, CBS-TV) which shed considerable light on the question. The stories told of how a CIA officer, Donald C. Rickard by name, under cover as a consular official in Durban, had tipped off the Special Branch that Mandela would be disguised as a chauffeur in a car headed for Durban. This was information Rickard had obtained through an informant in the ANC. One year later, at a farewell party for him in South Africa, at the home of the notorious CIA mercenary, Colonel "Mad Mike" Hoare, Rickard himself, his tongue perhaps loosened by spirits, stated in the hearing of some of those present that he had been due to meet Mandela on the fateful night, but tipped off the police instead. Rickard refused to discuss the affair when approached by CBS-TV.[3]

CBS-TV newsman Allen Pizzey did interview journalist James Tomlins on the air when the story broke in 1986. Tomlins, who was in South Africa in 1962, stated that Rickard had told him of his involvement in Mandela's capture.[4]

On June 10, 1990, *The Atlanta Journal and Constitution* reported that an unidentified, retired US intelligence officer had revealed that within hours of Mandela's arrest, Paul Eckel, then a senior CIA operative, had told him: "We have turned Mandela over to the South African security branch. We gave them every detail, what he would be wearing, the time of day, just where he would be. They have picked him up. It is one of our greatest coups."[5]

After Mandela's release, the White House was asked if Bush would apologize to the South African for the reported US involvement in his arrest at an upcoming meeting between the two men. In this situation, a categorical denial by the White House of any American involvement in the arrest would have been *de rigueur*. However, Spokesman Marlin Fitzwater replied: "This happened during the Kennedy administration.... don't beat me up for what the Kennedy people did."[6]

The CIA stated: "Our policy is not to comment on such allegations." This is what the Agency says when it feels that it has nothing to gain by issuing a statement. On a number of other occasions, because it thought that it would serve their purpose, the CIA has indeed commented on all kinds of allegations.

While Mandela's youth and health ebbed slowly away behind prison walls, Donald Rickard retired to live in comfort and freedom in Pagosa Springs, Colorado.

Chapter 24

The CIA and Drugs...
Just say "Why not?"

*In my 30-year history in the Drug Enforcement Administration
and related agencies, the major targets of my investigations
almost invariably turned out to be working for the CIA.*

Dennis Dayle, former chief of an elite DEA enforcement unit.[1]

1947 to 1951, France

Corsican and Mafia criminal syndicates in Marseilles, Sicily and Corsica—benefiting from CIA arms, money, and psychological warfare—suppressed strikes and wrestled control of labor unions from the Communist Party. In return, the CIA smoothed the way for the gangsters to be left unmolested, and unindicted, and to reestablish the heroin racket that had been restrained during the Second World War—the famous "French Connection" that was to dominate the drug trade for more than two decades and was responsible for most of the heroin entering the Unites States.[2]

1950s to early 1970s, Southeast Asia

The Nationalist Chinese army, defeated by the Communists in 1949 and forced into exile, became part of an army formed by the CIA in Burma to wage war against Communist China. The Agency closed its eyes to the fact that their new clients were becoming the opium barons of The Golden Triangle (parts of Burma, Thailand and Laos), the world's largest source of opium and heroin. Air America, the CIA's principal airline proprietary, flew the drugs all over Southeast Asia, to sites where the opium was processed into heroin, and to trans-shipment points on the route to Western customers.[3]

During the US military involvement in Vietnam and Laos, the CIA worked closely with certain tribal peoples and warlords engaged in opium cultivation. In exchange for tactical or intelligence support from these elements, the Agency protected their drug operations. Air American pilots were again engaged in flying opium and heroin throughout the area to serve the personal and entrepreneurial needs of the CIA's various military and political allies, with Air America/CIA personnel at times lining their own pockets as well; on occasion, the proceeds also helped finance CIA covert actions off budget; ultimately, the enterprise turned many GIs in Vietnam into heroin addicts.

The operation was not a paragon of discretion. Heroin was refined in a laboratory located on the site of CIA headquarters in northern Laos. After two decades of American military intervention, Southeast Asia had become the source of 70 percent of the world's illicit opium and the major supplier for America's booming heroin market.[4]

1973-80, Australia

The Nugan Hand Bank of Sydney had close, not to say intimate, ties to the CIA. Among the bank's officers were a network of US generals, admirals and former (or "former") CIA men, including William Colby, recently the Agency's director, who was one of the bank's lawyers. Bank co-founder Michael Hand had been a Green Beret and CIA contract agent in Laos, working with Air America. Many of the depositors whose money first helped the bank get started were Air America employees.

The bank rapidly expanded, with branches in Saudi Arabia, Europe, Southeast Asia, South America and the US. It became one of the banks of choice for international drug traffickers (whom Nugan Hand actively solicited), money launderers, arms dealers, and the CIA (which used the bank for its payouts for covert operations). In 1980, amidst several mysterious deaths, the bank collapsed, $50 million in debt.[5]

1970s and 1980s, Panama

For more than a decade, Panamanian strongman, General Manuel Noriega, was a highly paid CIA asset and collaborator, despite knowledge by US drug authorities as early as 1971 that the general was heavily involved in drug trafficking and money laundering. Noriega facilitated "guns-for-drugs" flights for the Contras, the CIA proxy army fighting in Nicaragua, providing protection and pilots, safe havens for drug cartel officials, and discreet banking facilities for all. Yet US officials, including CIA Director William Webster and several Drug Enforcement Administration (DEA) officers, sent Noriega letters of praise for his efforts to thwart drug trafficking (albeit only against competitors of his Medellin Cartel patrons). William Casey, who became CIA Director in 1981, declared that he didn't denounce Noriega for his relationship with drug traffickers because the Panamanian "was providing valuable support for our policies in Central America, especially Nicaragua".[6]

When a confluence of circumstances led to Noriega falling into political disfavor in Washington, the Bush administration was reluctantly obliged to turn against him. In 1989, during the US invasion of Panama, American forces kidnapped and imprisoned the general. Washington falsely ascribed the invasion to the war on drugs, whereas several foreign-policy imperatives actually lay behind the operation. Drug trafficking through Panama continued unabated under the new US-installed government.[7] Had Noriega become addicted to communism rather than drug money, the

Marines would have landed in Panama City long before.

As further indication of how US officials have been, in actuality, relatively undisturbed about drug trafficking as such—in stark contrast to their public pose—consider the case of the former Panamanian ambassador-at-large in Washington, Ricardo Bilonick. He helped smuggle nearly 40,000 pounds of Colombian cocaine into the US in the early 1980s, but because he could serve a "higher" political purpose by turning state's witness against Noriega, he got off with a three-year sentence, compared to Noriega's 40 years. At his trial, Bilonick received letters of reference from former president Jimmy Carter, former under secretary of state William D. Rogers, and a former US ambassador to Panama.[8] There are thousands of men and women languishing in American prisons, charged with cocaine offenses, who—in TOTAL—did not traffic in as much cocaine as Bilonick did.

1980s, Central America

Washington's philosophy was consistent: let 'em traffic in drugs, let 'em murder, rape and torture, let 'em burn down schools and medical clinics...as long as they carry out our wars, they're our boys, our good ol' boys.

Obsessed with overthrowing the leftist Sandinista government in Nicaragua, Reagan administration officials tolerated and abetted drug trafficking as long as the traffickers gave support to the Contras. In 1989, the Senate Subcommittee on Terrorism, Narcotics, and International Operations (the Kerry committee) concluded a three-year investigation by stating:

> There was substantial evidence of drug smuggling through the war zones on the part of individual Contras, Contra suppliers, Contra pilots, mercenaries who worked with the Contras, and Contra supporters throughout the region.... U.S. officials involved in Central America failed to address the

drug issue for fear of jeopardizing the war efforts against Nicaragua.... In each case, one or another agency of the U.S. government had information regarding the [drug] involvement either while it was occurring, or immediately thereafter.... Senior U.S. policy makers were not immune to the idea that drug money was a perfect solution to the Contras' funding problems.[9]

In Costa Rica, which served as the "Southern Front" for the Contras (Honduras being the Northern Front), there were several different CIA-Contra networks involved in drug trafficking, including that of CIA asset John Hull, an American whose farms along Costa Rica's border with Nicaragua were the main staging area for the Contras. Hull and other CIA-connected Contra supporters and pilots teamed up with George Morales, a major Miami-based Colombian drug trafficker who later admitted to giving more than $4 million in cash to the Contras. Morales' planes were loaded with weapons in Florida, flown to Central America and then brought back with cocaine on board.[10]

In 1989, after the Costa Rica government indicted Hull for drug trafficking, a DEA-hired plane clandestinely and illegally flew him to Miami. The US repeatedly thwarted Costa Rican efforts to extradite Hull back to Costa Rica to stand trial. Another Costa Rican-based drug ring involved anti-Castro Cubans whom the CIA had hired as military trainers for the Contras. Many of the Cubans had long been involved with the CIA and drug trafficking. They used Contra planes and a Costa Rican-based shrimp company, which laundered money for the CIA, to move cocaine to the United States.[11]

In Honduras, in exchange for the government allowing the US to convert the country into a grand military base, the CIA and DEA turned a virtually blind eye to the extensive drug trafficking of Honduran military officers, government officials and others. The CIA enlisted Alan Hyde, a leading Honduran trafficker—the "godfather of all criminal activities", according to US government reports—to use his boats to transport Contra supplies. In exchange, the Agency discouraged counter-narcotics efforts against Hyde. A CIA cable stated that Hyde's "connection to [CIA] is well documented and could prove difficult in the prosecution stage."[12]

There were other way stations along the cocaine highway, such as the Guatemalan military intelligence service, closely associated with the CIA, and which harbored many drug traffickers; and Ilopango Air Force Base in El Salvador, a key component of the US military intervention against the country's guerrillas. Former DEA officer, Celerino Castillo, stationed in El Salvador, has written of how Contra planes flew north loaded with cocaine, landed with impunity in various spots in the United States, including an Air Force base in Texas, then returned laden with cash to finance the war. "All under the protective umbrella of the United States Government."

The operation at Ilopango was run by Felix Rodriguez (aka Max Gomez), who reported to Vice President George Bush (President Reagan's "drug czar") and to Oliver North of Reagan's National Security Council staff, where North oversaw Contra operations. (Reagan, after all, had hailed the Contras as the "moral equivalent of our Founding Fathers".) An entry from North's diary, August 9, 1985, reads: "Honduran DC-6 which is being used for runs out of New Orleans is probably being used for drug runs into U.S."

The CIA owned one of Ilopango's airport hangers, and the National Security Council ran another. When Castillo informed DEA headquarters of the details on cocaine flights from El Salvador to the US, his employer effectively ignored the reports; eventually, Castillo was forced out of the agency.[13]

When some authority in the US wasn't clued in about one of the arriving drug flights, and made an arrest, powerful strings were pulled on behalf of dropping the case, acquittal, reduced sentence, or deportation. Reportedly, a US Customs Agent was reassigned from his Texas post back to Washington because he was investigating Contra drug deals too vigorously. There is also the case of Honduran general José Bueso Rosa, who was convicted of conspiring to murder the president of Honduras, the plot being financed by a huge cocaine deal. Senior Reagan administration officials intervened with a Federal judge to obtain leniency for Bueso in return for his services to the Contras. He received five years, while other defendants in the case were sentenced to as much as 40 years.[14]

The connections were everywhere: Four companies that distributed "humanitarian" aid to the Contras but were "owned and operated by narcotics traffickers", and under investigation in the United States for drug trafficking, received State Department contracts of more than $800,000.[15] Southern Air Transport, "formerly" CIA-owned, and later under Pentagon contract, was deeply involved in the drug running as well.[16]

A former US Attorney in Miami told the Kerry committee that Justice Department officials told him that representatives of their department, the DEA, and the FBI met in 1986 "to discuss how Senator Kerry's efforts" to push for the hearings "could be undermined".[17]

To make it easier for the CIA to ignore, while benefiting from, the drug trafficking all about them, in 1982 Agency Director William Casey negotiated an extraordinary secret "memo of understanding" with Attorney-General William French Smith to spare the CIA from any legal responsibility to report drug trafficking operations of anyone working for it.[18] This agreement was not fully rescinded until 1995.

1990s, South America

Venezuelan general Ramón Guillén Davila was indicted by a federal grand jury in Miami in 1996 for smuggling as much as 22 tons of cocaine into the United States between 1987 and 1991. At the time he was engaged in this activity, Guillén was the head of the Venezuelan National Guard anti-drug bureau and was what the *Miami Herald* called "the CIA's most trusted man in Venezuela". The CIA, over the objections of the DEA, had approved the "controlled" shipments of cocaine to the United States as some kind of vague operation to gather information about the Colombian drug cartels. It has not been reported what kind of success this operation had, but at least on one occasion, in 1990, a ton of Guillén's cocaine made it to the streets of America. The CIA actually acknowledged this one, categorizing it as "poor judgment and management on the part of several CIA officers".[19]

1980s to early 1990s, Afghanistan

CIA-supported Moujahedeen rebels engaged heavily in opium cultivation while fighting against the Soviet-supported government. The Agency's political protection and logistical assistance enabled the growers to markedly increase their output. CIA-supplied trucks and mules, which had carried arms into Afghanistan, were used to transport opium to heroin laboratories along the Afghan-Pakistan border. The output is estimated to have provided up to one half of the heroin used annually in the United States and three-quarters of that used in Western Europe. US officials admitted in 1990 that they had failed to investigate or take action against the drug operation because of a desire not to offend their Pakistani and Afghan allies.[20] As in earlier drug-related actions, CIA officers may also have gotten their hands on a portion of the drug money, using it to help finance their operations, or even themselves. In

1993, an official of the DEA called Afghanistan the new Colombia of the drug world.[21]

1986 to 1994, Haiti

While working to keep right-wing Haitian military and political leaders in power, the CIA looked away from their drug trafficking. Joseph Michel Francois, No. 3 man in the military government of 1991-1994, was regularly briefed by the DEA, who shared intelligence with him on suspected drug smuggling operations in Haiti; this, while Francois was himself a leading drug lord, working with the Colombian Medellin cartel. Francois was part of a new organization, the National Intelligence Service (SIN), created by the CIA in 1986, purportedly to fight the cocaine trade, though SIN officers, Francois and others, themselves engaged in the trafficking.[22]

1980s, The United States and the Cocaine Import Agency

In addition to the cases cited above of drug-laden planes landing in the US unmolested by authorities, there is the striking case of Oscar Danilo Blandón and Juan Norwin Meneses, two Nicaraguans living in California. To support the Contras (particularly during a period in which Congress banned funding for them), as well as enriching themselves, the two men turned to smuggling cocaine into the US under CIA protection. This led to the distribution of large quantities of cocaine into Los Angeles' inner city at a time when drug users and dealers were trying to make the costly white powder more affordable by changing it into powerful little nuggets of "crack". The Nicaraguans funneled a portion of their drug profits to the Contra cause while helping to fuel a disastrous crack explosion in Los Angeles and other cities, and enabling the Los Angeles gangs to buy automatic weapons, sometimes from

Blandón himself.

The ties between the two Nicaraguans and the CIA were visible not far beneath the surface, as the following indicate:

When Blandón was finally arrested in October 1986 (after Congress had resumed funding for the Contras and his services were much less needed), and he admitted to crimes that have sent others away for life, the Justice Department turned him loose on unsupervised probation after only 28 months behind bars and subsequently paid him more than $166,000 as an informer.

According to a legal motion filed in a 1990 police corruption trial in Los Angeles: in a 1986 raid on Blandón's money-launderer, the police carted away numerous documents purportedly linking the US government to cocaine trafficking and money-laundering on behalf of the Contras. CIA personnel appeared at the sheriff's department within 48 hours of the raid and removed the seized files from the evidence room. At the request of the Justice Department, a federal judge issued a gag order barring any discussion of the matter.

When Blandón testified in 1996 as a prosecution witness in a drug trial, the federal prosecutors obtained a court order preventing defense lawyers from delving into his ties to the CIA. Though Meneses was listed in the DEA's computers as a major international drug smuggler and was implicated in 45 separate federal investigations since 1974, he lived openly and conspicuously in California until 1989 and never spent a day in a US prison. The DEA, US Customs, the Los Angeles County Sheriff's Department, and the California Bureau of Narcotic Enforcement all complained that a number of the probes of Meneses were stymied by the CIA or unnamed "national security" interests.

Lastly, the CIA-Contra-drugs nexus brings us the case of the US Attorney in San Francisco who gave back $36,800 to an arrested Nicaraguan drug dealer, which had been found in his possession. The money was returned after two Contra leaders sent letters to the court swearing that the drug dealer had been given the cash to buy supplies "for the reinstatement of democracy in Nicaragua". The letters were hurriedly sealed after prosecutors invoked the Classified Information Procedures Act, a law designed to keep national security secrets from leaking out during trials. When a US Senate subcommittee later inquired of the Justice Department the reason for this unusual turn of events, they ran into a wall of secrecy. "The Justice Department flipped out to prevent us from getting access to people, records—finding anything out about it," recalled Jack Blum, former chief counsel to the Kerry committee, which investigated allegations of Contra cocaine trafficking. "It was one of the most frustrating exercises that I can ever recall."[23]

> "The more I think about it, it's the difference between manslaughter and murder. It's the intent. The intent was not to poison black America but to raise money for the Contras, and they [the CIA] didn't really care what it came from. If it involved selling drugs in black communities, well, this was the price of admission."
>
> Gary Webb[24]

Chapter 25

Being the World's Only Superpower Means Never Having to Say You're Sorry

I will never apologize for the United States of America.
I don't care what the facts are.

George H. W. Bush[1]

Cuba

Cuba, said US District Judge James Lawrence King on December 17, 1997, "in outrageous contempt for international law and basic human rights, murdered four human beings in international airspace." He then proceeded to award $187.6 million to the families of the Florida-based Cuban pilots who had been shot down in February 1996 by Cuban jets while on an air mission, destination Cuba.[2] (In actuality, the Cuban government had done no more than any government in the world would have done under the same circumstances. Havana regarded the planes as within Cuban airspace, of serious hostile intent, and gave the pilots explicit warning: "You are taking a risk." Planes from the same organization had gone even further into Cuban territory on earlier occasions and had been warned by Cuba not to return.)

In November 1996, the federal government gave each of the families a down payment of $300,000 on the award, the money coming out of frozen Cuban assets.[3]

Such was justice, anti-communist style.

Totally ignored by the American government, however, was

Cuba's lawsuit of May 31, 1999, filed in a Havana court demanding $181.1 billion in US compensation for death and injury suffered by Cuban citizens in four decades of "war" by Washington against Cuba. The document outlined American "aggression", ranging from backing for armed rebel groups within Cuba and the Bay of Pigs invasion in 1961, to subversion attempts from the US naval base of Guantanamo and the planting of epidemics on the island.

Cuba was demanding $30 million in direct compensation for each of the 3,478 people it said were killed by US actions and $15 million each for the 2,099 injured. It was also asking $10 million each for the people killed, and $5 million each for the injured, to repay Cuban society for the costs it has had to assume on their behalf. That was "substantially less" than the amount per person fixed by US Judge King in the pilots' case, the document pointed out.

Cuban officials delivered the papers for the suit to the US Interests Section in Havana, but the Americans refused to accept them.[4] The Cuban government then took its case to the United Nations, where it has been in the hands of the Counter-Terrorism Committee since 2001. This committee is made up of all 15 members of the Security Council, which of course includes the United States, which may account for the inaction on the matter.

Vietnam

On January 27, 1973, in Paris, the United States signed the "Agreement on Ending the War and Restoring Peace in Vietnam". Among the principles to which the United States agreed was the one stated in Article 21: "In pursuance of its traditional policy [sic], the United States will contribute to healing the wounds of war and to postwar reconstruction of the Democratic Republic of Vietnam [North Vietnam] and throughout Indochina."

Five days later, President Nixon sent a message to the Prime

Minister of North Vietnam in which he stipulated the following:

"(1) The Government of the United States of America will contribute to postwar reconstruction in North Vietnam without any political conditions. (2) Preliminary United States studies indicate that the appropriate programs for the United States contribution to postwar reconstruction will fall in the range of $3.25 billion of grant aid over 5 years."[5]

Nothing of the promised reconstruction aid was ever paid. Or ever will be.

However—deep breath here—Vietnam has been compensating the United States. In 1997 it began to pay off about $145 million in debts left by the defeated South Vietnamese government for American food and infrastructure aid. Thus, Hanoi is reimbursing the United States for part of the cost of the war waged against it.[6]

How can this be? The proper legal term is "extortion". The enforcers employed by Washington included the World Bank, the International Monetary Fund, the Export-Import Bank, the Paris Club, and the rest of the international financial mafia. The Vietnamese were made an offer they couldn't refuse: Pay up or subject yourself to exquisite forms of economic torture, even worse than the considerable maiming you've already experienced at the hands of our godfathers.[7]

At the Vietnamese embassy in Washington (a small office in an office building), the First Secretary for Press Affairs, Mr. Le Dzung, told the author in 1997 that this matter, as well as Nixon's unpaid billions, are rather emotional issues in Vietnam, but the government is powerless to change the way the world works.

Nicaragua

Under siege by the United States and its Contra proxy army for several years, Nicaragua filed suit in 1984 in the World Court

(International Court of Justice), the principal judicial organ of the United Nations, located in The Hague, Netherlands, for relief from the constant onslaught, which included mining its harbors. The Court ruled in 1986 that the US was in violation of international law for a host of reasons, stated that Washington "is under a duty immediately to cease and to refrain from all such acts [of hostility]" and "is under an obligation to make reparation to the Republic of Nicaragua for all injury".

Anticipating the suit, the Reagan administration had done the decent and right thing: It announced, on April 6, 1984, three days before Nicaragua's filing, that the US would not recognize the World Court's jurisdiction in matters concerning Central America for a two-year period.

Apart from the awesome arbitrariness of this proclamation, the court's ruling of June 27, 1986 actually came after the two-year period had expired, but the United States ignored it anyway. Washington did not slow down its hostile acts against Nicaragua, nor did it ever pay a penny in reparation.[8]

Libya

The April 1986 American bombing of Libya took the lives of scores of people and wounded another hundred or so. The dead included Libyan leader Moammar Qaddafi's young daughter; all of Qaddafi's other seven children as well as his wife were hospitalized, suffering from shock and various injuries. A year later, 65 claims were filed with the White House and the Department of Defense under the Federal Tort Claims Act and the Foreign Claims Act, on behalf of those killed or injured. The claimants, who were asking for up to $5 million for each wrongful death, included Libyans, Greeks, Egyptians, Yugoslavs and Lebanese.[9] Before long, the number of claimants reached to about 340, but none of their claims got anywhere in the American judicial system, with the Supreme

Court declining to hear the case.[10]

Panama

For several years following the American invasion of 1989, with its highly destructive bombing and ground combat, many individual Panamanians tried in various ways to receive compensation for the death or injury of themselves or family members, or the wreckage of their home or business. But their legal claims and suits were met by an implacable US government. One American law firm filed claims on behalf of some 200 Panamanians (all non-combatants), under provisions of the Panama Canal treaty, first in Panama with US military officials, who rejected the claims; then in two suits filed in US courts, all the way up to the Supreme Court, with each of the courts declining to hear the cases.[11]

During the years 1990 to 1993, some 300 Panamanians petitioned the Inter-American Commission on Human Rights of the Organization of American States (OAS) for a finding that the United States had violated many of their rights and was liable for "just compensation". In 1993, the Commission ruled the petition "admissible". But as of the year 2005, it was still pending as to its "merits", which were being "studied".[12] It should be born in mind that over the years, the United States has wielded inordinate influence in the OAS, far more than any other member. Witness Washington's success in getting Cuba suspended from the organization in 1962 and kept out to the present time despite repeated, growing, and publicly-expressed support for Cuba's reinstatement by other OAS members.

There was a report some years ago that a few small payments— seemingly somewhat arbitrary—had been made "on the ground" by US officials to Panamanians in Panama. But in December 1999, the State Department Press Office dealing with Panama stated that "the United States has not paid any compensation for combat-related deaths or injuries or property damage due to Operation Just Cause" (this being the not-tongue-in-cheek name given to the American invasion and bombing).[13] Some of the American aid given to Panama since 1989, the State Department added, has been used by Panama for such purposes. The State Department puts the matter thusly, it would appear, to make it clear to the world that they do not feel any guilt or responsibility for what they did to the people of Panama and will not succumb to any kind of coercion, legal or moral, to pay any compensation.

On December 20, 1999, the tenth anniversary of the American invasion, hundreds of Panamanians took to the street to demand once again that the US pay damages to civilian victims of the bombing.

Sudan

The El-Shifa pharmaceutical plant had greatly raised Sudanese medicinal self-sufficiency while producing about 90 percent of the drugs used to treat the most deadly illnesses in the desperately poor country. But on August 20, 1998, the United States saw fit to send more than a dozen Tomahawk cruise missiles screaming into the plant, in an instant depriving the people of Sudan of their achievement.

Based on a covertly acquired soil sample, Washington claimed that the plant was producing chemical weapons. At the same time the US gave the world the clear impression that the factory's owner, Saleh Idris, was a close associate of terrorists and was involved in money laundering. Washington proceeded to freeze $24 million in Idris's London bank accounts. But the US was never able to prove any of its assertions, while every piece of evidence and every expert testimony that surfaced categorically contradicted the claim about chemical weapons.[14] The case fell apart completely, and in the meantime, Idris sued to recover his money as well as compensation for his pulverized plant.

Finally, in May 1999, the United States unfroze Idris's accounts rather than contest his suit because they knew they had no case. However—as far as what's publicly known—the US has yet to offer any kind of formal or official apology to Sudan or to Idris for the plant's destruction, or for the serious harm done to his reputation, and has yet to compensate him for the loss of the plant and the loss of business; nor the plant's employees for the loss of their jobs and income, or the ten people who were injured. The degree of Washington's arrogance in the whole matter was stunning, from the initial act on. "Never before," observed former CIA official Milt Bearden, "has a single soil sample prompted an act of war against a sovereign state."[15]

Iraq

The American government and media had a lot of fun with an obvious piece of Iraqi propaganda—the claim that a biological warfare facility, bombed during the Gulf War in 1991, had actually been a baby food factory. But it turned out that the government of New Zealand, whose technicians had visited the site repeatedly, and various other business people from New Zealand who had had intimate contact with the factory, categorically confirmed that it had indeed been a baby food factory. The French contractor who had built the place said the same. But Chairman of the Joint Chiefs of Staff, Colin Powell, insisted: "It was a biological weapons facility, of that we are sure."[16] As to American compensation, there was none.

China

After the United States bombed the Chinese embassy in Belgrade in May 1999, killing three people inside the building, Washington apologized profusely to Beijing, blaming outdated maps among other problems. But this, it appears, was just a cover for the fact that the bombing wasn't actually an accident. Two reports in *The Observer* of London in October and November, based on NATO and US military and intelligence sources, revealed that the embassy had been targeted after NATO discovered that it was being used to transmit Yugoslav army communications. The Chinese were doing this after NATO jets had successfully silenced the Yugoslav government's own transmitters.[17]

Over and above the military need, there may have been a political purpose served. China is clearly the principal barrier to US hegemony in Asia, if not elsewhere. The bombing of the embassy was perhaps Washington's charming way of telling Beijing that this is only a small sample of what can happen to you if you have any ideas of resisting or competing with the American juggernaut. Being able to have a much better than usual "plausible denial" for carrying out such a bombing may have been irresistible to American leaders. The chance would never come again.

All of US/NATO's other bombing "mistakes" in Yugoslavia were typically followed by their spokesman telling the world: "We regret the loss of life." These same words were used by the IRA in Northern Ireland on a number of occasions over the years following one of their bombings which appeared to have struck the wrong target. But their actions were invariably called "terrorist".

Guatemala

On March 10, 1999, in a talk delivered in Guatemala City, President Clinton said that US support for repressive forces in Guatemala "was wrong, and the United States must not repeat that mistake." But the word "sorry" did not cross the president's lips, nor did the word "apologize", nor the word "compensation".[18] Forty years of unholy cruelty to a people for which the United States was preeminently responsible was not worth a right word or a penny.

This was the first visit by an American president to Guatemala since Lyndon Johnson went there in 1968, during the height of the oppression by Washington's client-state government. Johnson did not of course say that the current US policy in Guatemala was wrong, when it would have meant a lot more than Clinton saying so 31 years later. LBJ did, however, inform his audience that he had heard that Guatemala was called "the land of eternal spring".[19]

Greece

Clinton's visit to Greece in November 1999 brought out large and fiery anti-American demonstrations, protesting the recent American bombing of Yugoslavia and the indispensable US support for the torturers *par excellence* of the 1967-74 Greek junta. During his one-day stop, the president found time to address a private group—"When the junta took over in 1967 here," he told his audience, "the United States allowed its interests in prosecuting the Cold War to prevail over its interest—I should say its obligation—to support democracy, which was, after all, the cause for which we fought the Cold War. It is important that we acknowledge that." National Security Council spokesman David Leavey was quick to point out that the president's statement about the former junta was "not intended as an apology."[20]

Questions arise. How can it be that the US fought the Cold War to "support democracy" and wound up supporting not only the Greek dictators but dozens of other tyrannies? Were they all simply "wrong" actions, all "mistakes", like in Guatemala? At what point do we conclude that a consistent sequence of "mistakes" demonstrates intended actions and policy? Moreover, if US "interests" in the Cold War "prevailed" over the cause of democracy, we must ask: What are these "interests" that are in conflict, or at least not harmonious, with democracy, these "interests" which are routinely invoked by American statesmen, but never given a proper name?

Finally, we have the words of President Clinton spoken in Uganda in March 1998:

> During the cold war when we were so concerned about being in competition with the Soviet Union, very often we dealt with countries in Africa and in other parts of the world based more on how they stood in the struggle between the United States and the Soviet Union than how they stood in the struggle for their own people's aspirations to live up to the fullest of their God-given abilities.[21]

What is going on here? Guatemala, Greece, Africa, other parts of the world...Was the president disowning a half-century of American foreign policy? Was he saying that the United States brought all that death, destruction, torture and suffering to the world's multitudes for no good reason? That all we were diligently taught about the nobility of the fight against the thing called "communism" was a fraud?

We'll never know what William Clinton really thought about these things. He may not know himself. But we do know what he did. As discussed in the Introduction and in the Interventions chapter, we know that he continued the very same kind of policies he was, in the above examples, repudiating. And some day, decades hence, another American president may acknowledge that what Clinton did in Iraq, Colombia, Mexico, Yugoslavia and elsewhere, and what George W. Bush did in Iraq and Afghanistan and elsewhere, was "wrong" or "mistaken". But that future president, even as he utters the words, will be doing the "wrong" thing himself in one corner of the world or another. And for the same "interests".

Chapter 26

The United States invades, bombs, and kills for it...but do Americans really believe in free enterprise?

S ince the end of the cold war, prominent American economists and financial specialists have been advising the governments of Eastern Europe and the former Soviet Union on the creation and virtues of a free-enterprise system.

The US-government-financed National Endowment for Democracy is busy doing the same on a daily basis in numerous corners of the world.

The US-controlled World Bank and International Monetary Fund will not bestow their financial blessings upon any country that does not aggressively pursue a market economy.

The United States refuses to remove its embargo and end all its other punishments of Cuba unless the Cubans terminate their socialist experiment and jump on the capitalist bandwagon.

Before Washington would sanction and make possible his return to Haiti in 1994, Haitian President Jean-Bertrand Aristide had to guarantee the White House that he would shed his socialist inclinations and embrace the free market.

It would, consequently, come as a shock to the peoples of many countries to realize that, in actuality, most Americans do not believe in the free-enterprise system. It would, as well, come as a shock to most Americans.

To be sure, a poll asking something like: "Do you believe that our capitalist system should become more socialist?" would be met with a resounding "No!"

But, going above and beyond the buzz words, is that how Americans really feel?

Supply and demand

Following the disastrous 1994 earthquake in Los Angeles came the cry from many quarters: Stores should not be raising prices so much for basic necessities like water, batteries, and diapers. Stores should not be raising their prices at all at such a time, it was insisted. It's not the California way and it's not the American way, said Senator Dianne Feinstein. More grievances arose because landlords were raising rents on vacant apartments after many dwellings in the city had been rendered uninhabitable. How dare they do that? people wailed. The California Assembly then proceeded to make it a crime for merchants to increase prices for vital goods and services by more than ten percent after a natural disaster.[1]

A similar tale followed the destruction caused by Hurricane Isabel in September 2003. In the Washington, DC area and points south, exorbitant prices were being demanded for generators, batteries, gasoline, ice, water pumps, tree-removal services, etc. The governor and attorney general of Virginia called on the legislature to pass the state's first anti-price-gouging law after receiving about 100 complaints from residents. North Carolina had enacted an anti-gouging law just shortly before.[2]

In the face of all this, one must wonder: Hadn't any of these people taken even a high-school course in economics? Hadn't they learned at all about the Law of Supply and Demand? Did they think the law had been repealed? Did they think it should be?

Even members of congress don't seem to quite trust the workings of the system. They regularly consider measures to contain soaring drug and health-care costs and the possible regulation of the ticket distribution industry because of alleged price abuses.[3] Why don't our legislators simply allow "the magic of the marketplace" to do its magic?

The profit motive

President Calvin Coolidge left Americans these stirring words to ponder: "Civilization and profits go hand in hand." Hillary Clinton, however, while the First Lady, lashed out at the medical and insurance industries for putting their profits ahead of the public's health. "The market," she declared, "knows the price of everything but the value of nothing."[4]

Labor unions regularly attack companies for skimping on worker health and safety in their pursuit of higher profit.

Environmentalists never sleep in their condemnation of industry putting profits before the environment.

According to a survey in 2005, 70 percent of Americans think that the pharmaceutical companies are more concerned "about making profits" than developing new drugs.[5]

Judges frequently impose lighter sentences upon lawbreakers if they haven't actually profited monetarily from their acts. And they forbid others from making a profit from their crimes by selling book or film rights, or interviews. The California Senate enshrined this into law in 1994, one which directs that any such income of criminals convicted of serious crimes be placed into a trust fund for the benefit of the victims of their crimes.[6]

President George H. W. Bush, in pardoning individuals involved in the Iran-Contra scandal, stated: "First, the common denominator of their motivation—whether their actions were right or wrong—was patriotism. Second they did not profit or seek to profit from their conduct."[7]

No less a champion of free enterprise than former senator Robert Dole said, in an attack upon the entertainment industry during his 1996 presidential campaign, that he wanted "to point out to corporate executives there ought to be some limit on profits.... We must hold Hollywood accountable for putting profit ahead of common decency."[8]

That same year, the mayor of Philadelphia, Ed Rendell, bemoaning the corporations move to the suburbs—for what he admitted were "perfectly rational" reasons—declared: "If we let the free market operate unconstrained, cities will die."[9]

Finally, we have a congressional debate in May 1998 about imposing sanctions against countries that allow religious persecution. The sanctions were opposed by US business interests, prompting Rep. Tom Coburn (R-Okla.) to declare: "We've got to figure out what we believe in our country. Do we believe in capitalism and money or do we believe in human rights?"[10]

But how can the system conceivably function as it was designed to without the diligent pursuit of profit? Not merely profit, but the *optimization* of profit. Surely an attorney like Hillary Clinton knows that corporate officers can be sued by stockholders for ignoring this dictum. Yet she and so many others proceed to blast away at one of the pillars of the capitalist temple.

Private entrepreneurship and ownership

Likewise, the American Medical Association has taken aim at another of the temple's honored pillars—patents, that shrine to the quintessential entrepreneur, the inventor. The AMA issued a blistering condemnation of the increasingly popular practice of patenting new surgical and medical procedures, saying it was unethical and would retard medical progress.[11] Is Thomas Edison rolling over in his grave?

A few years ago, the people of Cleveland felt very hurt and betrayed by the owner of the Browns moving his football team to Baltimore. But is it not the very essence of private ownership that the owner has the right to use the thing he owns in a manner conducive to earning greater profit? Nonetheless, Senator John Glenn and Representative Louis Stokes of Ohio announced their plan to introduce legislation to curb such franchise relocation.[12]

Competition and choice

And where is the appreciation for America's supposedly cherished
ideal of greater "choice"? How many citizens welcome all the junk
mail filling their mailboxes, all the email spam they have to wade
through each day, or having their senses pursued and surrounded
by omnipresent advertisements and commercials? People moan the
arrival in their neighborhood of the national chain that smothers and
drives out their favorite friendly bookstore, pharmacist, or coffee
shop, squawking about how "unfair" it is that this "predator" has
marched in with hobnail boots and the club of "discount prices".
But is this not a textbook case of how free, unfettered competition
should operate? Why hasn't the public taken to heart what they're
all taught—that in the long run competition benefits everyone?

Ironically, the national chains, like other corporate giants
supposedly in competition, are sometimes caught in price-fixing
and other acts of collusion, bringing to mind John Kenneth
Galbraith's observation that no one really likes the market except
the economists and the Federal Trade Commission.

The non-profit alternative

The citizenry may have drifted even further away from the system
than all this indicates, for American society seems to have more
trust and respect for "non-profit" organizations than for the profit-
seeking kind. Would the public be so generous with disaster relief
if the Red Cross were a regular profit-making business? Would
the Internal Revenue Service allow it to be tax-exempt? Why does
the Post Office give cheaper rates to non- profits and lower rates
for books and magazines which don't contain advertising? For an
AIDS test, do people feel more confident going to the Public Health
Service or to a commercial laboratory? Why does "educational"
or "public" television not have regular commercials? What would

Americans think of peace-corps volunteers, elementary-school teachers, clergy, nurses, and social workers who demanded in excess of $100 thousand per year? Would the public like to see churches competing with each other, complete with ad campaigns selling a New and Improved God?

Pervading all these attitudes, and frequently voiced, is a strong disapproval of greed and selfishness, in glaring contradiction to the reality that greed and selfishness form the official and ideological basis of our system.

It's almost as if no one remembers how the system is supposed to work any more, or they prefer not to dwell on it. Where is all this leading to? Are the Eastern European reformers going to wind up as the last true believers in capitalism?

It would appear that, at least on a gut level, Americans have had it up to here with free enterprise; indeed, the type of examples given above can be found in the media very regularly. The great irony of it all is that the mass of the American people are not aware that their sundry attitudes constitute an anti-free enterprise philosophy, and thus tend to go on believing the conventional wisdom that government is the problem, that big government is the biggest problem, and that their salvation cometh from the private sector, thereby feeding directly into pro-free enterprise ideology.

Thus it is that those activists for social change who believe that American society is faced with problems so daunting that no corporation or entrepreneur is ever going to solve them at a profit carry the burden of convincing the American people that they don't really believe what they think they believe; and that the public's complementary mindset—that the government is no match for the private sector in efficiently getting large and important things done—is equally fallacious, for the government has built up an incredible military machine (ignoring for the moment, what it's used for), landed men on the moon, created great dams, marvelous national parks, an interstate highway system, the peace corps, student loans, social security, insurance for bank deposits, protection of pension funds against corporate misuse, the Environmental Protection Agency, the National Institutes of Health, the Smithsonian, the G.I. Bill, and much, much more. In short, the government has been quite good at doing what it wanted to do, or what labor and other movements have made it do, like establishing worker health and safety standards and requiring food manufacturers to list detailed information about ingredients.

Activists have to remind the American people of what they've already learned but seem to have forgotten: that they don't want *more* government, or *less* government; they don't want *big* government, or *small* government; they want government *on their side*.

None of the above, of course, will deter The World's Only Superpower from continuing its *jihad* to impose capitalist fundamentalism upon the world.

A couple of more reasons why the *jihad* may have tough going

Nearly half of adult Americans surveyed by the Hearst Corporation in 1987 believed Karl Marx's aphorism: "From each according to his ability, to each according to his need" was to be found in the US Constitution.[13]

Mark Brzezinski, son of Zbigniew, was a post-Cold War Fulbright Scholar in Warsaw: "I asked my students to define *democracy*. Expecting a discussion on individual liberties and authentically elected institutions, I was surprised to hear my students respond that to them, democracy means a government obligation to maintain a certain standard of living and to provide health care, education and housing for all. In other words, socialism."[14]

Chapter 27

A Day in the Life of a Free Country

The question is irresistibly upon us.

How do they get away with it?

How does the United States orchestrate economies, subvert democracy, overthrow sovereign nations, torture them, chemicalize them, biologize them, radiate them...all the less-than-nice things detailed in this book, often in the full glare of the international media, with the most stunning contradictions between word and deed...without being mercilessly condemned by the world's masses, by anyone with a social conscience, without being shunned like a leper? Without American leaders being brought before international tribunals, charged with crimes against humanity?

It's no mystery about the silence and collusion, if not the adoration, of other governments and their leaders. It takes buying out only a few men with sleek jet fighters or tons of wheat, canceled debts, the World Bank, the IMF; they've been intimidated, threatened, extorted, bribed, allowed to remain in power, had their egos massaged, their nationalism patronized, and had membership in the exclusive private clubs of NATO, the World Trade Organization, and the European Union dangled before them. Only the occasional oddball Fidel Castro-type is willing to risk being shunned by respectable international high society by acting on principle against the United States.

But what keeps the vast majority of humanity, including the countless victims, from rising up in protest, spewing gross scorn and skepticism, if not bullets?

Being enamored of the United States—a former colony that made good, with its wondrous New World promise of a new life—goes well back into the nineteenth century, and reached new heights with the victory over fascism in the Second World War, then higher yet with America's science-fiction technical wizardry, epitomized by walking on the moon. Soviet Cold War propaganda made scarcely a dent. Nor did Cold War truths. Or any truths.

For decades after the close of the Second World War, Western visitors to the Soviet Union and Eastern Europe regularly brought back tales from their professional counterparts as well as the man in the street—the citizens refused to believe that there was homelessness in America or that there was no national health insurance; they were convinced that that was simply communist propaganda. They believed that in the US and Britain, government decisions were never made secretly, and that if a politician told a single lie he would be removed from office, citing Nixon as an example..."We sometimes get copies of the Daily Mail [the London tabloid] from your embassy—it is good to read unbiased world news."[1]...After the close of the Cold War, the chief of the Soviet general staff told the US chairman of the Joint Chiefs of Staff how impressed he was that enlisted people in the US military were not afraid to speak out and were not intimidated by their officers ...[2]

Over the years, a number of Third-World leaders, under imminent military and/or political threat by the United States, have made appeals to Washington officials, even to the president in person, under the apparently hopeful belief that it was all a misunderstanding, that America, storybook America, was not really intent upon crushing them and their movements for social change.

In 1945 and 1946, Vietnamese leader Ho Chi Minh, a genuine admirer of America, wrote at least eight letters to President Truman and the State Department asking for America's help in winning Vietnamese independence from the French. He wrote that world peace was being endangered by French efforts to reconquer Indochina and he requested that "the four powers" (US, USSR, China, and Great Britain) intervene in order to mediate a fair settlement and bring the Indochinese issue before the United Nations.[3] He received no reply, for he was some sort of communist.

The Guatemalan foreign minister in 1954, Cheddi Jagan of British Guiana in 1961, and Maurice Bishop of Grenada in 1983 all made their appeals to be left in peace.[4] All were crushed.

In 1961, Che Guevara offered a Kennedy aide several important Cuban concessions if Washington would call off the dogs of war. To no avail.[5]

In 1994, we had the case of the leader of the Zapatista rebels in Mexico, Subcommander Marcos. "Marcos said," it was reported, "he expects the United States to support the Zapatistas once US intelligence agencies are convinced the movement is not influenced by Cubans or Russians." "Finally," Marcos said, "they are going to conclude that this is a Mexican problem, with just and true causes."[6] With all due respect to the considerable courage of Señor Marcos, one must seriously question his degree of contact with history, reality, and gringos. For many years, the United States has been providing the Mexican military with all the training and tools needed to kill Marcos' followers and, quite possibly, before long, Marcos himself.

In 2002, before the coup in Venezuela that ousted Hugo Chavez, some of the plotters went to Washington to get a green light from the Bush administration. Chavez learned of this visit and was so distressed by it that he sent officials from his government to plead his own case in Washington. The success of this endeavor can be judged by the fact that the coup took place shortly thereafter.[7]

Syria today appears to be the latest example of this belief that somewhere in Washington, somehow, there is a vestige of human-like reasonableness that can be tapped. The Syrians turn over suspected terrorists to the United States and other countries and accept prisoners delivered to them by the US for the obvious purpose of them being tortured to elicit information. The Syrians make it clear that they do these things in the hope of appeasing the American beast; this while the United States continues speaking openly of overthrowing the Syrian government and imposes strict sanctions against the country.

Was there anything Czechoslovakia could have done to prevent a Nazi invasion in 1938? Or Poland in 1939?

When US bombs fell on Serbia in the spring of 1999, many Serbians expressed their shock and amazement that America—beloved, admired America—could do such a thing. The *Washington Post* interviewed a family in Belgrade: "They regard themselves as pro-American," said the paper. "It is very difficult for us to hate America," the husband declared. "We have always aspired to an American way of life, not a Russian way of life." Added the *Post*: "The fact that the United States is bombing their country shocks and bewilders them."[8] A Serbian poet from the Kosovo capital of Pristina, one Alexander Simovich, was deeply upset by the US bombing which was devastating the city and his life. Yet, we were told that he "loves Bob Dylan and jazz and lyrical poets. In the moments when he still allows himself to dream, he is living in another country, like the United States."[9]

In Russia, most people strongly opposed the bombing and were shocked that it was the United States that was mainly responsible. The US media informed us repeatedly that the level of anti-American sentiment in Russia at this time was easily the greatest in memory. It was as if the Russians were discovering for the first time that the United States had a violent side to it. Such innocence, it must be said, is virtually a form of insanity.

When the Chinese embassy in Belgrade was torn apart by American missiles, the reaction amongst Chinese was disbelief, as they marched in protest. A graduate student at Beijing University said his first thought was that the Americans couldn't have done it. A terrorist must have been to blame. "I feel very sad. I have watched so many American movies and other things. I believe America has so much that is so humane, and so just."

"You were the ideal for so many of us," added a senior Chinese official. "And now your stupid bombs have killed our people."

This attitude was not confined to Chinese who have not set foot in the United States. A Chinese graduate of Stanford University declared that "We used to think the United States was a model. But now you've killed our people. This is the end of our honeymoon with America."[10]

This naiveté, this love affair with the mystique of "America", while certainly touching in a way in this tired old world, is not of immaculate conception. The United States, the inventor and perfecter of modern advertising and public relations, the world's leading producer and distributor of films, TV programs, books, magazines and music, with US Information Service libraries in more than 100 countries, and Voice of America with more than a hundred million listeners...the United States, the world's only information superpower, has flooded the media and the hearts and minds of the earth's multitude with this mystique, playing it for all it's worth, for generations.

Historian Christopher Simpson, in his study, *Science of Coercion,* observed:

> Military, intelligence, and propaganda agencies such as the Department of Defense and the Central Intelligence Agency helped bankroll substantially all of the post-World War II generation's research into techniques of persuasion, opinion measurement, interrogation, political and military mobilization, propagation of ideology and related questions."[11]

"It's a free country."
The thought comes with mother's milk.
"It's a free country."

How many times does someone growing up in the United States have to hear those words before it settles comfortably, deep in the "received truth" lobe of the brain?

"It's a free country."

How many in the world have made this adage a basic element of their love affair with America?

"It's a free country."

In the minds of many Americans and foreigners, whether consciously or not, this gives the United States the moral right to do what it does in and to the rest of the world.

"It's a free country."

The following is offered as a corrective.

Overtly and covertly, legally and illegally, the military-industrial complex has joined forces with the prison-industrial complex, linked further to the omnipresent national security-police complex, all clasping hands tightly with the War on Drugs and the War on Terrorism in a declaration of War on the American People and the Bill of Rights. This Authority Juggernaut—enamored with its own perpetuation, glorification, and enrichment—has convinced the American public that without its storm troopers all hell would break loose and the safety and security of the citizenry would be on a life-support machine. In this undertaking, the Juggernaut has had the indispensable assistance of intimidated legislatures, an uniconoclastic judiciary, compliant media, and the president: first, Bill Clinton, who—in the words of civil-liberties columnist Nat Hentoff—"in this century...has inflicted the most harm on our constitutional rights and liberties"[12], followed by George W. Bush, who has matched or exceeded Clinton for harm done to the justice system, albeit in a new century.

On any given day, a day like today in fact, or one during last month, or last year, much of the following—*all of it derived directly from actual happenings or disclosures of recent years*—is taking place somewhere in the United States. Time and again we have been assured that certain practices have been terminated, only to discover that—perhaps with slight modifications—they are still being carried out.

It should be kept in mind that what is presented below deals essentially with violations of civil liberties and human rights, and does not include the numerous forms of corporate abuse which are economic in nature or which adversely affect people's health or safety.

Note: This list was compiled in 2000. However, virtually all of it, in one form or another, is still true in 2005, only worse, due to the aftermath of the September 11, 2001 attacks, the so-called War on Terrorism, the wars in Afghanistan and Iraq, and the Bush administration's draconian legislative attack on civil liberties called the Patriot Act.

None are more hopelessly enslaved than those who falsely believe they are free.

Johann Wolfgang von Goethe

- In every state, the police or the National Guard and, at times, active-duty army troops, are conducting relentless helicopter drug-surveillance over people's homes and property, setting up roadblocks, interrogating, detaining, harassing, and terrifying residents with displays of excessive power.

- In hundreds of American cities, young people are being subjected to a nighttime curfew law; many have a daytime curfew as well.

- The CIA, FBI and other federal agencies are refusing to respond to subpoenas for documents issued by attorneys who need them for the defense of their clients in national security cases in state courts.

- The CIA is opening and reading mail to and from selected countries. The FBI is peeking at our correspondence, domestic and international, for a host of its own priorities.

- In Western states, police and US Border Patrol agents, are stopping pedestrians and motorists purely because they look Hispanic, and asking them to prove that they're lawful residents of the United States.

- Motorists are being stopped on highways for drug checks, blacks and Hispanics being the most likely to be stopped because of the race-based drug-courier profile being employed. Blacks are being strip searched on streets by police, who then shine a flashlight at their genital and anal areas.

- The Immigration and Naturalization Service (INS) is holding children (under age 18), mainly from Latin America and China, for months at a time in prison-like conditions, not informing them of their rights, interfering with their attempts to obtain lawyers, and failing to facilitate contact with relatives; detaining them perhaps to force their illegal alien parents to come for them, so they can be taken into custody.

- Private corporations are recording employees' phone calls and voice mail, reading their computer files and email, getting logs of what websites they've looked at, videotaping them as they work, observing them in bathrooms and locker rooms with two-way mirrors or hidden cameras, tracking their whereabouts by having them use electronic pass keys, bugging their offices, subjecting them to airport-style electronic searches, testing their urine for drugs, doing extensive security checks on their backgrounds—- all this whether or not they have ever behaved poorly on the job, or whether their work involves any danger to anyone.

- At the Naval Academy in Annapolis, a random group of students is having to undergo urinalysis each week. At other schools, students are obliged to take a urine test in order to join the track team, join the chess club, go to the prom, go on a field trip, or drive to and from school; some of these school policies have been approved by courts.

- New Jersey state troopers are enlisting hotel workers along the New Jersey Turnpike to tip them off about suspicious guests who, among other things, pay for their rooms in cash or receive a flurry of phone calls; hotel managers are allowing troopers, without a warrant, to leaf through the credit card receipts and registration forms of guests; the troopers are giving surveillance seminars to train employees to scrutinize guests who fit the profile of drug traffickers, the profile including race and speaking Spanish.

- The Federal Emergency Management Agency (FEMA) is keeping up to date its list of aliens, radicals and other undesirables who will be rounded up and detained in times of "national emergency".

- Juveniles imprisoned at one of the nation's more than 50 so-called "boot camps" are forced to go on endurance runs until blood has soaked their shoes; one has already died from it; at other times, the youngsters are subjected to shackles or handcuffs.

- Women are being arrested for using crack cocaine while pregnant, even if their baby is perfectly normal at birth. Indeed the idea of the "crack baby" may well be a myth.

- Task forces of international, federal, military, state, and local law enforcement and intelligence agencies, as well as private entities, are employing increased interaction, abundant funds, new laws, new technologies, and new octopus-like data bases to spy on and harass activists of many stripes: Irish and Middle-East support groups, human rights, immigrants' rights, civil liberties, prison reform, minorities, labor, environmental, animal rights, nuclear power, anti-war, and anti-imperialism, even if there is no evidence of violence or illegal activities.

The FBI and police are noting license plate numbers of people attending meetings and demonstrations, photographing people, paying informers to infiltrate groups, breaking into offices to steal mailing and contributor lists, rifling through files, and carrying out "harassment arrests" (i.e., charges later dropped). Individual members of these groups are receiving FBI visits at their homes and workplaces, or the Bureau is sending anonymous letters to the person's colleagues implying that s/he is actually an informer, as well as assorted poison-pen letters to employers, landlords, and spouses designed to produce optimal distress.

- Airport passengers are being detained for hours, even days, and missing flights because they fit a "terrorist profile" based on their nationality, ethnicity, appearance, airport behavior, travel itinerary, or other criteria. They are being strip searched, including body cavity searches, X-rayed, and forced to take laxatives so their bowel excretions can be examined.

- The FBI is urging librarians to report on the books taken out by patrons with foreign-sounding names, particularly scientific and technical books. (When this program was first revealed and criticized, the FBI proceeded to do checks on the critics.)

- The Drug Enforcement Administration (DEA) is demanding that a publisher provide it with the names of people who bought a marijuana cultivation book.

- The police are confiscating the cars of customers of prostitutes, sometimes after a female police officer has lured the man into offering her money for sex. It matters not if the car does not belong to the man.
  Other police officers somewhere are forcing prostitutes to perform sex acts by threatening to arrest them if they don't comply.

- Women desiring an abortion are finding increasingly daunting obstacles placed in their path by state and federal authorities.

- The FBI or the police are carrying out a sting operation in order to arrest a black elected official regarded as too charismatic or "uppity". (The repeated case of former Washington, DC mayor Marion Barry is highly instructive.)

- People are being rejected for housing and employment because of their race.

- Numerous foreign academics and activists are being refused entry to the US to attend a conference due to their ideology and/or the ideology of the conference not being to the liking of the US State Department.

- Language minorities are facing discrimination and hostility from the "English Only" movement.

- US government *agents provocateur* are encouraging some people, as in the World Trade Center bombing or within militia groups, to carry out a bombing or other terrorist act.

- *The judge sentences you to prison. Then the prison officials sentence you to hell*...Prisoners are being handcuffed or hogtied and forced to lap their food like dogs from plates shoved under their faces...non-violent drug offenders thrown in with dangerous murderers, rapists, and robbers, despite court orders to segregate them...guards kicking inmates in the groin, siccing dogs on them...female prisoners being beaten and raped by guards, sold for sex to male prisoners, taken off the grounds to work as prostitutes, forced to perform stripteases for corrections officers (14 states do not outlaw sexual contact between correctional staff and prisoners), women's sex acts photographed by guards, prisoners of both genders kept naked or in their underwear, and monitored by the opposite sex...male prisoners slain, with impunity... guards using tear gas, Mace, and pepper spray against prisoners in handcuffs or locked in their cells...prisoners not protected from assaults, physical and sexual, by other prisoners...guards instigating fights between prisoners... inmates kept in shackles, belly chains, and handcuffs at all times when outside their cells, even in the shower...chain gangs resurrected...guards who report abuses risk reprisals from prison officials...the California Correction Officers union makes large political contributions to public officials and prosecutors so that the guards can continue to act with impunity.

• Increasingly, those incarcerated in the US are seeing their rights and privileges taken away or seriously curtailed in regard to academic classes, vocational training, reading materials, sports, exercise, prison law libraries, access to free legal advice, ease of appealing their cases, access to media. They are being charged for room and board, for doctor visits, forbidden to receive packages, forced to shave off beards and long hair and remove earrings; their phone use limited to a few minutes a week, visits to one hour a month, visiting family members treated rudely and subjected to humiliating searches and disrobings, prisoners being transferred to other prisons very far from their families; HIV-positive and terminally ill prisoners denied special care, asthmatics not monitored, those on anti-psychotic medications miss their doses, hypertensives cannot get proper diets; prisoners confined to cells for all but a few hours a week; lights on in cells 24 hours a day.

- In a new prison being built 3,000 feet up in Big Stone Gap, Virginia, windows in each cell command spectacular views of the valley below. Prison officials are planning to smoke the windows so inmates can't see out.

- Various levels of government agencies are seizing bank accounts of men who supposedly are "deadbeat dads", but it's later determined that they aren't.

- Educational institutions are being forced to allow military recruiters on campus to avoid losing government grants for student aid and other purposes.

- The US military is carrying out one of its many urban exercises, such as this one described in Massachusetts: "Last week Navy Seals landed from helicopters on top of some buildings, rappelled down the buildings, and had fun and games shooting and throwing dummy explosives around. They woke half the city of Lowell. Early that evening our house shook and the windows rattled violently as several helicopters flew over at no more that 200 feet."
In some of their exercises in the United States, the military uses live ammunition.

- A driver, stopped by the police, tapes the encounter. When he goes to the local police station to complain about his treatment, he is asked to hand the tape over. He's then charged with illegal wiretapping.

- Intercity busses and trains are being boarded by DEA agents to conduct searches of passengers' belongings. Passengers are assured that it's all "voluntary".

- Law enforcement authorities of various stripes are routinely confiscating a computer from the home of someone charged with drug something or other...or whatever...They take the computer back to the office where the good ol' boys can have a thigh-slappin' time reading the personal mail. There's no telling when they'll get around to returning the computer.

- In the Miami area and sections of New Jersey, those who don't toe the anti-Castro party line are being subjected to a wide range of abuses. Suggesting a rapprochement with Cuba, calling for an end to the US embargo, arranging for travel to the island, shipping medicines there, etc., has on hundreds of occasions led to bombings, shootings, death threats, murder, beatings, being driven out of business, fired from a job, forced off the air. Perpetrators of these acts have enjoyed a virtual immunity from prosecution.

- In contrast to Washington's hands-off treatment for anti-Castro terrorists, under the Antiterrorism and Effective Death Penalty Act of 1996, there are 30 foreign "terrorist" organizations which are held in official disdain. The law prohibits persons from "knowingly providing material support or resources to a designated foreign terrorist organization". Thus it is that donating toys to an orphanage operated by Hamas in Jordan, or books to a school run by a

Kurdish independence organization, or collecting money for the families of Irish prisoners can be regarded as "association with a known terrorist organization", and be subject to federal prosecution.

Under this legislation, tens of thousands of legal US residents, many here for a decade or more, with families and children born in the US, are being deported or being refused re- entry into the country because of such associations, or because they were once convicted of a crime, even though they've served their sentence, and regardless of how long ago it was; many were convicted of misdemeanors for which no sentence was imposed other than probation of one year, but that is sufficient for expulsion. The INS formerly could look at individual cases and keep out only people judged potentially dangerous. Now, regardless of all other circumstances, the person must be deported. Sometimes they are apprehended and deported when they apply for citizenship.

- The INS is bursting into the homes of Palestinians, legally resident in the US, and dragging them out for distributing the magazine of a Palestinian organization or raising funds for various Palestinian causes which are not involved with violence. They will be incarcerated for an indefinite term, with an indefinite fate, without criminal charges being filed against them. (Aliens, the Justice Department has long believed, and the Supreme Court has now confirmed, do not have the full protection of the Bill of Rights.)

- Various kinds of government agents or private investigators are covertly checking through your garbage, either behind your house or at the dump.

- A Federal judge is sentencing an American citizen to six months in a "halfway house" and 300 hours of community service because he drove a Libyan official, who had been denied a visa, from Mexico to Texas, or in some equally innocuous way, treated a citizen from an Officially Designated Enemy country with simple human dignity.

- The police are beating up and arresting strikers and escorting scab workers into plants, thus taking the side of the employer, as the police have done virtually without exception during 150 years of industrial conflict in the United States.
Corporations are using many of the more than 10,000 private security firms, which employ some 1.5 million guards, to suppress strike action and intimidate union organizers.

- Law enforcement officers in northern California, taking the side of logging interests once again, are pressing cotton swabs saturated with pepper spray (600 times hotter than cayenne pepper) into the eyes of non-violent people chained to each other, who are protesting the felling of ancient redwoods; protestors are shrieking and writhing in pain as the solution takes effect.
People are dying in police custody in cases where pepper spray is a contributing factor.

- Banks, telephone companies, utility companies, credit card companies, airlines, bus companies, rental car outlets, storage facilities, hotels and motels, and all manner of other private institutions are providing various local, state and federal authorities with all the information about their customers they desire under the ever-expanding legal authorities being granted to law enforcement bodies with scarcely any public hearings or debate.
The War on Drugs is requiring banks, brokers, casinos and other financial institutions to monitor their customers' financial transactions and report any "unusual" or "suspicious" activity.

The information is all fed into the Treasury Department's Financial Crimes Enforcement Network whose computers spend their days making linkages between individuals and bank accounts, businesses, real estate and other assets.

• States are selling confidential wages, driving, and other information about their residents to private information companies and other enterprises.

• Scenarios along the lines of the following from Savannah, Ga, are probably taking place elsewhere: Without warning, a team of armed county and school system officers periodically entered the schools, ordered everyone into the hallways, used dogs to sniff the students' belongings, and scanned the students' bodies with metal detectors. One of the high-school teachers was very upset by this—"Because I teach the Constitution", she explained—and made her feelings known to the authorities. A police officer told her principal that because of her "attitude" problem, she might have to be detained or restrained during future surprise raids. During a subsequent raid, the teacher's son was the only student out of 1,500 to be individually searched. Later, cars in the parking lot were searched, and the police claimed to have found a marijuana cigarette in the teacher's car. The Board of Education suspended her and she was later fired.

• In various schools students are being suspended for: bringing a bottle of the nonprescription painkiller Advil to school; dying their hair an "unacceptable" color; giving a classmate a Midol tablet for relief of menstrual cramps; bringing "drugs" to school—lemon drops; bringing a gift-wrapped bottle of wine as a Christmas gift for a teacher; another punished for carrying a small paring knife to cut her lunch fruit; yet another, a 9-year-old boy, punished for waving his drawing of a gun in class; a six-year-old boy sent home for planting a kiss on a girl's cheek; eight-year-old girls strip searched in school, looking for stolen money (not found); pre-schoolers to 6th grade students given genital exams as part of their physicals; high schools employing random Breathalyser testing to ferret out students who have imbibed alcohol; a 14-year-old girl strip-searched and suspended for two weeks because she told her classmates she could understand how the Columbine shooters felt; and high school students questioned by police who wanted to know if a chemistry textbook was for bomb-making.

This while an eleven-year-old boy is being arrested and accused of incest because a neighbor saw him touching his younger sister "sexually" in their yard. He was held six weeks in a juvenile detention center and shackled in court on at least one occasion. The boy and his parents said he had pulled down his five-year-old sister's underwear to help her urinate.

And two 10-year-old boys who put some soap in their teacher's water bottle are being charged with a felony.

- A high-school teacher is being suspended without pay for teaching mathematics using real-life problems, such as: "Jerome wants to cut his half-pound of heroin to make 20 percent more profit. How many ounces of cut will be needed?"

- Juveniles in reform schools are being hogtied and thrown into isolation cells for weeks at a time; placed in straightjackets; standing with noses pressed against a wall for as long as 16 hours a day; handcuffed naked to beds. Juveniles are being jailed with adult criminals even for just being runaways.

- Prisoners in a state correctional facility who staged a peaceful demonstration against the transfer of other inmates to out-of-state gulags against their will, are being punished with up to a year of solitary; and their time in solitary will not count towards their sentences according to the Department of Corrections.

- A federal court, created by the Foreign Intelligence Surveillance Act (FISA) of 1978, is receiving applications for authorization of electronic surveillance within the United States and is rubber-stamping them. In its first 20 years, the court received some 10,000 applications from the Justice Department on behalf of the FBI and the National Security Agency. By all accounts, only one was rejected, on a technicality.

  There exists no public record of any kind about the individual cases, nor any oversight. The Clinton administration has expanded the court's mandate to allow it to approve physical break-ins, enabling the Justice Department to bypass the usual warrant procedure in an open court, which would necessitate some accounting of the items to be seized, and an explanation of probable cause that a crime had been committed.

  The targets of these wiretaps and burglaries can be under surveillance merely because of belonging to or supporting an organization whose politics are looked upon with disfavor by the US government. Federal agents can now obtain the phone numbers of all incoming and outgoing calls on any lines used or called by suspected foreign agents.

- Cars of those arrested for drunken driving are being seized by the police. At times the police try to keep the car even if the person is acquitted.

- People are being harassed, arrested, and/or having their

property confiscated for engaging in certain forms of gambling, even in their own homes. Other forms of gambling, which are legitimized by the local or state government, proceed happily unmolested.

• Hundreds of political prisoners are rotting away in American prisons. As US-based human rights groups have testified before the Human Rights Commission of the United Nations in Geneva, these people are being held "as a direct result of actions undertaken in furtherance of a political or social vision". They go back to the black liberation struggles of the 1960s and 70s, particularly members of the Black Panthers; others are Native American activists, anti-nuclear activists, opponents of US interventionist policies in Puerto Rico, Central America, and elsewhere. A number of these prisoners were set up by FBI dirty tricks under the notorious COINTELPRO (counter-intelligence program), aimed at "neutralizing" Black Panthers and white radicals.

Many have used violence against property, and a few toward police, but persons who commit politically motivated offenses in furtherance of leftist causes receive substantially, often shockingly, harsher treatment than those who commit similar acts for monetary or right-wing reasons. Many were sentenced to more than 50 years for actions, such as possession of explosives, without there being any victims. If the usual sentence for such an act in a particular court or state is 10 years, at the beginning of year 11—certainly by year 15—these people are political prisoners.

It is often not the "worst" prisoners that are thrown into solitary confinement, but rather these political prisoners, as well as the jailhouse lawyers and prisoner activists.

The Congressional Black Caucus, in October 1997, issued

a declaration to remind the world of the existence of these political prisoners.

- Aliens who have come to the US from oppressive countries, seeking political asylum, are winding up in Kafkaesque nightmares; wasting away in prison under intolerable conditions, without criminal charges being filed against them, some dying because of unattended health problems, forgotten about until perhaps Amnesty International or some other human rights organization takes up their case. The FBI and the INS are using secret evidence—which neither the accused nor their attorneys have a right to examine—to detain these people and ultimately deport them, even if they are married to an American citizen. The aliens are often those who decried human rights abuses in their home country and fled torture and other retribution from their government, which may be putting pressure on Washington to silence and return them by providing the evidence in question.

  Many are refused entry to the US because they lack proper documents, when in fact many escape their homeland with false papers. As of 1999, the INS was holding more than 10,000 asylum seekers. In February of that year, the Washington representative of the U.N. High Commissioner for Refugees called upon the United States to stop detaining such people. Many may be regarded as political prisoners.

- The Boy Scouts are rejecting some young man as a member because he is an atheist, or rejecting an adult as a troop leader because the person is homosexual.

- Some of the more than 10,000 FBI agents are spending their time enticing people on the internet to purchase child porno, or the G-men are pretending online to be a 13-year-old girl in order to lure a man to a meeting. When the man shows up, he's arrested.

- Many foreigners, in the US legally, are sitting in prisons, charged with a crime, without their country's consulate having been informed, without the prisoner being told that he has the right to contact his consulate. Some of them are sitting on death row.

- The Internal Revenue Service (IRS), acting as judge, jury and executioner, is subjecting taxpayers to nightmarish collection processes, ordering them to pay taxes they don't owe, failing to credit them for payments made, seizing their cars and bank accounts, boosting tax penalties to meet office quotas, and generally wreaking havoc in peoples' lives; an audit is being carried out upon an individual because he or she has upset someone in a very high position in the government.

- Monetary rewards are being paid out to students who report other students for smoking, drinking alcohol, using drugs or violating other school rules.
  DARE and other school-based drug programs are teaching children to turn in their parents for marijuana or other drug violations.
  The mayor of New York has urged citizens to take pictures of people going into sex-video stores and topless bars.
  Other informant schemes call for people to turn in others for not wearing seatbelts, for telling ethnic or racist jokes, and for failing to recycle their garbage properly.

- First-time drug offenders, carrying no weapons, including many who were simply couriers or played peripheral roles in drug trafficking, and others with no record of violence or involvement in sophisticated criminal activity, are being sentenced to very long prison terms, with no chance of parole.

- Under "three-strikes" laws, people are being sentenced to 25-to-life terms for petty theft, despite that fact that the three- strikes laws were designed for violent crimes.

- The grand jury system is running amok. Virtually all federal cases use it to obtain indictments. Neither the accused nor his or her lawyer is there, so they can't confront accusers. The system is used as an instrument of terror—relatives testifying against one another with no confidentiality privilege with respect to family members other than husbands and wives: parents called to testify against their children, children against their parents, brother against sister. It lacks due process. It's another secret tool of an expanding executive branch.

- Those wishing to experiment with their mind in the privacy of their home, those seeking transcendence and nirvana, are being punished by the state for their sin. Young men are being sentenced to up to 20 years in prison for possession of less than a gram of LSD, with no evidence presented of them having done any harm to any other person.

- Human Rights Watch is charging state governments, as it did in New York, of violating international law by sentencing drug dealers to prison terms similar to those given to violent offenders. A person convicted in New York of selling two ounces of cocaine receives a mandatory sentence of 15 years to life, the same penalty meted out to a murderer.

- More states are joining the frenzy to make publicly available the names, addresses, biographies (often with detrimental erroneous information), and photos of convicted sex offenders for the rest of their lives, driving these people from their neighborhoods and jobs; this is being done regardless of whether the popular a priori view of sex offenders being untreatable is true or not, or whether they're undergoing therapy or not.

- Many hundreds of schoolbooks are being dropped from curriculums because of complaints by parents, religious groups and others. Books in public libraries are under attack as well, books which no one is obliged to read—Catcher in the Rye, Huckleberry Finn, Oliver Twist, The Grapes of Wrath, The Diary of Anne Frank, I Know Why the Caged Bird Sings, and numerous other lesser known novels, as well as countless books of history, social studies, geography, even home economics. School newspapers, other curriculum materials, music, and art, are also being targeted.

- Individuals who wish to end their lives with dignity and with a minimum of suffering are being denied the assistance of a doctor by state legislatures, the Catholic Church, and citizens' groups. In Oregon, after passage by 60 percent of a referendum allowing doctor-assisted suicide, the DEA warned that physicians who help someone commit suicide will risk their licenses to write prescriptions; whether this is ever enforced or not, the threat will have its effect.

- Numerous people who could get exceedingly welcome relief from dreadful symptoms by the use of marijuana are denied the legal right to do so. In states where voters have passed initiatives legalizing the medical use of marijuana, the authorities are throwing up obstacles to make its practice as difficult as they can make it. In Washington, D.C., Congress has in effect nullified the passage of such a referendum.
Cancer patients in great pain are being denied sufficient morphine to relieve their suffering because the War on Drugs has inhibited doctors from prescribing as much as is needed.

- Hundreds of cities are employing highly armed and trained Special Weapons and Tactics Teams (SWAT), based on military special operations models, and told they're part of a "war" on crime; ready to terrorize the enemy (the citizens) with automatic assault rifles, tanks and grenade launchers, called out even in non-crisis situations; choosing a neighborhood and swooping onto street corners, forcing pedestrians to the ground, searching them, running warrant checks, taking photos, and entering all the new "intelligence" into a state database from computer terminals in each patrol car. As they carry out this exercise, they do not trip over many members of the Fortune 500.

- A known militant, but non-violent, opponent of the president is being removed by the Secret Service from a site where the president is going to speak, then released after the speech.

- Defendants and prisoners appearing in court, who don't know their place, are being given 50,000 volt shocks with a torture device known as an electronic security belt.

- Young men are registering with Selective Service, making themselves subject to be drafted for a future war of "national security"—as defined solely by the government, no opposing arguments accepted. Failure to register is punishable by a large fine, imprisonment, and/or permanent loss of all federal financial aid and employment.

  Those already in the service are being subjected by the military to a process aimed at breaking down their deep-seated reluctance to kill people they don't know and don't hate, so as to make them willing to risk their lives fighting in one of these "national security" wars, the purpose of which they don't understand at all (or, perhaps, they understand it only too well). They are being forced, under threat of court martial, discharge, deportation if not a citizen, and in violation of international human rights standards, to take experimental drugs and vaccines, whose effects on health are unknown.

- Aliens are being denied citizenship for refusing to agree to bear arms in defense of the United States because of their pacifist beliefs, a reason not acceptable to the INS, which insists on a religious basis.

For a citizen to qualify as a conscientious objector, it means being opposed to participation in all wars, not a selective objection to a particular war, no matter how repulsive it may appear to the individual. (A female Kansas doctor, who was an Army Reserve captain, and refused to serve in the Gulf War, insisting that it was a "public health catastrophe", was kept in military prison for eight months, and Kansas medical authorities moved to revoke her medical license.)

- DEA, INS, FBI, Bureau of Alcohol, Tobacco and Firearms (ATF), Secret Service, US Forest Service, National Park Service, Sheriff's Department, National Guard, and/or other official cowboys, wearing black suits, ski masks, and the like, forming massively armed mobs of screaming, swearing agents, helicopters chopping above, battering down doors, raiding people's homes, smashing up furniture, beating up residents, handcuffing them, manhandling pregnant women, terrifying children, separating them from their parents, shooting people dead, looking for drugs or individuals which often are not there—this *jihad* being the outcome of no more than a tip from an informant.

Heavily-armed bounty hunters, with the force of law behind them, are carrying on in a similar manner to kidnap a person, sometimes killing someone, sometimes the "wrong" person.

Operators of "pirate" radio stations are also being invaded, with FCC agents, federal marshals, a SWAT team, customs agents, and local police comprising the attacking force.

- Forced labor is thriving: people compelled to work off their welfare grants, with no prospect of real employment, sometimes at sub-minimum wages, or no wages at all; convicted defendants sentenced to "community service"; conscientious objectors obliged to do alternative service, for a period longer than military service, thus being punish for exercising their conscience; inmates denied vital privileges if they refuse to work in prison, many producing for private companies, who get away with paltry wages, no benefits, no unions. (Some prison-made products are being exported, exactly what the US has condemned China for.)

- US embassies abroad are surveilling selected American travelers, fingered by a joint effort of the FBI and the State Department Passport Office.

- The INS and the US Border Patrol at the Mexican border are killing or physically mistreating large numbers of would-be immigrants. In INS centers around the country, thousands of immigrants are being held under inhumane conditions, including heads pushed into toilets, forced drugging, and being made to kneel naked and chant "America is Number One."
Immigrants in prison are also being forced to recite "America is Number One", as they walk by guards who punch and kick them.

- The INS is illegally seizing files of social agency employees working with undocumented immigrants. Lawyers and others working on behalf of victims of abuse are finding it almost impossible to file a complaint and receive a response from the INS or the Border Patrol. Media and human rights groups are virtually excluded.

- Demonstrations against detention centers and other INS practices are being brutally squashed in Los Angeles by a phalanx of local and federal armed forces—riot squads, mounted units, ATF agents, INS commando units, water cannons, tear gas...many protestors are being injured and arrested; some of those not carrying proper documents are being deported directly from a police station.

- Indigent defendants are waiting in jail for many months before the court appoints a lawyer, and then a further wait before they have a chance to speak with the lawyer.

- The notion of bail is rapidly eroding. We're raised to believe that for other than a capital offense, reasonable bail must be offered. We have a long history of not holding people in custody until their guilt has been determined. That's not true anymore. We call the new concept "preventive detention".

- Citizens are being sentenced to inordinately long prison terms, often for life, for providing information, or merely *attempting* to do so, to a country not named the United States of America. The disclosure of the information—in some cases already publicly available, or declassified before the arrest—would typically cause no actual harm at all to the United States, nor to anyone else on earth, except that the act of passing it to an alien nation grates on the sensibilities of those who professionally play the secrets game, the patriots game, and the enemies game. These professional players are fond of announcing that the "betrayal" has caused "irreparable harm" or "incalculable damage" to US national security. In some cases, the information has been passed only to the FBI, in a sting operation, yet the duped person is put away for decades.

- Workers in the Defense Department's "Area 51", in the Nevada desert, are suffering and dying from inhaling toxic chemicals that spew from the burning of hazardous wastes in huge open pits. Severe, persistent respiratory distress, cancers, aching guts, ugly crusty scales, cracked and bleeding skin, "tissues filled with industrial toxins rarely seen in humans"... But because of the ultra secrecy surrounding Area 51, they can't obtain information about what chemicals they've been exposed to in order to get appropriate medical treatment, and they can't claim workers' compensation because Area 51 can't be investigated. The place is subject to no law of the land save national security.

- Black-uniformed officers in laced-up black boots, wearing black berets, with name tags missing, are descending without warning on a prison, hauling prisoners, some without clothes, from their beds, shackling them and beating them, jumping on their backs; an inmate's head is driven into a wall, a sickening cracking sound, the prisoner screams, blood splatters the wall and the ground. All to demonstrate that the Correction Commissioner doesn't "coddle" prisoners.

- Human Rights Watch and the American Civil Liberties Union (ACLU) are finding once again that the United States is violating Article 10 of the International Covenant on Civil and Political Rights, ratified by the US in 1992, which requires that all prisoners and detainees "be treated with humanity and with respect to the inherent dignity of the human person". (In fiscal year 1999, there were 2,324 brutality claims against the New York Police Department, which kills someone every ten days on average, often unarmed, at times in handcuffs, or in jail; police officers guilty of such actions are not being disciplined; some are later promoted.)

- You're exercising your precious freedom to vote and the only candidates presented to you with more than a snowball-in-hell's chance of winning are those whose ideologies enable them to raise about a half million dollars to contest a seat in the House, about five million for the Senate, and about a hundred million for the White House. Or, increasingly, the candidates themselves are multi-millionaires.

- In California, teenagers are being stopped, harassed, photographed, and questioned by police purely because their clothing is thought to be gang attire, or of gang colors.
  In the early morn, sheriff's deputies are descending upon the homes of parents of suspected gang members, warning them that if they don't take responsibility for their children, they could face criminal charges, even jail.

- As in Detroit, New York, Philadelphia, Los Angeles and Indianapolis in recent years, police in large cities are exhibiting a remarkable level of disdain for the laws of the land: giving false information to courts to secure search warrants, or acting without warrants, committing perjury on the stand, allowing the results of botched tests of drugs to be used in criminal cases, staging drug raids in order to steal drugs, money, guns, and other valuables, taking money and drugs from dealers in exchange for immunity, robbing and beating people on the streets of their precinct.
  And exhibiting the same disdain for individual rights in numerous search-and-destroy missions against private homes: using special "shock-lock" shotgun rounds to blow apartment doors off their hinges, or shooting off the door

locks, tossing in "flash- bang grenades," which produce explosions that terrify and disorient people, illegally searching the inhabitants, menacing them with their guns, firing shots at people without cause, killing people, planting drugs or other false evidence on innocent people and arresting them, tampering with evidence, forcing people outside almost naked, filing false arrest reports, or sometimes filing no charges at all after all this, assaulting or threatening people who make charges against them.

- New cases are being added to the more than 60,000 people suing the city of New York for being illegally strip-searched after being arrested for minor offenses.

- Public relations firms, hired by large corporations and business associations, are utilizing hefty fees, lawyers, detectives, spies, and phony "grassroots" campaigns to influence the media and public opinion against food, environmental, and other activists and authors who pose a threat to one of their special-interest clients, trying to make the activists look foolish, if not criminal, as they exercise their political rights.

- NBC television is canceling an appearance by a nuclear activist because she has criticized General Electric, which owns the network. Another nuclear activist or author, or opponent of military spending, is unwelcome at CBS because it belongs to Westinghouse; while yet another finds doors closed at ABC because of having treated the Disney conglomerate with less than reverence; ditto at CNN, owned by the AOL-Time Warner octopus; while the advertisers are increasingly influencing the content of the news stories.

- During a new US invasion abroad, the media is being

severely restricted as to what it can report to the American people about the war; reporters are required to submit their copy to the Pentagon censor, and are told where they can go, what they can film, who they can interview; those who don't toe the line are transferred by their employer under heavy Pentagon pressure.

- The FBI is placing ads in Vietnamese-language and Russian-language newspapers in the US asking immigrants to report on suspected spies amongst their number.

- A prison inmate's sacramental confession to a Catholic priest is surreptitiously being taped by prison officials. The personal mail of inmates, including those awaiting trial, is being read.

- The FBI is staging photos used in a trial, and its crime laboratory is producing scientifically flawed, misleading or altered evidence benefiting the prosecutor's case against a defendant, even allowing a judge to be impeached on false charges. A Bureau official is destroying an internal report critical of an FBI action in a particular case and not disclosing its existence to prosecutors or defense attorneys; or the Bureau is allowing inaccurate and/or incomplete "expert" testimony during court proceedings, tilting it in such a way as to incriminate the accused. A veteran FBI agent who blows the whistle on such goings-on is being harassed and suspended.

- Police are setting up more and more cameras to observe the citizenry on public streets.

- Police sting operations are ensnaring gay men and charging them with "soliciting lewdness", under a state anti-sodomy law, which prohibits homosexual couples, but not heterosexual couples, from having consensual oral sex in private. Married men leaving gay sex clubs are being photographed by police, who then extort money from them by threatening to inform their wives or bosses.

- Students are being suspended by their schools for refusing to stand up for the American flag or recite the Pledge of Allegiance; or for something they wrote in the school newspaper or on their own personal home webpage.

- The INS is sending letters to immigrants who have been applying to legalize their status. The letters tell the immigrants to come to the federal building, bring some identification, and the INS will give them a work permit good for a year. When the immigrants eagerly arrive at the INS office, they are promptly arrested and deported.

- Police are stopping cars on the road, stealing money and other goods from the passengers, or taking bribes to refrain from making (false) arrests.
  Police officers, now armed with a Supreme Court ruling, are searching the belongings of a passenger in a car simply because they suspect the driver has done something wrong.

- Undercover vice squads in Arizona, wearing black ski masks, are seizing hundreds of copies of an adult newspaper from vending machines.

- Mentally ill people are languishing in prisons all over the country, receiving no treatment and often suffering physical and sexual abuse from other inmates and guards.

- Some persons judged to be mentally ill, retarded, or in other ways regarded as "misfits" are being sterilized without their knowledge in secluded corners of various state institutions.

- The DEA, other federal and state agents, and police are

seizing houses, boats, cars, airplanes, real estate, furnishings, bank accounts, and other assets belonging to people suspected of involvement in drug trafficking, or belonging to their spouses, often without a conviction, and whether or not the assets seized were tied to the alleged crime. In one state, a man is losing his home and his business for selling two grams of cocaine. In another, numerous cars are being confiscated from new car dealerships for failing to report all cash transactions involving more than $10,000. Elsewhere, a 75-year-old grandmother is being dispossessed of her home for the sins of her fugitive, drug-dealing son.

The government agencies are selling these assets and using the proceeds for anything from patrol cars to parties. The expected value of forfeitures is at times a determining factor in the question of who to raid. Police are routinely planting drugs and falsifying police reports to establish probable cause for cash seizures. Plea bargains are struck that commonly favor drug kingpins willing to surrender their assets and penalize "mules" with nothing to trade. As of early 1999, there was $2.7 billion in the federal government's "Asset Forfeiture Fund" alone.

- The concept of equal access to legal remedy and justice is being invalidated every day after a decade of deep government cutbacks to the legal aid program, thus robbing the poor of what is often their sole defense against unscrupulous landlords, scam artists, battering spouses, home foreclosure, consumer fraud, and many other legal predicaments.

- People going to police stations to lodge complaints against officers are being unceremoniously ushered out.

- Police in Los Angeles are carrying out a pre-dawn commando raid of more than 100 homes in a fishing expedition for individuals and contraband, yielding very little but many frightened and upset residents.

- In many cities, the homeless are being rounded up in parks and other sites supposedly open to the public and taken to places where respectable citizens, particularly tourists, will not be forced to cast eyes upon them.

- People who bring food to the homeless in public parks are being arrested, charged with giving out food without a permit, trespassing, or whatever else the authorities can think of; cooking equipment and vehicles are being confiscated.

- An FBI sting operation is entrapping police officers in Washington, D.C. and elsewhere by offering them bribes to escort supposed drug couriers, resulting in the officers being sentenced to as much as 55 years in prison without the possibility of parole—a veritable life sentence.

- In many states, thousands of people are having their driver's licenses suspended for six months for any drug conviction, whether or not their offenses were related to operation of a motor vehicle.
  In some localities, students are being denied a driver's license because their grades and/or attendance records are not good enough.

- Numerous individuals are being harassed and/or arrested because of a "positive alert" from a drug-sniffing dog even though law enforcement and scientific circles have known for many years that most US currency has some amount of cocaine or other drug stuck to it—in Los Angeles it was found that more than 75 percent of all the paper money in circulation was so tainted.

- Several other extreme police brutality cases like Rodney

King in Los Angeles and Abner Louima in Brooklyn are taking place, but there are no video cameras or witnesses observing, or the victim dies and his death is ruled accidental or a heart attack.

- A public official who questions the War On Drugs is paying an awful price, like former Surgeon General Jocelyn Elders whose son was sentenced to 10 years prison for selling one-eighth of an ounce of cocaine to an undercover police officer. His arrest took place five months after the sale, on a warrant issued a week after his mother suggested that the government study the legalization of drugs.

- Then there's the thing called Waco.

The prison society

Government statistics released at the end of 2003 indicated that there were nearly 2.1 million human souls confined to prisons and jails in the Land of the Free, more than in any other country in the world. The new figures represented a 31-year continuous rise in the number of inmates in the United States; this despite the fact of sustained, falling crime rates over the previous decade. The incarceration rate of 714 per 100,000 residents placed the United States first among nations in this regard. Russia was second with a rate of 548 per 100,000. Rates of incarceration for some other industrialized nations included England/Wales, 141; Canada, 116; Australia, 114; France, 95; Japan, 58.[13]

Perhaps the most outrageous, and the saddest, aspect of this prison picture is that almost half a million of the inmates have been put away for victimless crimes, principally drug related.

What may keep most Americans from being shocked by the bursting prisons, police violence, the shredding of the Bill of

Rights, and much of the rest described above is that they have yet to feel the consequences, either personally or through someone close to them. America's foreign groupies, in the meantime, remain blissfully ignorant of these violations and in need of a reality transplant.

Notes

Opening Quotes

1 *Washington Post*, October 23, 1999, p.17
2 Sept.1, 1997, cover story, p.160 ff.
3 *New York Times*, January 29, 1992, p.16
4 *Washington Post*, November 4, 1997, p.13
5 *Public Papers of the Presidents of the United States* (GPO), 1996, Vol. I, p.654, April 28, 1996
6 Washington Office of Amnesty International, *Human Rights & US Security Assistance*, 1996, p.1

Introduction

1 Senate Committee on Veterans' Affairs, *Is Military Research Hazardous to Veterans' Health? Lessons Spanning Half a Century*, December 8, 1994, p.5
2 Ibid., passim. Also see chapter 15 in the present book.
3 *Washington Post*, October 2 and 23, 1996 and July 31, 1997 for the estimated numbers of affected soldiers.
4 *Journal of the American Medical Ass*ociation, September 1, 1999, p.822.
5 *Washington Post*, October 19, 1999, p.3
6 John Kenneth Knaus, *Orphans of the Cold War* (New York, 1999), p.312. Knaus was the CIA officer who spoke to the Dalai Lama.
7 *Le Nouvel Observateur* (France), January 15-21, 1998, p.76, translation from the French by the author. There are at least two editions of this magazine; with the perhaps sole exception of the Library of Congress, the version sent to the United States is shorter than the French version, and the Brzezinski interview was not included in the shorter version.
8 *Washington Post*, January 13, 1985, p.30
9 "60 Minutes", May 12, 1996
10 For the full text of the relevant part of his memo, see *The Economist* (London), February 8, 1992, p.66 (US edition)
11 *Washington Post*, April 25, 1999, p.28
12 John Judis, "K Street Gore", *The American Prospect*, July- August 1999, p.18-21; *Washington Post*, June 18, 1999, December 4, 1999, p.18
13 *New York Times*, June 13, 1999
14 Ibid., February 14, 1991, p.16
15 *U.S. News & World Report*, February 21, 1966, p.112
16 "An Oriana Fallaci Interview: Otis Pike and the CIA", *New Republic* (Washington, DC), April 3, 1976, p.10
17 Speaking at the National Press Club, Washington, DC, June 25, 1999.

18   Phrase borrowed from media critic Norman Solomon

19   NPR Morning edition, Mara Liasson, June 11, 1999

20   Adolf Hitler, *Mein Kampf* (Houghton Mifflin Co., Boston, 1971; original version 1925) Vol. 1, chapter 10, p.231

21   See essay by author on this subject at: http://members.aol.com/bblum6/abomb.htm

22   *Los Angeles Times*, September 2, 1991, p.1

23   *Vital Speeches of the Day*, May 1, 1990, p.421, speech delivered March 23, 1990.

24   For excellent and concise summaries of how and why the United States planned and achieved world domination, see Noam Chomsky, *What Uncle Sam Really Wants* (Odonian Press, Berkeley, 1992) and Michael Parenti, *Against Empire* (City Lights Books, San Francisco, 1995)

25   Mark Falcoft, "Why Allende Fell", *Commentary* (New York), July 1976, p.42

26   See, e.g., Tim Weiner, "Military Accused of Lies Over Arms", *New York Times*, June 28, 1993, p.10; Tim Weiner, *Blank Check* (New York, 1990), p.42-43, for CIA's inflated figures re Soviets; Anne H. Cahn, "How We Got Oversold on Overkill", *Los Angeles Times*, July 23, 1993, about a GAO study; Douglas Jehl & Michael Ross, "CIA Nominee Faces Charges He Slanted Data", *Los Angeles Times*, September 15, 1991, p.1; Arthur Macy Cox, "Why the U.S., Since 1977, Has Been Misperceiving Soviet Military Strength", *New York Times*, October 20, 1980, p. 19 (Cox was formerly an official with the State Department and the CIA)

27   *The Guardian* (London), January 1, 1999

28   *New York Times*, February 3, 1992, p.8

29   *The Guardian* (London), December 6, 1986 ("NATO rebuffs Russian approach"; includes the "inappropriate and potentially divisive" quote); *Los Angeles Times*, March 10, 1989 (op-ed by John Tirman); Ibid., October 25, 1989 ("U.S. Rejects Soviet Bid to Drop Alliances"); Ibid., October 26, 1989, p.7; TASS News Agency, March 9, 2000; Associated Press, June 16, 2001 ("Putin Cites 1954 NATO Document")

30   *New York Times*, January 7, 1983, p.4; *The Guardian* (London), December 6, 1986 (first quote); *Los Angeles Times*, October 25, 1989, p.7 (second quote), and October 26.

31   *AIR FORCE Magazine* (Arlington, VA), March 1991, p.81

32   *Washington Times*, August 24, 1999, p.1; the words are those of the newspaper and may be a paraphrase of the original.

33   *In Defense of Women* (1920)

34   Vorin Whan, ed. *A Soldier Speaks: Public Papers and Speeches of General*

of the Army Douglas MacArthur (1965)

35   State Department, "Patterns of Global Terrorism, 2003", released April
      2004, can be read on their website.

36   "Pentagon's Planning Guidance for the Fiscal Years 1994-1999", *New
      York Times*, March 8, 1992, p.14

37   From the study's Introduction, p.8. The *Boston Globe,* March 2, 1998, p.5
      contains almost the entire passage.

38   Parenti, op. cit., p.80

Chapter One

1   *Miami Herald*, September 12, 2001

2   Agence France Presse, November 19, 2002

3   *The Guardian* (London), December 19, 2001, article by Duncan
      Campbell

4   *Washington Post*, August 1, 2003, p.4

5   *New York Times*, August 22, 1998, p.15

6   *Washington Post*, June 23, 2004 and June 28, p.19

7   "Bush Administration Eliminating 19-year-old International Terrorism
      Report", Knight Ridder Newspapers, April 15, 2005

8   Jim Dwyer, et al., *Two Seconds Under the World* (New York, 1994),
      p.196; see also the statement made in court by Ramzi Ahmed Yousef, who
      planned the attack, *New York Times*, January 9, 1998, p.B4

9   *Washington Post*, October 3, 2002, p.6

10   Agence France Press, December 23, 2002; *Washington Post*, November 9,
      2002

11   *Los Angeles Times*, November 13, 2002, p.6

12   Associated Press, November 7, 2002

13   Associated Press, June 19, 2004

14   BBC News, April 15, 2004

15   Associated Press, November 7, 2002

16   Voice of America News, April 21, 2003

17   *Washington Post*, June 15, 2002

18   US Department of Defense, Defense Science Board 1997 Summer Study
      Task Force on DOD Responses to Transnational Threats, October 1997,
      Final Report, Vol.1

19   *New York Times*, March 26, 1989, p.16

20   Colin Powell with Joseph E. Persico, *My American Journey* (New York,
      1995), p.291

21   *Boston Globe*, October 12, 2001, p.28

22   *Washington Post*, March 27, 2003
23   Ibid., June 4, 2003, p.18
24   *Washington Post*, July 23, 2004
25   *New York Times*, November 24, 2004
26   *Imperial Hubris*, p.x and passim
27   *Washington Post*, June 26, 2004
28   *Los Angeles Times*, July 2, 2004, op-ed by "Anonymous"
29   Pentagon briefing, June 30, 2003
30   *Washington Post*, June 29, 2003
31   Ibid., July 24, 2003, p.7
32   Ibid., August 8, 2003
33   Ibid., June 17, 2004, p.14

Chapter Two

1   *Washington Post*, March 14, 1996
2   *Los Angeles Times*, August 4, 1996
3   *Washington Post*, August 15, 1996, p.32
4   *Covert Action Information Bulletin* (Washington, DC), #64, Spring 1998,
      p.29-30
5   Mary Anne Weaver, *The New Yorker,* November 13, 1995, p.62 and 64
6   *Los Angeles Times*, August 2, 1993, p.12
7   Mary Anne Weaver, "Blowback", *The Atlantic Monthly,* May 1996, p.28
8   *Washington Post*, September 6, 1996
9   *Los Angeles Times*, August 6, 1996, p.12
10   *New York Times*, March 8, 1995, p.12; March 9, p.6
11   *Los Angeles Times*, August 4, 1996, p.1
12   Ibid., p.17
13   *Slovo* (Russian daily newspaper published in New York), August 27, 1999;
      Los Angeles Times, August 4, 1996, p.1; *New York Times*, September 20,
      1999, p.9
14   *Los Angeles Times*, August 4, 1996, p.1
15   *New York Times Magazine*, March 13, 1994, p.54
16   Ibid.
17   Ibid.; *Los Angeles Times*, August 2, 1993, p.12
18   *Los Angeles Times*, August 4, 1996
19   Ibid., March 7, 1992, p.14 and August 5, 1996
20   Ibid., August 5, 1996, p.11
21   Weaver, *Atlantic Monthly,* op. cit.; *Los Angeles Times*, August 6, 1996,
      p.11

22　　*Washington Post*, May 26, 1996
23　　Ibid., August 28, 1999, p.14
24　　*Los Angeles Times*, August 4, 1996, p.2

Chapter Three

1　　Amnesty International, in a report of January 17, 1994, entitled "KUWAIT: Three years of unfair trials" (AI Index: MDE 17/01/94), states that it "expressed its concern on 1 July 1993 that the trial of 14 defendants, 12 of whom face the possibility of death sentences, accused of participation in an alleged assassination attempt on former United States President George Bush, failed to satisfy international minimum standards." The report makes repeated references to the use of torture by the Kuwaiti government of people accused of collaboration with the occupying Iraqis in 1990. The subsequent convictions and "confession" of one of the Bush-case defendants may be seen in this context.
See also *The Guardian* (London), June 29, 1993, p.9 and June 7, 1994, p.9 for further discussion of the questions surrounding the arrests and trial.
2　　*Washington Post*, June 27, 1993
3　　*Sunday Times* (London), July 6, 1975, p.1. Narut at the time was working at a US naval hospital in Naples, Italy, and made his remarks at a NATO-sponsored conference held in Oslo, Norway the week before.
4　　The Select Committee to Study Governmental Operations with Respect to Intelligence Activities (US Senate), *Interim Report: Alleged Assassination Plots Involving Foreign Leaders*, November 20, 1975, p.285
5　　*Los Angeles Times*, October 5, 1988, "CIA Reportedly Got 'License to Kill' Terrorists"
6　　*Washington Post*, October 5, 1988, summarizes some of Reagan's executive orders
7　　*Los Angeles Times*, October 14, 1989, p.16
8　　Council on Foreign Relations study, http://cfrterrorism.org/policy/assassination.html
9　　Ibid.
10　　William Corson, *The Armies of Ignorance* (New York, 1977), p.347

Chapter Four

1　　Part of a May 23, 1997 release by the CIA of 1,400 pages of classified documents concerning the 1954 coup in Guatemala. It is 20 pages long.

2   One of seven manuals from the Army's Foreign Intelligence Assistance Program, entitled "Project X"; written originally in English in the mid-1960s, later translated into Spanish; provided to Latin American and other Third World countries' military intelligence trainees; also used at School of the Americas; in use until at least 1991; various paragraphs in the original texts were revised by the Pentagon during the 1970s and 80s; released to the public by the Pentagon, September 20, 1996.

3   Another of the seven manuals referred to in note 2.

4   Inter Press Service (a well-known and respected Third World news agency headquartered in Rome), March 10, 1997, on the internet

5   KUBARK was a code name used by the CIA, with no particular significance. This is a Vietnam-era training manual, written for use by Americans against the enemy, not for training foreign military services. Also see *New York Times*, February 9, 1997

6   Much of the material in this manual derives from the KUBARK manual, discussed above. Both HRETM and KUBARK were declassified January 24, 1997. They deal exclusively with interrogation. The Pentagon has stated that HRETM was altered in 1984-85 to discourage torture. This was after a furor was raised in Congress and the press about CIA training techniques used in Central America. For further excerpts see *Baltimore Sun*, January 27, 1997 and the website of School of the Americas Watch -- http://www.soaw.org

7   For a complete list of the methods of sabotage, see Holly Sklar, *Washington's War on Nicaragua* (Boston, 1988), p.183-4. For some of the illustrations and Spanish text, see *Covert Action Information Bulletin* (Washington, DC), #22, Fall 1984, p.28

8   *New York Times*, October 17, 1984, p.1 and 12; Sklar, p.177-87

9   Sklar, 186

Chapter Five

1   *Baltimore Sun*, June 11, 1995, p.10A

2   *Washington Post*, August 3, 1999, p.10

3   James Becket, *Barbarism in Greece* (New York, 1970), p.xi

4   Article 2, S2. The convention was proposed in 1984, put in force 1987, ratified by the United States 1994

5   *Baltimore Sun*, op. cit.

6   Amnesty International, *Report on Torture* (London 1973), p.77

7   Becket, op. cit., p. 15

8   Becket, op. cit., p.16, see also p.127

9   Kermit Roosevelt, *Countercoup: The Struggle for the Control of Iran*
        (McGraw-Hill paperback, 1981), p.9.   Roosevelt was a CIA officer
        operating in Iran in the 1950s.
10   Leaf was chief CIA analyst on Iran for five years before resigning in 1973,
        interviewed by Seymour Hersh in the *New York Times*, January 7, 1979.
11   Robert Fisk, article in *The Independent* (London), August 9, 1998, p.19
12   Thomas Powers, *The Man Who Kept the Secrets: Richard Helms and the
        CIA* (Pocket Books, New York, 1979) p.155, 157
13   Donald Duncan, *The New Legions* (London, 1967) p.156-9; Duncan
        describes the Green Beret "interrogation" class he was in.
14   David Wise, "Colby of CIA -- CIA of Colby", *New York Times Magazine*,
        July 1, 1973, p.33-4
15   Telford Taylor, *Nuremberg and Vietnam: an American Tragedy* (New York
        Times, 1970), p.148-53
16   Richard Harris, *Death of a Revolutionary: Che Guevara's Last Mission*
        (New York, 1970) p.185-6
17   A.J. Langguth, *Hidden Terrors* (New York, 1978) p.285-7; (Langguth
        was Saigon Bureau Chief for the *New York Times* in 1965); also see *New
        York Times*, August 15, 1970
18   Langguth, p.289
19   Manuel Hevia Cosculluela, *Pasaporte 11333: Ocho Años con la CIA*
        (Havana, 1978), p.284-7. Hevia was a Cuban agent who worked under
        cover with Mitrione in Uruguay.
20   *San Francisco Chronicle*, November 2, 1981
21   Langguth, passim; see index under "torture".
22   Allan Nairn, "C.I.A. Death Squad", *The Nation*, April 17, 1995, p.511-13
23   *Washington Post*, May 12, 1996, p.C1; *Los Angeles Times*, March 31,
        1995, p.4
24   From "Statement of Sister Dianne Ortiz, May 6, 1996", distributed by
        her supporters in Lafayette Park opposite the White House while she was
        conducting a silent vigil there.
25   *New York Times*, January 11, 1982, p.2.
26   The National Guardsman, identified only as "Manuel", was interviewed
        in the television documentary "Torture", produced and directed by
        Rex Bloomstein for Thames Television Ltd. (Great Britain) in 1986
        with the cooperation of Amnesty International. Video copy in author's
        possession.
27   *Baltimore* Sun, lengthy series of articles on US support for Battalion 316,
        June 11-20, 1995; and January 27, 1997, "Torture Was Taught By CIA";
        also see *New York Times*, October 24, 1998 and *The Nation*, November 10,

1997, p.20-22 (David Corn)

28 Philip Wheaton, *Panama Invaded* (New Jersey, 1992), p.14-15; this is from testimony recorded by the staff of the Central American Human Rights Center of San José, Costa Rica, taken in Panama on Jan. 29, 1990 from a Red Cross contact.

29 Readers can contact the author at bblum6@aol.com for the source of anything mentioned in this section. See also Karen Greenberg and Joshua Dratel, eds., *The Torture Papers: The Road to Abu Ghraib* (Cambridge University Press, New York, 2005); Steven Strasser, ed., *The Abu Ghraib Investigations* (New York, 2004); Seymour Hersh, "Torture at Abu Ghraib", *The New Yorker,* May 5, 2004; Human Rights Watch, *Getting Away with Torture* (April 2005)

30 Adapted from a remark by Kenneth Roth, Executive Director of Human Rights Watch

31 *Washington Post,* January 14, 2005, April 19, 2005, April 23, 2005 ("Top Army Officers Are Cleared in Abuse Cases")

32 Peter Beaumont, "Abu Ghraib abuse firms are rewarded", *The Observer* (London), January 16, 2005

33 White House press release, May 3, 2004

34 Associated Press, February 10, 2005

35 *Newsweek,* March 22, 1976, p.28 and 31

36 "Chicago Police Used Torture, Report Alleges", *Los Angeles Times,* February 8, 1992, p.1 and 14.

37 Holly Burkhalter, "Torture in U.S. Prisons", *The Nation,* July 3, 1995, p.17-18. Burkhalter at the time was the Washington director of Human Rights Watch.

38 See also "Torture in the United States" a 1998 report by The Coalition Against Torture and Racial Discrimination -- http://www.woatusa.org/ CAT/catreport/intro.html

39 *Washington Post,* October 28, 1996. The provision is part of the Antiterrorism and Effective Death Penalty Act of 1996.

40 *Los Angeles Times,* May 13, 1992; *Washington Post,* July 3, 1995

41 Associated Press, April 25, 2005

Chapter Six

1 See Interventions and other sections of this book. Also see Christopher Simpson, *Blowback* (New York, 1988), John Loftus, *The Belarus Secret* (New York, 1982), Martin Lee, *The Beast Reawakens* (Boston, 1997)

2 *Washington Post,* November 21, 1971, p.13

3   *Los Angeles Times*, September 13, 1988, p.19. For further discussion of this issue, see Russ Bellant, "Old Nazis and the New Right: The Republican Party and Fascists", *Covert Action Information Bulletin* (Washington, DC), #33, Winter 1990, p.27-31

Chapter Seven

1   *New York Times*, September 20, 1999, p.6
2   Course 0-47, taught at SOA while it was still in the Panama Canal Zone, Defense Department Document 5489, p.5, February 3, 1977, as cited in Penny Lernoux, *Cry of the People: The Struggle for Human Rights in Latin America -- The Catholic Church in Conflict With U.S. Policy,* (Penguin Books, New York, 1982), p.167n; for other course descriptions, see p.180-1, 471-3
3   *New York Times*, September 28, 1996, p.22
4   *Washington Post*, February 5, 1968
5   SOA Watch, http://www.soaw.org/new/
6   Mark Danner, *The Massacre at El Mozote* (Vintage Books, 1994)
7   *Washington Post*, November 16, 1999, p.31, op-ed column by Leo J. O'Donovan, S.J.
8   See the website of School of the Americas Watch -- http://www.soaw.org -- Also see *Covert Action Quarterly* (Washington, DC), #46, Fall 1993, p.15-19
9   February 8, 1990, before the Senate Committee on Armed Services
10   For further discussion, see Latin America Working Group (Washington, DC), *Just the Facts: A civilian's guide to U.S. defense and security assistance to Latin America and the Caribbean*, which tells everything one would want to know about training Latin militaries in the US and abroad -- bases, military exercises, human-rights restrictions, and much more; can be read in full at http://www.ciponline.org/facts
     Also see the excellent series in the *Washington Post,* July 12-14, as well as December 13 and 14, 1998
11   *New York Times*, November 18, 1999
12   Press release of School of the Americas Watch, March 25, 2004, http://www.soaw.org/
13   Michael Klare and Nancy Stein, "Police Terrorism in Latin America", *NACLA's Latin America and Empire Report* (North American Congress on Latin America, New York), January 1974, p.19-23, based on State Department documents obtained by Senator James Abourezk in 1973; ibid., July-August 1976, p.31; also see Jack Anderson, *Washington Post,*

October 8, 1973, p.C33; A.J. Langguth, *Hidden Terrors* (New York, 1978), p.242-3.

14   *New York Times*, January 23, 1975, p.38; January 26, 1975, p. 42; *NACLA*, op. cit., July-August 1976, p.31-2; Langguth, p.301.

15   See Lawrence Rockwood & Amelia Simpson, "Training the world's police", *Foreign Policy in Focus* report, Institute for Policy Studies (Washington, DC), 2000.

16   Thomas E. Skidmore, *Politics in Brazil, 1930-1964* (Oxford University Press, New York, 1967), p.330; also see James Kohl and John Litt, *Urban Guerrilla Warfare in Latin America* (The MIT Press, Cambridge, Mass., 1974), p.39, for further discussion of the strong pro-US, anti-leftist bias of the college's curriculum.

17   Phyllis R. Parker, *Brazil and the Quiet Intervention, 1964* (University of Texas Press, Austin, 1979) p.98, cable to State Department, March 4, 1964.

Chapter Eight

1   *The New Yorker*, June 19, 1995, p.48

2   *Washington Post*, December 4, 1996, p.1

3   Leonard A. Cole, *Clouds of Secrecy: The Army's Germ Warfare Tests over Populated Areas* (Maryland, 1990), p.12-14

4   *Washington Post*, September 21, 1999, p.1

5   United Nations General Assembly Resolution: "Establishment of a nuclear-weapon-free zone in the region of the Middle East", December 4, 1990, Resolution No. 45/52.

6   *New York Times*, January 24, 1991, p.11

7   *Ibid.*, March 23, 1991

8   Michael Bilton and Kevin Sim, *Four Hours in May Lai* (Viking, New York, 1992), p.175, 209-13

9   *LA Weekly* (Los Angeles), March 9-15, 1990, p.12

10   *New York Times,* January 9, 1971, p.3

11   Telford Taylor, *Nuremberg and Vietnam: an American Tragedy* (New York, 1970), p.140-43

12   *Far Eastern Economic Review* (Hong Kong), October 30, 1997, p.15, 20

13   *Sunday Telegraph* (London), July 18, 1999, interview with Pinochet

14   *Washington Post*, May 25, 1998, p.B4

15   This and most of the other material concerning the complaints to the Tribunal mentioned here were transmitted to the author by Mandel and other complainants.

16   Press Release from Chief Prosecutor Louise Arbour, The Hague, May 13, 1999.

17   *The Observer* (London), December 26, 1999; *Washington Times*, December 30 and 31, 1999; *New York Times*, December 30, 1999

18   *Washington Post*, May 24, 1999, p.1

19   *New York Times*, May 13, 1999, p.1

20   NATO press conference, Brussels, May 25, 1999

21   *Washington Post*, April 22, 1999, p.18

22   Ibid., September 20, 1999, p.1

23   *New York Times*, December 2, 1998, p.1; January 3, 2000

Chapter Nine

1   *The Miami Herald*, November 16, 1997.

2   *Washington Post,* August 27, 2004, April 13, 2005

3   *The Miami Herald*, March 26, 1983

4   Ann Louise Bardach, "Our Man's in Miami. Patriot or Terrorist?", *Washington Post*, April 17, 2005

5   CounterPunch Wire, June 11, 2004. Cuban television broadcast segments of the program, which had aired on Miami TV Channel 41.

6   Associated Press, Tampa, Fla., July 16, 1997

7   Unless otherwise indicated, information about the individual cases can be found in the following: *Miami Herald,* October 21, 1998, p.11A; *Boston Globe,* May 2,3 &4, 1999; press releases of The Center for Justice and Accountability (San Francisco) and the Center for Constitutional Rights (New York), which have been involved in lawsuits against several of the individuals named; *Covert Action Quarterly* (Washington, DC), #65, Fall 1998, p.45. The most current information can be found at the website of Center for Justice and Accountability -- www.cja.org/

8   Guatemalan Human Rights Commission (Washington, DC), *Human Rights Update*, April 21, 1995

9   Noam Chomsky, *Z Magazine*, March 1992, p.9, based on an interview given by Gramajo to the *Harvard International Review.*

10   EFE (Spanish news agency), dispatch from Miami, November 20, 1999

11   According to the Center for Justice and Accountability (San Francisco). These men have claimed that they themselves were victims of torture, by the North Vietnamese and/or the National Liberation Front. It was during their treatment in the US for this experience that they recounted their own culpability. The CJA does not wish to reveal their names because this information was obtained in a clinical setting.

12   *Los Angeles Times*, many articles throughout the 1980s and later; e.g., August 4, 1985, II, p.1; May 8, 1986, II, p.1; October 17, 1987, II, p.8 (editorial); March 24, 1990, p.33; see also Asia Resource Center (Washington, DC), "Vietnamese Death Squads in America? A Casebook", in *Asia Insights*, Summer 1986, passim

13   *New York Times*, September 22, 1998, p.12

14   This discussion is derived from "Torture in the United States", a paper produced by the World Organization Against Torture, USA (Washington, DC) -- now known as The World Organization For Human Rights, USA -- October 1998, part 7, "Extraditions", written by Neil Tow.

15   *Washington Post*, February 5, 1997, p.28

16   Associated Press, February 7, 1999

Chapter Ten

1   For an overview, see John Pilger, "The Long Secret Alliance: Uncle Sam and Pol Pot", *Covert Action Quarterly* (Washington, DC), #62, Fall 1997, p.5-9; Philip Short, *Pol Pot: An Anatomy of a Nightmare* (New York, 2004), p.420-21; plus other sources listed below.

2   Elizabeth Becker, *When the War Was Over: Cambodia and the Khmer Rouge Revolution* (Public Affairs, NY, 1998), p.435

3   *Los Angeles Times*, December 5, 1980, I-B, p.1

4   Linda Mason and Roger Brown, *Rice, Rivalry and Politics: Managing Cambodian Relief* (Univ. of Notre Dame Press, 1983), p.135-6

5   William Shawcross, *The Quality of Mercy: Cambodia, Holocaust and Modern Conscience* (London, 1984), p.289, 395

6   *New York Times*, November 16, 1989, p.16

7   *Washington Post*, July 8, 1985, p.18

8   *Newsweek*, October 10, 1983, p.41

9   *Los Angeles Times*, February 27, 1991

10   *San Francisco Examiner*, August 12, 1990, p.18

11   *Los Angeles Times*, February 27, 1991

12   *Washington Post*, September 5, 1995

13   Jack Colhoun, "U.S. Supports Khmer Rouge", *Covert Action Information Bulletin* (Washington, DC), #34, Summer 1990, p.37-40; *Washington Post*, January 10, 1999, op-ed by Peter Goodman; *New York Times*, October 18, 1989, p.29

14   *Weekly Compilation of Presidential Documents* (GPO), April 16, 1998, p.663

Chapter Eleven

1   *The Nation*, September 26, 1994, p.304
2   RFE/RL Newsline, April 9, 2003 (Radio Free Europe/Radio Liberty is a "private" international communications service in Europe and Asia funded by the US government.)
3   *Washington Post*, January 1, 2003, Australian Broadcasting Company, January 1, 2003, Agence France Presse, September 19, 2003
4   Associated Press, "France Confirms It Denied U.S. Jets Air Space, Says Embassy Damaged", April 15, 1986
5   U.S. Commission on National Security/21st Century, *New World Coming* (Phase I Report), September 15, 1999, p.3
6   *Journal of the American Medical Association*, August 25, 1999, p.761

Chapter Twelve

1   Marc. W. Herold, professor, University of New Hampshire, "Uranium Wars: The Pentagon Steps Up Its Use of Radioactive Munitions", www.cursor.org/stories/uranium.htm. Given the propensity of the Taliban and other opponents of the US occupation of Afghanistan to use mountains, caves, and underground bunkers for concealment, the use by American forces of DU to blast through such fortifications was to be expected.
2   International Action Center (New York), *Metal of Dishonor: Depleted Uranium*, p.3-40, 134-149 and elsewhere for a detailed discussion of the properties of DU, its health dangers, and the circumstances under which US military personnel and Iraqis may have been exposed to it; p.140-44 for a discussion of the airborne transport of uranium particles.
    See also *The Bulletin of the Atomic Scientists*, November/December 1999, p.42-5, and *Radioactive Battlefields of the 1990s: The United States Army's Use of Depleted Uranium and Its Consequences for Human Health and the Environment*, by the Depleted Uranium Citizens' Network (of the Military Toxics Project), Lewiston, ME, January 16, 1996; www.antenna.nl/wise/uranium/dmtp.html
3   Bill Mesler, "The Pentagon's Radioactive Bullet", *The Nation* (New York), October 21, 1996, p.12-13.
4   *The Washington Report on Middle East Affairs*, July/August 1995
5   Ibid.
6   *New York Daily News*, April 3, 2004, column by Juan Gonzalez; *The Army Times* (Virginia), April 9, 2004, article by Jane McHugh
7   *Sunday Herald* (Glasgow, Scotland), April 4, 1999

8   *Washington Post*, May 29, 1999, August 19, 1999, May 11, 2003
9   "Recent Military Accidents In Vieques, Puerto Rico", paper prepared by
        the office of Puerto Rico's Congressional representative, Carlos Romero-
        Barceló, May 1999; *Orlando Sentinel* (Orlando, Florida), May 1, 1999,
        p.18; Pacifica Radio, "Democracy Now", July 21, 1999
10   *The Albuquerque Tribune*, January 26, 1994, p.A1; *Uranium Battlefields
        Home & Abroad: Depleted Uranium Use by the U.S. Department of
        Defense*, March 1993, a joint publication of various environmental and
        community organizations in New Mexico; U.S. Army Environmental
        Policy Institute, *Health and Environmental Consequences of Depleted
        Uranium Use in the U.S. Army: Technical Report*, June 1995, Appendix
        B
11   *Radioactive Battlefields*, op. cit., p.3

Chapter Thirteen

1   Rachel Stohl, "Cluster Bombs Leave Lasting Legacy", report of the Center
        for Defense Information (Washington, DC), August 5, 1999.
2   Handicap International (European NGO, co-winner of the 1997 Nobel
        Peace Prize), "The dangers of cluster munitions", www.handicap-
        international.org.uk
3   *Washington Post*, August 3, 1999
4   *Christian Science Monitor*, June 9, 1999, p.11
5   Ibid.
6   *The Guardian* (London), June 23, 1999, p.12
7   Rachel Stohl, op. cit.
8   Paul Watson, "Unexploded Weapons Pose Deadly Threat on the Ground",
        Los Angeles Times, April 28, 1999, p.5
9   Handicap International, "Living with UXO [Unexploded Ordnance]",
        1997. See also International Committee of the Red Cross, "Explosive
        Remnants of War: The Lethal Legacy of Modern Armed Conflict," June
        2003, p.6.
10   From a paper entitled "Cluster Munitions: Toward a Global Solution", by
        Steve Goose of Human Rights Watch, January 2004.
        For further information on cluster bombs, see:
        a) Human Rights Watch website -- http://www.hrw.org/ -- (go to "Arms")
        b) Marc Herold, "Steel Rain: An analysis of Cluster Bomb use by the US
        in four recent campaigns", found at: http://cursor.org/stories/archivistan.
        htm
        c) Marc Herold, *Blown Away: The Myth and Reality of Precision Bombing*

(Common Courage Press, 2004)
d) Cluster Munitions Coalition: http://www.cmc-international.org/

Chapter Fourteen

1   Robert Harris and Jeremy Paxman, *A Higher Form of Killing: The Secret Story of Gas and Germ Warfare* (London, 1982), p.xi

2   Leonard A. Cole, *Clouds of Secrecy: The Army's Germ Warfare Tests over Populated Areas* (Maryland, 1990), p.18

3   *Baltimore Sun*, August 15, 1980, p.7

4   Stephen Endicott and Edward Hagerman, *The United States and Biological Warfare: Secrets from the Early Cold War and Korea* (Indiana University Press, 1998), p.166-7
     In January 1998, a Japanese newspaper claimed to have a dozen documents from a Moscow archive that suggested that the Chinese claims about biological warfare were no more than a hoax initiated by the Soviets. (Ibid., p.248-9) But this counter-claim raises as many questions as it answers, not the least of which is why has the mammoth US publicity machine not said a word about this incredibly advantageous "find"? Nor has Washington apparently asked the Russians to open the archives so the documents can be authenticated. For a discussion of this issue, see the review of the Endicott and Hagerman book by Peter Pringle in *The Nation*, May 3, 1999, p.29-32.

5   Endicott and Hagerman, op. cit., p.xi, 49-50, 218

6   *San Francisco Chronicle*, October 8, 1979, p.13; *Washington Post*, October 9, 1979, p.6

7   Endicott and Hagerman, op. cit., p. 63

8   *San Francisco Chronicle*, April 24, 1980; *Washington Post*, November 17, 1999

9   The Michigan Agent Orange Commission, *Physician's Information for Care of Vietnam Veterans Exposed to Agent Orange and Other Chemicals*, June 1991, p.4-8; Harris and Paxman, p.192-3.

10   According to Dr. Barry Commoner, director of the Center for Biology of Natural Systems at Washington University, St. Louis, *The Guardian* (London), February 17, 1984.

11   Robert Dreyfuss, "Apocalypse Still", *Mother Jones* magazine (San Francisco), February 2000, p.42ff

12   James Ridgeway, *Village Voice*, Feb. 5, 1991, p.30; *New York Times*, September 9, 1965

13   John Cookson and Judith Nottingham, *A Survey of Chemical and*

Biological Warfare (London, 1969), p.15-17

14   Ibid., p.30

15   April Oliver and Peter Arnett, "Did the U.S. Drop Nerve Gas?", *Time*, June 15, 1998, p.37-9

16   *The Washington Post Magazine*, November 29, 1998, p.20 ff.

17   "Tailwind: Rebuttal to the Abrams/Kohler Report", July 22, 1998, can be found on the Internet.

18   John Lindsay-Poland, "Toxic Aftertaste", *The Progressive*, (Madison, Wisconsin), December 1998, p. 24-27; see also *Washington Post*, January 10, 2000, p.14-5

19   *The Dallas Morning News*, August 20, 1999

20   Philip Wheaton, *Panama Invaded* (New Jersey, 1992), p.16-17, citing the monthly magazine *El Periódico* (Panama City), February 1990, p.8, "Bombardean Pacora con substancias quimicas".

21   *New York Times*, April 28, 1966, p.1.

22   Taylor Branch and George Crile III, "The Kennedy Vendetta", *Harper's* magazine (New York), August 1975, p.52

23   *Washington Post*, March 21, 1977, p.A18.

24   Warren Hinckle and William Turner, *The Fish is Red: The Story of the Secret War Against Castro* (Harper & Row, New York, 1981), p.293, based on their interview with the participant in Ridgecrest, California, September 27, 1975.

25   *San Francisco Chronicle*, January 10, 1977.

26   Bill Schaap, "The 1981 Cuba Dengue Epidemic", *Covert Action Information Bulletin* (Washington, DC), No. 17, Summer 1982, p.28-31

27   Reported on their website: www.cdc.gov/ncidod/dvbid/dengue/index.htm#history

28   Jane Franklin, *Cuba and the United States: A Chronological History* (Ocean Press, Melbourne and New York, 1997), p.170. This book states that 188 people died from the dengue epidemic (p.174)

29   *San Francisco Chronicle*, October 29, 1980, p.15

30   *Science* (American Association for the Advancement of Science, Washington, DC), January 13, 1967, p.176

31   *Covert Action Information Bulletin* (Washington, DC), No. 22, Fall 1984, p.35, the trial of Eduardo Victor Arocena Perez, Federal District Court for the Southern District of New York, transcript of September 10, 1984, p.2187-89.

32   For further details of the State Department's side of the issue, see *New York Times*, May 7, 1997, p.9

33   Response to author's query, July 29, 1997, by FAA spokesperson Hank

Price.

34　　UN General Assembly document A/52/128, April 29, 1997

35　　Human Rights Watch report on CBW, 1999.

36　　See, e.g., *San Francisco Chronicle*, July 27, 1981.

37　　*Washington Post*, September 16, 1977, p.2

38　　Aljazeera.com, March 4, 2005. The press conference was attended by more than 20 Iraqi and foreign media networks, including the *Washington Post* and the Knight-Ridder service.

39　　*Los Angeles Times*, June 18, 1990, p.1

40　　There's an abundance of documentation of this. See, e.g., Seth Shulman, *The Threat at Home: Confronting the Toxic Legacy of the U.S. Military* (Beacon Press, Boston, 1992), passim.

Chapter Fifteen

1　　*New York Times*, January 22, 1999, p.12

2　　*Biological Testing Involving Human Subjects by the Department of Defense, 1977*, Hearings before the Subcommittee on Health and Scientific Research of the Committee on Human Resources, US Senate, March 8 and May 23, 1977, p.270

3　　Leonard A. Cole, *Clouds of Secrecy: The Army's Germ Warfare Tests over Populated Areas* (Maryland, 1990), chapter 1

4　　*San Francisco Chronicle*, October 8, 1979, p.13; *Washington Post*, October 9, 1979, p.6; *Scientific American,* June 1999, p.70-75

5　　Cole, chapters 7 and 8; *San Francisco Examiner,* December 22, 1976, p.1; December 23, 1976, p.1; September 17, 1979, p.3; October 19, 1980

6　　Cole, Appendix 3, p.170

7　　Associated Press, March 18, 2005

8　　*San Francisco Chronicle,* December 22, 1976, p.1; April 3, 1981, p.12

9　　Ibid., April 3, 1981; *Baltimore Sun*, August 15, 1980, p.7; Cole, p.60-64

10　　Cole, p.63-65

11　　*Washington Post*, June 9, 1980, p.11

12　　*San Francisco Chronicle*, October 14, 1980, p.12

13　　Airport and White House: *Washington Post*, December 5, 1984, p.B1

14　　*New York Times*, September 19, 1975, p. 14

15　　*San Francisco Chronicle*, December 17, 1979, p.5

16　　For details of this experiment and the scientists' objections, see Leonard Cole, *The Eleventh Plague* (New York, 1997), p.28-31, based on US Army Chemical Corps, *Summary of Major Events and Problems*, fiscal year 1959, p.101-3; see also *San Francisco Chronicle,* October 29, 1980, p.15

17   *San Francisco Chronicle*, December 4, 1979, p.12

18   Cole, *Clouds of Secrecy*, p.65-9

19   *New York Times*, September 19, 1975, p.14

20   *Washington Post*, December 5, 1984, p.B1

21   *Biological Testing* ... , op. cit., p.134. A lengthy list of the open-air CBW testing locations (but without details) can be found on pages 124-140, although for some reason the list doesn't include the occasions where zinc cadmium sulfide was used.

22   Department of Defense "Fact Sheets" released in 2001-2; see this site and related links: www.deploymentlink.osd.mil/current_issues/shad/shad_intro.shtml; Also see Associated Press, October 9, 2002

23   *New York Times*, May 24, 2002

24   Associated Press, October 9, 2002

25   Article by Williscroft, April 10, 2002

26   US General Accounting Office (GAO), *Nuclear Health and Safety: Examples of Post World War II Radiation Releases at U.S. Nuclear Sites,* November 1993, passim.

27   Senate Committee on Veterans' Affairs, *Is Military Research Hazardous to Veterans' Health? Lessons Spanning Half a Century*, December 8, 1994, passim

      US General Accounting Office (GAO), *Human Experimentation: An Overview on Cold War Era Programs*, September 28, 1994, passim;

      Final Report of the Senate Select Committee to Study Governmental Operations with Respect to Intelligence Activities (The Church Committee), Book 1, *Foreign and Military Intelligence,* April, 1976, p.385-422

      Eileen Welsome, *The Plutonium Files: America's Secret Medical Experiments in the Cold War*, (New York, 1999) passim

      Jonathan Moreno, *Undue Risk: Secret State Experiments on Humans* (W.H. Freeman & Co., 1999), passim

      John Marks, *The Search for the 'Manchurian Candidate': The CIA and Mind Control* (Dell, New York, 1979), passim

      Martin Cannon, "Mind Control and the American Government", *Lobster* magazine (Hull, England), #23, 1992, p.2-10

      Aaron Epstein, "At Holmesburg Prison, 320 human guinea pigs", *Philadelphia Inquirer,* November 25, 1979, p.1 ff.

28   From a review of *The Plutonium Files*, op. cit., by Deborah Nelson, *Bookworld (Washington Post),* November 21, 1999, based on chapter 22 of the book.

29   *Washington Post*, June 9, 1999

30 Hearings before a House Subcommittee of the Committee on Appropriations, "Department of Defense Appropriations for 1970"

Chapter Sixteen

1 Jack Anderson, *Washington Post*, October 25, 1969, p.F11; *Washington Post*, April 14, 1998
2 *Los Angeles Times*, August 1, 1998
3 *Covert Action Quarterly* (Washington, DC), #63, Winter 1998, p. 29
4 *U.S. Chemical and Biological Warfare-Related Dual Use Exports to Iraq and their Possible Impact on the Health Consequences of the Persian Gulf War*, Senate Committee on Banking, Housing and Urban Affairs with Respect to Export Administration, reports of May 25, 1994 and October 7, 1994.
5 Amy E. Smithson, "Rudderless: The Chemical Weapons Convention at 1 1/2", published September 1998 by the Henry L. Stimson Center (Washington, DC), as part of their Chemical and Biological Weapons Nonproliferation Project; the report or an Executive Summary of it can be read at: www.stimson.org/pubs.cfm?ID=28

Chapter Seventeen

1 *Imperialism and Social Classes*, (1955, first published in 1919), p.51
2 *America and the World Revolution and Other Lectures* (Oxford University Press, New York, 1962), p.92-3
3 Alfred W. McCoy, *The Politics of Heroin: CIA Complicity in the Global Drug Trade* (Lawrence Hill Books, NY, 1991), p.54-63; Sallie Pisani, *The CIA and the Marshall Plan* (University Press of Kansas, 1991), p.99-105 and elsewhere
4 *New York Times*, May 5, 1947, p.1; May 11, IV, p.5; May 14, p.14 and 24; May 17, p.8; May 18, IV, p.4; May 20, p.2; Howard K. Smith, *The State of Europe* (London, 1950), p.151 (includes Ramadier quote; similar quote in *New York Times*, May 20).
5 *The Guardian* (London), November 29, 1983
6 *Washington Post*, September 30, 1999, p.1; October 14, p.14; December 29, p.19
7 Stewart Steven, *Operation Splinter Factor* (London 1974), passim. For those familiar with the story, it will be of interest that under the Freedom of Information Act the author received a document from the CIA which

reveals that the State Department knew about Noel Field's imprisonment in Hungary for almost the entire five years it was publicly claiming it had no knowledge of his fate.

8   Operation Gladio: Daniele Ganser, *NATO's Secret Armies: Operation Gladio and Terrorism in Western Europe* (Frank Cass Publishers, London, 2005)

9   *Washington Post*, November 14, 1999, for some aspects of the situation at that time; also see *Amnesty International Annual Report* for Guatemala 1997, 1998, 1999 on AI's website; and the *Washington Post*, April 13, 2005 for how little has changed.

10 *New York Times*, April 29, 1959, p.1

11 See John Gerassi, *The Coming of the New International* (New York, 1971), p.245-56, for an overview of the situation, including a long "self-criticism" by the Iraqi Communist Party.

12 Claudia Wright, *New Statesman* magazine (London), July 15, 1983, p.20. She doesn't say how the Soviets found out about the plan.

13 *Los Angeles Times*, April 14, 1991, p.M1

14 *Le Monde* (France), February 5, 1963, p.5

15 Roger Morris (former member of the National Security Council under Presidents Johnson and Nixon), *New York Times*, March 14, 2003; United Press International (UPI), April 10, 2003

16 State Department statement: *Christian Science Monitor*, February 13, 1963, p.3

17 *The Guardian* (London), January 1, 1994, p.5

18 Ralph McGehee, *Deadly Deceits: My 25 years in the CIA* (New York, 1983), passim. McGehee spent much of his CIA career in Thailand; The Committee of Concerned Asian Scholars, *The Indochina Story* (Random House, New York, 1970), p.64-69; New *York Times*, November 27, 1966, p.4; *Washington Post*, November 20, 1966, p.22; December 7, 1966.

19 *Washington Post*, August 23, 1966

20 Bush quote: *Washington Post*, May 21, 1997, column by Nora Boustany

21 Based on a Dave Barry line

22 CIA internal memorandum of February 25, 1966, declassified March 7, 1977, received by the author as a result of a Freedom of Information Act (FOIA) request.

23 Cable News Network en Español, July 23, 1998; *El Diario-La Prensa* (New York) July 24, 1998; *Clarin* (Buenos Aires) July 22, 1998, p.45

24 Numbers of victims: *New York Times*, January 3, 2000

25 FBI: *New York Times*, February 10, 1999, p.6; Kissinger: US government document, 1976, described in article by Lucy Komisar, *The Progressive*

(Madison, Wisconsin), May 1999

26   *New York Times*, July 23 1986, p.1; *Baltimore Sun*, November 12, 1995, p.1D; *Covert Action Information Bulletin* (Washington, DC), #12, April 1981, p.24-27; William Minter, *Apartheid's Contras* (London, 1994), chapter 6 and passim. See also "Mandela" and "United Nations" chapters herein.

27   Staff Report of the Select Committee on Intelligence, US House of Representatives, 1975, "the Pike Report". This report can be read in book form: *CIA -- The Pike Report* (Spokesman Books, Nottingham, England, 1977), p.56, 195-8, 211-17

28   *Washington Post*, October 9, 1974, p.36; *New York Times*, September 25, 1975, p.1; Evans and Novak column in *Washington Post*, October 26, 1974, p.19 (NATO information); *Facts on File*, March 1, 1975, p.131 (NATO exercises). Also see the Elections chapter under Portugal.

29   For a detailed history of the East Timor question, 1975-78, see Noam Chomsky and Edward S. Herman, *The Washington Connection and Third World Fascism, Volume I* (Boston, 1979), p.129-204

30   Daniel Moynihan with Suzanne Weaver, *A Dangerous Place* (Boston, 1978), p.247.

31   Allan Nairn, "US Complicity in Timor", *The Nation* (New York), September 27, 1999, p.5-6; "U.S. trained butchers of Timor", *The Observer* (London), September 19, 1999

32   *New York Times*, October 31, 1995, p.3. The official was described as someone who deals often on Asia policy. He apparently was referring to Suharto in terms of economic policy, but to make such a remark about a man with the blood of a million or more people on his hands does say something about one's political ideology.

33   Holly Sklar, *Washington's War on Nicaragua* (South End Press, Boston, 1988), see "Honduras" in index; Philip Wheaton, *Inside Honduras: Regional Counterinsurgency Base* (Ecumenical Program in Central America and the Caribbean [EPICA], Washington, DC, 1982), passim

34   *New York Times*, May 25, 1988, p.8

35   See Elections chapter under Nicaragua

36   Dianna Melrose, *Nicaragua: The Threat of a Good Example?* (Oxfam, Oxford, UK, 1985), p.14

37   *San Francisco Examiner*, March 22, 1987, p.1

38   *New York Times*, December 2, 1989, p.1

39   *Los Angeles Times*, September 28, 1991

40   *Sunday Tribune* (Durban, South Africa), November 29, 1981, p.1 and 52

41   "60 Minutes", CBS, June 15, 2003; Mark Curtis, *The Guardian* (London),

October 10, 2003; Jacques Duplouich, *Le Figaro* (France), June 22, 2004; John Pilger, *The Guardian* (London), October 2, 2004

42   Bob Woodward, *VEIL: The Secret Wars of the CIA 1981-1987* (New York, 1987), p.78-9, 124-5, 215; *New York Times*, April 8, 1982, p.3

43   Fred Halliday, "Russians help to beat leftwing guerrillas", *The Guardian* (London), May 3, 1984, p.7; *New York Times*, March 19, 1980, p.1

44   *New York Times*, May 23, 1980, p.1

45   *The Milwaukee Journal,* August 12, 1980, based on the observations of three American Peace Corps workers in South Korea. Two of the three wrote an article on the events in Korea for *Covert Action Information Bulletin* (Washington, DC), #11, December 1980, p.9-15

46   State Department quote: *The Milwaukee Journal, op. cit.* For an overall discussion of the US relationship to South Korea and the 1980 uprising, see Tim Shorrock, "Debacle in Kwangju", *The Nation,* December 9,1996, p.19-22; *Washington Post*, March 5, 1996, p.5; Bill Mesler, "Korea and the US: Partners in Repression", *Covert Action Quarterly* (Washington, DC), #56, Spring 1996, p.53- 57

47   *New York Times*, February 2, 1981, p.8; February 3, p.6

48   Woodward, p.96-7, 157-58, 215; Jonathan Bearman, *Qadhafi's Libya* (Zed Books, London, 1986), p.216-225

49   *New York Times*, February 11, 2000, p.30, editorial

50   See the author's essay on this subject, "The Bombing of PanAm Flight 103: Case Not Closed", at: http://members.aol.com/bblum6/panam.htm

51   Speech at the Pacific Islands Luncheon, Kahala Hilton Hotel, Hawaii, February 10, 1982, cited in a September 1989 paper, "Possible Foreign Involvement in the Fiji Military Coup", p.2, by Owen Wilkes, editor of *Peacelink* and *Wellington Pacific Report,* both of New Zealand.

52   Ibid, p.6-7

53   *The Nation*, August 15/22, 1987, p.117-20; *San Francisco Chronicle*, June 17, 1987; *The National Reporter* (Washington, DC), Fall 1987, p.33-38; *Covert Action Information Bulletin* (Washington, DC), #29, Fall 1987, p.7-10

54   *The Sydney Morning Herald* (Australia), May 16, 1987, p.1

55   The Independent Commission of Inquiry on the U.S. Invasion of Panama, *The U.S. Invasion of Panama: The Truth Behind Operation 'Just Cause'* (South End Press, Boston, 1991), passim; Philip Wheaton, ed., *Panama Invaded* (The Red Sea Press, New Jersey, 1992), passim; in addition to the chapter in *Killing Hope.*

56   Inducing the Soviet intervention: See Brzezinski's remarks in the Introduction. Also, Robert Gates (former CIA Director), *From the*

Shadows (New York, 1996), p.178 -- "[President] Carter began numerous covert actions to counter Soviet advances ... Well before the invasion of Afghanistan, he approved intelligence findings aimed at countering the Soviets ... [in] Afghanistan."

57   *Washington Post*, November 23, 1999

58   National Endowment for Democracy, Washington, DC, *Annual Report, 1990* (October 1, 1989-September 30, 1990), p.23-4.

59   Ibid., 1991, p.41-43

60   *Los Angeles Times*, June 13, 1991, p.14

61   National Endowment for Democracy, Washington, DC, *Annual Report, 1991* (October 1, 1990 - September 30, 1991), p.42

62   *Los Angeles Times*, March 9, 1992, p.14

63   Alex de Waal, "US War Crimes in Somalia", *New Left Notes* (London), July/August, 1998; Stephen Shalom, "Gravy Train: Feeding the Pentagon by Feeding Somalia", November 1993, at www.zmag.org/zmag/articles/shalomsomalia.html; *Los Angeles Times (*oil companies*)*, January 18, 1993, p.1; *Washington Post*, October 6, 1993; Mark Bowden, *Black Hawk Down* (1999), passim

64   *Washington Post,* June 24, 1996

65   *The Dallas Morning News*, March 18, 1998. For greater discussion of this and other aspects of the US intervention in Colombia, see the Colombia Support Network website: www.colombiasupport.net

66   *Miami* Herald, October 7, 1997, p.8a; *Washington Post*, February 24, 2000, p.1

67   *New York Times*, November 11, 1998, p.24

68   *Washington Post*, October 4, 1997

69   National Security Archive Update, August 2, 2004, "U.S. intelligence listed Colombian president Uribe among 'important Colombian narco-traffickers' in 1991." Find it at: www.gwu.edu/~nsarchiv/

70   CNN.com, August 27, 2000

71   Associated Press, May 5, 2005

72   *Washington Post,* February 18, 1999

73   *Amnesty Action* (AIUSA, NY), Winter 1997, p.1 and 8, reiterating the details of the 1994 report; *Washington Post*, March 30, 2004

74   *Colombia Bulletin: A Human Rights Quarterly* (Colombia Support Network, Madison Wisconsin), Spring 1997, p.29, article by Carlos Salinas of Amnesty International.

75   *Public Papers of the Presidents of the United States* (Government Printing Office), 1996, Vol. I, p.614, April 21

76   *New York Times*, March 21, 1999, p.1. "Ethnic cleansing" is what it was

labeled by the International Criminal Tribunal for the Former Yugoslavia.

77   *Washington Post*, November 8, 1998, p.3

78   *The Independent* (London), April 24, 1999, p.1

79   Ibid.

80   *Washington Post*, January 23, 2000, p.1; World Socialist Web Site -- www. wsws.org/ -- "The coup in Ecuador: a grim warning", February 2, 2000; Z Magazine (Massachusetts), February 2001, p.36-7

81   See, e.g., testimony of John Maresca, Unocal Corporation, before the Subcommittee on Asia and the Pacific, of the House Committee on International Relations, February 12, 1998

82   *New York Times*, March 2, 2003, Section 4, p.2

83   *New York Times*, November 3, 2001

84   *Washington Post*, February 23, 2002, p.18

85   *Financial Times* (London), September 26, 2001

86   *Washington Post*, April 13, 2002, p.1

87   Ibid.

88   Ibid., p.17

89   State Department press statement, April 12, 2002

90   *The Times* (London), April 17, 2002; *Washington Post*, April 17, 2002, p.8, April 18, p.17 ($100,000)

91   *Washington Post*, April 21, 2002, p.1

92   Ibid., April 14, 2002, p.1

93   National Endowment for Democracy, *Annual Report* 2000, 2001, 2002

94   Statement of Jean-Bertrand Aristide, March 5, 2004, from exile in the Central African Republic, Pacific News Service (San Francisco), same date.

95   Cox News Service, March 1, 2005

Chapter Eighteen

1   *Miami Herald*, October 17, 1997, p.22A

2   Joseph Burkholder Smith (former CIA officer), *Portrait of a Cold Warrior* (New York, 1976), chapters 7, 15, 16, 17; Raymond Bonner, *Waltzing With a Dictator: The Marcoses and the Making of American Policy* (New York, 1987), p.39-42; *New York Times* editorial, October 16, 1953, p.26

3   David Wise and Thomas Ross, *The Invisible Government* (New York, 1965,) p.337; Wilbur Crane Eveland, *Ropes of Sand: America's Failure in the Middle East* (W.W. Norton & Co., New York, 1980), p.249-50

4   Smith, p.210-11

5   Dwight Eisenhower, *The White House Years: Mandate for Change, 1953-*

1956 (New York, 1963), p.372

6   *The Guardian* (London), December 28, 1984, for a detailed description of the raw cynicism behind the policy to oust Jagan, based on British government documents released in 1984; *The Times* (London), October 7 and 10, 1953; *The Sunday Times* (London), April 16 and 23, 1967.

7   *New York Times*, October 9, 1994, p.1, March 31, 1997, p.11; *Los Angeles Times*, March 20, 1995, p.5

8   *Washington Post*, January 24, 1997

9   Duane Clarridge with Digby Diehl, *A Spy For All Seasons: My Life in the CIA* (New York, 1997), p.64-6. Clarridge went on to become a high official in the CIA.

10   *New York Times*, April 25, 1966, p.20.

11   Philip Agee, *Inside the Company: CIA Diary* (New York, 1975), p.321; A.J. Langguth, *Hidden Terrors* (New York, 1978) p.92

12   John Bartlow Martin, *Overtaken by Events: The Dominican Crisis From the Fall of Trujillo to the Civil War* (Doubleday, NY, 1966) p.226-8

13   Ibid., p.347-8

14   Georgie Anne Geyer, *Miami Herald*, December 24, 1966; Stephen Schlesinger and Stephen Kinzer, *Bitter Fruit: The Untold Story of the American Coup in Guatemala* (New York, 1982), p.236-44; *New York Herald Tribune*, April 7, 1963, article by Bert Quint, section 2, p.1

15   *Washington Post*, May 17, 1975; *New York Times*, May 17-18, 1975

16   *Covert Action in Chile, 1963-1973*, a Staff Report of The Select Committee to Study Governmental Operations with Respect to Intelligence Activities (US Senate), December 18, 1975, passim

17   *New York Times*, September 25, 1975, p.1, January 7, 1976, p.1; *The Guardian* (London), February 7, 1996 (review of book about Soares' links to CIA)

18   Ernest Volkman and John Cummings, "Murder as Usual", *Penthouse* magazine (New York), December 1977, p.112 ff.; David Corn, *Blond Ghost: Ted Shackley and the CIA's Crusades* (Simon & Schuster, NY, 1994), p.330; Robert Gates (former CIA Director), *From the Shadows* (New York, 1996), p.175

19   1984: *Los Angeles Times*, March 21, 1992, p.2; 1989: *U.S. News & World Report*, May 1, 1989, p.40; *Los Angeles Times*, April 23, 1989, p.1

20   *New York Times*, October 21, 1984, p.12, October 31, p.1

21   *Covert Action Information Bulletin* (Washington, DC) No. 22, Fall 1984, p.27, contains a reproduction of the advertisement

22   William I. Robinson, *A Faustian Bargain: U.S. Intervention in the Nicaraguan Elections and American Foreign Policy in the Post-Cold*

War Era (Westview Press, Colorado, 1992) passim; Jacqueline Sharkey, "Anatomy of an Election: How U.S. Money Affected the Outcome in Nicaragua," *Common Cause Magazine* (Washington, DC) May/June 1990

23   *The Guardian* (London), September 22, 1986; *Los Angeles Times*, October 31, 1993, p.1; *New York Times*, November 1, 1993, p.8

24   *Time* magazine, July 15, 1996, p.29-37; Fred Weir, veteran American correspondent in Moscow, analysis dated July 17, 1996, prepared for the Institute for Policy Studies (Washington, DC).
      Clinton quote: *Washington Star*, March 27, 1996, p.1, from a State Department cable that paraphrased the Clinton-Yeltsin talk.

25   *Washington Post*, April 6, 1997. The dollar amount is derived from the NED Annual Reports, 1991-1996.

26   *New York Times*, July 3, 1996, p.6

27   *Wall Street Journal*, July 3, 1996, p.10

28   *Intelligence Newsletter* (Paris), June 18, 1998. (Though scarcely known amongst non-specialists, this is a well-established and respected source of international intelligence information.)

29   *Los Angeles Times*, September 12, 1998, p.6; March 6, 1999, p.6; *The Guardian* (London), May 31, 1997, p.16

30   Agence France Presse, March 29, 2005; Associated Press, March 29, 2005

31   William Blum, *Freeing the World to Death: Essays on the American Empire* (Common Courage Press, 2004), p.171-174

32   Ibid., p.174

33   Ibid., p.168-171

34   Ibid., p.183-5

35   *Los Angeles Times*, September 23, 2004; *Washington Post*, December 22, 2001

36   *Los Angeles Times*, May 21, 2002

Chapter Nineteen

1   *The New York Times*, June 1, 1986

2   *Washington Post*, September 22, 1991

3   NED Annual Reports, 1994-96.

4   NED Annual Report, 1996, p.39

5   For further information on AIFLD, see: Tom Barry, et al., *The Other Side of Paradise: Foreign Control in the Caribbean* (Grove Press, NY, 1984), see AIFLD in index; Jan Knippers Black, *United States Penetration of*

Brazil (Univ. of Pennsylvania Press, 1977), chapter 6; Fred Hirsch, *An Analysis of Our AFL-CIO Role in Latin America* (monograph, San Jose, California, 1974) passim; *The Sunday Times* (London), October 27, 1974, p.15-16

6   NED Annual Report, November 18, 1983 to September 30, 1984, p.21
7   NED Annual Report, 1998, p.35
8   See NED annual reports of the 1990s.
9   Council on Hemispheric Affairs (Washington, DC), press release, June 13, 2002, www.coha.org; *Washington Post*, November 18, 2003; NED Annual Report, 1998, p.53; *Haiti Progres* (Port-au- Prince, Haiti), May 13-19, 1998
10   *New York Times*, March 31, 1997, p.11
11   *Washington Post*, February 16, 1987; also see *New York Times*, February 15, 1987, p.1
12   *San Francisco Examiner*, July 21, 1985, p.1
13   *New York Times*, July 13, 1998
14   For a detailed discussion of NED, in addition to the sources named above, see: William I. Robinson, *A Faustian Bargain: U.S. Intervention in the Nicaraguan Elections and American Foreign Policy in the Post-Cold War Era* (Westview Press, Colorado, 1992), passim

Chapter Twenty

The information about the voting on the resolutions is derived from the annual editions of the *Yearbook of the United Nations*.

1   *New York Times*, November 4, 1983, p.16
2   *Washington Post*, November 18, 1996
3   *The Guardian* (London), April 20, 2002; Chicago Tribune, April 20, 2002
4   *The Guardian*, July 31, 2002
5   Jim Lobe, "National sovereignty takes major hits in Yemen, Mauritius", Inter Press Service, November 11, 2002
6   Agence France Presse, March 22, 2002; George Monbiot column, *The Guardian*, April 16, 2002
7   *The Guardian*, January 20, 2005
8   *The Independent* (London), April 25, 2005
9   Shirley Hazzard, *Countenance of Truth: The United Nations and the Waldheim Case* (Viking, New York, 1990), p.7. Hazzard worked at the UN from 1952 to 1962.

10   *New York Times*, November 1, 1952, p.1
11   *The Guardian* (London), September 20, 1983. The next day the White House disowned Lichenstein's remark.
12   February 3, 1994 at The Global Structures Convocation in New York; *Washington Times*, October 16, 1998, Bolton's column; *The New Yorker*, March 21, 2005

Chapter Twenty-One

1   *Washington Post*, November 13, 1999
2   Overall discussions of ECHELON and related topics:
     a) Nicky Hager, *Secret Power: New Zealand's Role in the International Spy Network* (Craig Potton Publishing, Nelson, New Zealand, 1996), passim
     b) European Union report, "An Appraisal of the Technologies of Political Control", September 1998, in particular Section 7.4, can be read at http://cryptome.org/stoa-atpc-so.htm
     c) Report to the European Parliament, "Interception Capabilities 2000", April 1999, by Duncan Campbell, can be read at: www.iptvreports.mcmail.com/interception_capabilities_2000.htm
3   *The Observer* (London), June 28, 1992, p.4
4   *Sunday Times* (London), May 31, 1998, p.11
5   *The Telegraph* (London), Dec. 16, 1997
6   *The Independent* (London), April 11, 1998
7   *Electronic Telegraph (London), April 11, 1999*
8   *Washington Post*, February 26, 1995, p.1
9   Ibid., October 17, 1995
10   *Electronic Telegraph* (London), April 11, 1999
11   *Washington Post*, September 30, 1999, p.20
12   Hager, op. cit., p.94
13   "The working document for the Scientific and Technological Options Assessment [STOA] panel", May 14, 1999, can be found at: www.iptvreports.mcmail.com/interception_capabilities_2000.htm (STOA is an agency of the European Parliament); *Baltimore Sun,* December 10, 1995, article beginning on p.1
14   *Baltimore Sun,* December 10 and 15, 1995, part a of six-part series on the NSA; Wayne Madsen, "Crypto AG: The NSA's Trojan Whore?" *Covert Action Quarterly* (Washington, DC), #63, Winter 1998, p.36-42; *Der Spiegel* (Hamburg, Germany), September 2, 1996, p.206-11
15   Duncan Campbell's article of September 3, 1999 can be found on the

website of TechWeb: http://www.techweb.com/wire/29110640
16   Agence France Presse, February 18 and 21, 2000. Microsoft categorically denied all the charges and the French Defense Ministry said that it did not necessarily stand by the report, which was written by "outside experts".

Chapter Twenty-Two

1   Dominican Republic: See Elections chapter (18) for further information; Honduras: *New York Times*, May 25, 1988, p.8; Mexico: Ibid., April 20, 1990, p.1; Cypriot: *Washington Post*, April 18, 1999
2   Agence France Presse, April 7, 2005
3   Jane Mayer, "Outsourcing Torture", *The New Yorker*, February 14, 2005; Associated Press, June 26, 2003; *Wall Street Journal*, November 20, 2001; *Washington Post*, March 11, 2002 ("U.S. Behind Secret Transfer of Terror Suspects"); *New York Times*, March 6, 2005
4   Mayer, op. cit.; *Washington Post*, March 11, 2002, op. cit.
5   *The Sunday Herald* (Scotland), February 27, 2005, interview of Baer
6   *Los Angeles Times*, June 21, 1992, p.M1
7   Ibid.
8   *Washington Post*, October 15, 1999, p.23
9   Ronald Schneider, Communism in Guatemala 1944-1954 (Frederick A. Praeger, Publisher, New York, 1958), p.323
10   *New York Times*, November 6, 1983, pp.1,18,19; Casey: Bob Woodward, *VEIL: The Secret Wars of the CIA 1981-1987* (New York, 1987), p.294
11   *Los Angeles Times*, June 23, 1990
12   Philip Wheaton, Panama Invaded (New Jersey, 1992), p.45, 50-1; plus interview of Wheaton by author
13   *New York Times*, March 20, 1990, p.8
14   As told to the author in November 1999 by the Panamanian embassy in Washington.
15   *Washington Post*, November 22, 1998, p.2; March 3, 1999; October 27, 1999, p.27
16   Ibid., September 4, 1999, p.26
17   Haiti: *The Nation*, February 26, 1996, p.5; *Washington Post*, August 3, 1996; Agence France Press, February 9, 1996; *New York Times*, November 28, 1995. For the most detail, do a Google search under "The Campaign for the Return of the FRAPH/FADH Documents".
18   Human Rights Watch, World Report 2002, can be found on their website

Chapter Twenty-Three

1   *Los Angeles Times*, February 12, 1990
2   *New York Times*, July 23, 1986, p.1
3   *The Guardian* (London), August 15, 1986; *The Times* (London), August 4, 1986
4   CBS-TV interview with Tomlins, August 5, 1986; interview of Pizzey by author, April 25, 1999.
5   *The Atlanta Journal and Constitution*, June 11, 1990, p.1
6   *Los Angeles Times*, June 13, 1990, p.12

Chapter Twenty-Four

1   Peter Dale Scott & Jonathan Marshall, *Cocaine Politics: Drugs, Armies, and the CIA in Central America*, (University of California Press, Berkeley, 1991), p.x-xi. Dayle was speaking in 1991 at Fordham University in New York, as part of a panel concerning drugs, organized by the Christic Institute and other groups.
2   Alfred W. McCoy, *The Politics of Heroin: CIA Complicity in the Global Drug Trade* (New York, 1991), p.43-47, 53-62; Alexander Cockburn and Jeffrey St. Clair, *Whiteout: The CIA, Drugs and the Press* (Verso, New York/London, 1998), p.137-41
3   Christopher Robbins, *Air America*, (New York, 1985), chapter 9; McCoy, chapter 7 and elsewhere.
4   McCoy, chapters 4, 5 and 7; Robbins, chapters 5 through 9
5   Jonathan Kwitny, *The Crimes of Patriots: A True Tale of Dope, Dirty Money, and the CIA* (W.W. Norton & Co., New York, 1987) -- bank's drug connections: chapter 16 and elsewhere; bank's CIA connections: see index; McCoy, p.461-78; *The Village Voice* (New York), July 1-7, 1981; *CounterSpy* magazine (Washington, DC), November 1980-January 1981, p.30-33
6   Casey: *Los Angeles Times*, April 14, 1989, p.11, derived from the Kerry Report (see note 9 below)
7   *Cocaine Politics*, op. cit., chapters 6 and 10; John Dinges, *Our Man in Panama* (Random House, New York, 1991) passim; Murray Waas, "Cocaine and the White House Connection", *LA Weekly* (Los Angeles), September 30-October 6 and October 7-13, 1988; National Security Archive Documentation Packet: "The Contras, Cocaine, and Covert Operations" (1996; the Archive is in Washington, DC)
8   *Washington Post*, November 28, 1995, p.3
9   *Drugs, Law Enforcement and Foreign Policy*, a Report of the Senate

Committee on Foreign Relations, Subcommittee on Terrorism, Narcotics and International Operations, 1989, p.2, 36, 41 ("Kerry Report")

10   *Los Angeles Times*, April 8, 1988, p.12
11   Costa Rica/Hull/Cubans: Robert Parry, Lost History: Contras, Cocaine, the Press & "Project Truth" (Arlington, Virginia, 1999), p.220-223 and elsewhere; Cocaine Politics, op. cit., see "Anti-Castro Cubans" in index; Martha Honey, Hostile Acts: U.S. Policy in Costa Rica in the 1980s (University Press of Florida, Gainesville, 1994), chapters 8 to 10 and elsewhere;
      Martha Honey and David Myers, "U.S. Probing Drug Agent's Activities in Costa Rica," *San Francisco Chronicle*, August 14, 1991
12   *Cocaine Politics*, op. cit., chapters 2 and 3 and elsewhere; Hyde: Peter Dale Scott, *The Official Story: What the government has admitted about CIA ties to drug dealers* (Institute for Policy Studies, Washington, DC, 1999), p.28-9. This monograph is an analysis of two CIA and one Justice Department reports issued in 1997-8 in response to the many allegations of CIA drug connections. See also *Lost History*, op. cit., passim for an analysis of the government reports.
13   Ilopango: Celerino Castillo and Dave Harmon, *Powder Burns: Cocaine, Contras and the Drug War* (Mosaic Press, Canada, 1994), p.128-139 and elsewhere; North's diary: *Washington Post*, October 22, 1994, p.11; Guatemala: Frank Smyth, "In Guatemala, The DEA Fights the CIA", *New Republic*, June 5, 1995.
14   *New York Times*, April 14, 1989, p.8; *Cocaine Politics*, op. cit., p.60-62; Customs Agent: FBI debriefing of Dennis Ainsworth, California Contra supporter, January 21, 1987, p.8, part of National Security Archive Documentation Packet, op. cit.
15   Kerry Report, p.42-43; *New York Times*, April 14, 1989, p.8
16   *Cocaine Politics,* op. cit., p.17-18
17   *New York Times*, April 14, 1989, p.8
18   *Washington Post*, March 17, 1998
19   *Whiteout*, op. cit., p.95-7; *Wall Street Journal*, November 22, 1996; *New York Times*, November 19, 1996; *Miami Herald*, November 23, 1996, p.B1
20   McCoy, p.436-60; Tim Weiner, *Blank Check: The Pentagon's Black Budget* (Warner Books, New York, 1990), p.151-2; *New York Times*, June 18, 1986; *Covert Action Information Bulletin*, (Washington, DC) No. 28, Summer 1987, p.11-12; *Los Angeles Times*, November 4, 1989, p.14; *Washington Post*, May 13, 1990, p.1
21   *Los Angeles Times*, August 22, 1993

22   *New York Times*, Nov. 14, 1993; *The Nation*, October 3, 1994, p.346;
      Washington Post, March 8, 1997

23   In the United States: Gary Webb, *Dark Alliance: The CIA, The Contras,
      and the Crack Cocaine Explosion* (New York, 1998) passim; *San Jose
      Mercury News,* August 18-20, 1996, series by Gary Webb, from which his
      book springs;
      Cocaine Politics, op. cit., passim;
      Lost History, op. cit., passim;
      iF Magazine (Arlington, VA), March-April 1998, September-October
      1998, and other issues;
      The Official Story, op. cit., passim;
      New York Times, October 10, 1998, "CIA said to ignore charges of contra
      drug dealing in '80s"

24   *Eugene Weekly* (Oregon),January 15, 1999, interview with Webb

Chapter Twenty-Five

1   Speaking as vice president in the context of the shooting down of an
      Iranian passenger plane by an American ship, taking 290 lives, *Newsweek*,
      August 15, 1988

2   *Washington Post*, December 18, 1987

3   *New York Times*, November 11, 1996, p.12

4   Author's conversation with the Cuban Interest Section in Washington,
      DC

5   *U.S. Aid to North Vietnam*, Hearings Before the Subcommittee on Asian
      and Pacific Affairs, House Committee on International Relations, July 19,
      1977, Appendix 2.

6   *Los Angeles Times* and *New York Times*, March 11, 1997

7   For a discussion of this maiming, see John Pilger, "Vietnam: The Final
      Battle", *Covert Action Quarterly* (Washington, DC), #64, Spring 1998,
      p.54-65

8   Holly Sklar, *Washington's War on Nicaragua* (South End Press, Boston,
      1988), p.169-70, 314

9   *San Francisco Chronicle*, April 16, 1987, p.15

10   Interview of attorney Ramsey Clark, September 7, 1999, by the author.
      Clark had acted on behalf of many of the claimants. See also Clark's
      account in his book, *The Fire This Time*: *U.S. War Crimes in the Gulf*
      (New York, 1992), p.167-8

11   Interview of attorney John Kiyonaga of Alexandria, VA, September 10,
      1999; he and his brother David were the attorneys for these cases; see

their op-ed in the *Los Angeles Times*, April 1, 1990; see also *The Guardian* (London), July 28, 1990, p. 7; *San Francisco Examiner*, April 26, 1992, p.4

12   Interview of Elizabeth Abimershad of the IACHR-OAS in Washington, September 7, 1999 and Aurora Amezquita of the IACHR- OAS in February 2005. The case is Salas, et al. against United States of America, Case No. 10.573

13   Read to the author over the phone, December 22, 1999, by the State Department's Panama desk from an official press announcement.

14   *The Independent* (London), February 15, 1999, p.12; Seymour Hersh, "The Missiles of August", *The New Yorker*, October 12, 1998, p.34-41; *New York Times*, October 21, 1998, p.1 and 8

15   *Washington Post*, July 25, 1999, p.F1. For a fuller account of this matter, see William Blum, *Freeing the World to Death: Essays on the American Empire (2004),* chapter 7

16   *Peacelink* magazine (Hamilton, New Zealand), March 1991, p.19; *Washington Post*, February 8, 1991, p.1 (includes Powell remark)

17   "Nato bombed Chinese deliberately", *The Observer* (London), October 17, 1999; and November 28, 1999. Also see *Extra! Update* (Fairness & Accuracy in Reporting, New York), December 1999

18   *Weekly Compilation of Presidential Documents,* dated March 15, 1999, p.395

19   *Public Papers of the Presidents of the United States* (GPO), *1968-69, Vol. II*, p.800

20   The Associated Press, dispatch from Athens, Greece, November 20, 1999, by Terence Hunt; *Washington Post*, November 21, 1999

21   *Weekly Compilation of Presidential Documents*, March 24, 1998, p.491

Chapter Twenty-Six

1   *Los Angeles Times*, January 2, 1995, Assembly Bills 36X and 57X

2   *Washington Post,* September 24, 2003

3   *Los Angeles Times*, September 29, 1994; *Washington Post*, December 26, 1999, p.16

4   Speech in Austin, Texas, April 1993, unveiling her health-care campaign.

5   *Washington Post*, February 26, 2005

6   *Los Angeles Times*, January 2, 1995, Senate Bill 1330

7   *New York Times*, December 25, 1992

8   *Washington Post*, June 11, 1995

9   Ibid., July 5, 1996, column by E.J. Dionne Jr.

10   Ibid., May 15, 1998, p.9
11   Ibid., June 20, 1995
12   Ibid., November 30, 1995
13   *New York Times*, June 7, 1987, Section 11CN ("Connecticut Weekly Desk"), p.36
14   *Los Angeles Times*, September 2, 1994

Chapter Twenty-Seven

1   *The Guardian* (London), October 11, 1984; January 11, 1986, p.7
2   *Los Angeles Times*, August 26, 1991, p.6
3   *The Pentagon Papers* (NY Times edition, Bantam Books, 1971), pp.4, 5, 8, 26.
4   Guatemala: Stephen Schlesinger and Stephen Kinzer, *Bitter Fruit: The Untold Story of the American Coup in Guatemala* (Doubleday & Co., New York, 1982), p.183; Jagan: Arthur Schlesinger, *A Thousand Days* (Boston, 1965), p.774-9; Bishop: Associated Press, May 29, 1983, "Leftist Government Officials Visit United States"
5   *Miami Herald*, April 29, 1996, p.1
6   *Los Angeles Times*, February 24, 1994, p.7
7   *New York Times*, April 16, 2002
8   *Washington Post,* April 19, 1999, p.14
9   *Los Angeles Times*, April 4, 1999, p.4
10   *Washington Post,* May 9, 1999, p.1 and 22
11   Christopher Simpson, *Science of Coercion* (Oxford University Press, New York, 1994), p.4
12   *Washington Post,* January 2, 1999; see also constitutional lawyer Floyd Abrams' serious criticism of Clinton's policies on First Amendment issues, *New York Times Magazine*, March 30, 1997, p.42-4
13   "New incarceration figures: Rising population despite falling crime rates", The Sentencing Project (Washington, DC), www.sentencingproject.org/

The sources for the incidents listed in chapter 27 are not provided in order to avoid giving the false impression that these are all one-time occurrences. However, the reader can contact the author at bblum6@aol.com to request a source for any particular incident.

Index

About the Author

William Blum left the State Department in 1967, abandoning his aspiration of becoming a Foreign Service Officer, because of his opposition to what the United States was doing in Vietnam.

He then became one of the founders and editors of the *Washington Free Press,* the first "alternative" newspaper in the capital.

Mr. Blum has been a freelance journalist in the United States, Europe and South America. His stay in Chile in 1972-3, writing about the Allende government's "socialist experiment" and its tragic overthrow in a CIA-designed coup, instilled in him a personal involvement and an even more heightened interest in what his government was doing in various parts of the world.

In the mid-1970's, he worked in London with former CIA officer Philip Agee and his associates on their project of exposing CIA personnel and their misdeeds.

His book on U.S. foreign policy, "Killing Hope: U.S. Military and CIA Interventions Since World War II", first published in 1995 and updated since, has received international acclaim. Noam Chomsky called it "Far and away the best book on the topic."

In 1999, he was one of the recipients of Project Censored's awards for "exemplary journalism" for writing one of the top ten censored stories of 1998, an article on how, in the 1980s, the United States gave Iraq the material to develop a chemical and biological warfare capability.

In 2002, "West-Bloc Dissident: A Cold War Memoir" appeared. And in 2004, "Freeing the World to Death: Essays on the American Empire".

During 2002-2003, Blum was a regular columnist for the magazine "The Ecologist", which is published in London and distributed globally.

His books have been translated into 15 foreign languages.

He currently sends out a monthly newsletter, the Anti-Empire Report. To be put on the mailing list, send him an email. Previous issues of the report can be read on his website.

email: bblum6@aol.com
www.killinghope.org